MAKING KIDS SMARTER:

A Guide for Developing and Teaching Children Successfully

Pedro R. Portes, Ph.D.

Butler Books
Louisville, Kentucky

Acknowledgements

I would like to express great appreciation to all those parents, students, friends and family who helped and encouraged me to complete this book over the many years it took to do it, and particularly, Trish, my caring and devoted partner. Also, my thanks to Catherine McCliment, Madelon Zady, and Tracy Smith who helped in the editing of this work.

Cover Concept and Creative Direction:
Catherine McCliment

Photography, Digital Images, and Photo Editing:
Terry Head
Catherine McCliment

Page 128, 152 Photo Courtesy:
Timothy Korpela

Book Cover and Layout:
Terry Head

Copyright 1998

ISBN 1-884532-14-4

No part of this book may be reproduced in any form, mechanical, xerographic or electronic, without permission in writing from the author.
Printed in the U.S.A.

Portes Books c/o
Butler Publishing Company
2002 Ardsley Rd.
Louisville, KY 40292
Fax 502-852-0630

For Andre Sebastian, and for all children to more fully discover their potential and develop their talents.

y para Eva Rosa, la niña mas linda del mundo a quien queremos como esa alma tierna que vino para que pudiéramos despedir a Tita y quien seguirá la tradición de esta familia tan inteligente y creativa. y para su mami, mi queridísima Lisa que tiene todo el savoir-faire necesario para este mundo

Pedro N. Porta
7-14-04

Table of Contents

INTRODUCTION 11

Why Parents Need This Book 11
Author's Preface 11
Making Parents Smarter 14
Why Parents Education is Important 15
The Advantages of this Book 16

CHAPTER I: Cultivating Your Child's Superb Intelligence 19

Are You A Knowledgeable Gardener? 19
The Cultural Context Matters 19

CHAPTER II: What Intelligence Is 29

Let's Define It Before Increasing It. 29
What Is A Learning Set? 33
Two Questions Parents Should Ask 34
Activities Shape the Mind 36
Intelligence Explained 38
Children Are Driven 39
Facts about Intelligence 41
Birth Order and Intelligence 44
The Child-Parent Interaction Study 48
Divorce and Intelligence 50
What Intelligence Is Not. 55
Formal and Informal Zones of Intelligence & Development .. 57
Different Kinds of Intelligence 60

CHAPTER III: The Early Years 65

Infant Intelligence? 68
The First Year 70
The Second Year 75
Towards The Third Year 77

CHAPTER IV: The Preschool Years 79

Concept Matching 81
Concept Formation - Part I 82
Learning in the Preschool Years 82
Developmental Principle 88
If your Child is Older, is it Too Late? 91
Concept Formation - Part II 92
Language Development Makes the Mind 95
Teach Language Very Early 96
Precursors to Language: Cooing and Gurgling, then Babbling 97
The Fast Track 99

CHAPTER V: Strategies for Parenting Intelligently 103

Building A Positive Self-concept 105
Ownership & Control 106
Logical Consequences 108
Making Learning a Routine 108
The Spiral Curriculum 109
Back to Control 110
Response Cost 111
Catch the Child Doing Good (CCDG) 111
Grandma's Rule 112
Modeling 113
Why use praise and encouragement? 115
Positive Reinforcement (PR) 116
Extinction 118
More Strategies To Foster Intelligence 119
Dinner Conversations 122
Infancy and Trust 124
Toddler's Search for Independence 124

Preschoolers Need Initiative *125*
Early Schooling and Concrete Thought *126*
Adolescence and Abstract Thought *128*

CHAPTER VI: Childrearing Patterns and the Mind 133

The Disciplinarian-Authoritarian Style *133*
The Permissive Style *134*
The Democratic Style *135*
Reasoning/Sensitive Parent *136*
Inconsistent Parenting *136*
The Protective Parent *136*

CHAPTER VII: Learning and Motivation 139

Achievement Motivation *139*
How Children Learn To Be Motivated *140*
Competence *141*
Attribution of Success & Failure *141*
Four Ways Children Learn *142*
Learning Mechanisms *145*
Make The Connection or Set It Up. *147*
Intelligence and Learning *148*
Intelligence Defined *149*
Summary *153*
Building the Base for Intelligence *153*

CHAPTER VIII: Creating as Intelligence in Action 155

When does creativity start? *156*
Is Creativity Learned? *157*
Creativity defined *158*
Setting Up Your Child To Be Creative *161*
How to develop creativity *162*
The Big Picture *164*
The Family Backgrounds of Creative Persons *164*
Teachable Moments *167*

CHAPTER IX: Conclusions **173**

BIBLIOGRAPHY & RESOURCES: **182**
Organizations *190*
GLOSSARY: **192**

INTRODUCTION

Why Parents Need This Book
This book is designed to provide you, the parent, with:

1. A different approach based upon facts and the synthesis of theories of how intelligence is constructed.
2. Not only a "how to" guide, but also a plan for developing a unique style for smarter parenting, as well as for developing an intelligent culture in the home.
3. The best theory of intelligence in order to help expand children's genius.
4. An account that "gives psychology away," by showing what intelligence is and how it develops.
5. A revelation for parents of young children, enabling them to see that children's intelligence is actually being born before their eyes.
6. A plan of action for parents of older children who will be able to see how they can co-construct and guide their child's intelligence.

Author's Preface

In writing this book, a broad base of information and reliable research studies were compiled from various scientific fields relating to how children become intelligent. This book integrates knowledge from hundreds of studies that focus on children's mental development. It presents a holistic approach that challenges many popular views. Intelligence is not a fixed trait within the child but grows out of the social and cultural contexts in which parents raise their children on a day to day basis. Intelligence really consists of two main components. The first is that part which is already actualized and already under the child's own control. The other part is the potential in the process of being actualized and still dependent upon external assistance.

Intelligence is not fixed in the person, but rather, it is an interactive process which includes motivation, expectations and regulation patterns over which parents have a great deal of control. Intelligence is not just inside the head but also outside it.

This perspective challenges traditional psychological models of intelligence. It is based upon the views of many distinguished psychologists and educators as well as my own research. It is founded upon numerous studies which show how parents make the difference in children's intellectual development, how they help to construct and direct the intelligence that will become characteristic of the child in life. Children are born intelligent. The capacity to be genial, creative, exceptional or smart is there all along. But exceptional or smart in "what regard" you may ask? Well, children become intelligent in whatever portion of culture in which they are actively involved, like sports, Nintendo, science, crime, or art. If your children like and become active in a given mini- culture (e.g., reading, computing, skateboarding, or music), then they can develop expertise or intelligence in this pursuit. A child internalizes concepts and skills from activities in any given mini-culture. To internalize means to learn something well enough to be able to use that something in one's own way. Take for example music, in which one can compose after internalizing the basic symbols. However, what makes a difference in how far that intelligence develops and how well it is used? Intelligence depends mainly upon how parents nurture and guide it. This book is designed to show you how.

What Kind of Parent Are You?

Many parents have bright kids, and they are unaware of how they themselves were effective in facilitating the children's development across a number of key areas. Other parents who try to develop bright or above average kids fail, because they do not understand the key factors involved, (often frustrating the child as well as themselves in the process). They need to know how the model works. These are the same parents who tell me that they have tried everything, and nothing seems to work for their child, and then they conclude: "I guess my child doesn't have what it takes to be exceptional so why push it." Or they conclude prematurely: "I guess Kathy is not as smart as her older sister." As you will see, this is a very uninformed view, which is expressed by parents who are not with it. They don't have "it." While there is no need to push, there are basic ways to nurture children's minds intelligently. Although I cited skateboarding and music above, some areas of talent, of course, are more in line with the typical definition(s) of intelligence than others. So, parents need to know how to reinforce patterns of activities that lead to advanced development of intelligence as a whole. They need to be educated about recognizing the seeds of talent.

A major thesis in this book is that each family environment has its trademark and leaves a deep imprint upon the child. This trademark is like a signature, or is akin to a radio transmission frequency that regularly beams signals to the child's mind. Parent-child interaction style is like the typical wave pattern that is found in a family environment. Some patterns are more effective in developing intelligence. The rest of these chapters amplify this thesis.

A two-year-old learns concepts by being talked to over and over again about a small number of things. Development is easier to see at this stage than at later ones. For example, parents can see how a very young child develops the concept of

Introduction

TV or a program or book. The idea "hot" enters the vocabulary of a thirteen-month-old a few days after the parent draws attention to the concept. In fact, such conceptual development seems to take place in stages. A child, who can show you that he has learned a concept by pointing at, it is at stage one. Stage two is evident when the child uses the concept verbally, as when he says 'doggie' or 'milk, I want it.' In the third and most parentally captivating stage, the child incorporates the verbal concept into more and more sentences or contexts (situations). In this second year of life and thereafter, it is important to encourage the child to "play" or to use new concepts in various activities, and to give feedback and reinforcement. This encouragement will allow the child to adapt and to act upon the environment more effectively. In short, parents need to develop "an eye" for activities that can be turned into areas of learning expertise over time.

This book represents an effort to provide parents with a grasp of how the mind works, how it is formed, and how its development is enhanced or undermined for children at different stages. As a result, parents will be in a better position to nurture and guide more wisely the unfolding of great talents. In the text, parents are shown first how the mind is developed, so that they can effectively find ways to fit the present model to their child. At this point, I should like to emphasize that it is not enough to present the reader with a "how-to" list of techniques. Rather, parents need to know why certain methods work and are more helpful than others are. They need to have a general overview of the model before applying it to specific situations. Your child's intelligence will develop as much as you permit it. Encourage it and then some. Yes, children are innately brilliant, yet they can't reach their potential in uptight family contexts, in which parents' lack of knowledge about parenting effectively slows down the child's growth.

In this book, you will discover why intelligence is not fixed, and also how it is constructed gradually. You will hopefully understand how certain basic day to day routines (styles of interaction with children), impact upon the growth of different areas of the child's mind. You will be encouraged to become a co-designer and an architect of that 'construction' which is taking place in the child's mind.

A major purpose of this book is to make new findings in psychology readable so that you understand the implications for your particular family, regardless of your children's ages. Yet, the psychological phenomena described are not always easy to comprehend at first, so bear with it in these chapters even if you might feel a bit lost. You will probably have to read some parts of this book more than once. The book is designed not just to tell you what to do, but more so to change how you think as a parent and help you understand mental development.

Eventually, you will get the gist of it because the important points are presented clearly and in many different ways. The design of the book is such that, even if you don't get the key points one way, you will in another. The only condition is that you finish reading the book.

Reading this book will raise your kid's I.Q. score, but that is not the main goal. Yes, that will happen, but what is most important is that your child will have a smoother ride in adapting to whatever life has in store. Both of you will be wiser in understanding development. The main goal of this book is to help develop your child's natural genius, and to help you become more responsive, more adaptive, and more creative in rousing your child's intelligence from birth on through college. In becoming more knowledgeable about parenting, you raise children more intelligently, and you make it easier for their own intelligence to reach a fuller potential. So the goal is to empower children in ways that make their adaptation to the complexities of today's world easier. Consequently, through this parenting process, parents will not only give their kids "an edge," but they can also create a better world, a more intelligent world. After all, intelligence is about adapting to life in the best way possible.

I present you with an added incentive: You may also reduce college costs. After all, the brightest students are actually paid to attend the best universities. So your return on investing in this book is manifold. And the best thing about intelligent parenting is that it is no chore at all, once you "get it." Rather it is an art and a science. Intelligent parenting is a science in that parents learn to master a unique approach, and the product, an intelligent mind, is the best art form, the most valuable product in the universe.

Making Parents Smarter

So you think raising intelligent children can be done? As you will soon see, intelligent parents are the key to producing intelligent children, so doing what you are doing now reflects well upon you. You are trying to gather intelligence (data) so that you can be a more effective parent. You are also intelligent enough to know that most parents do what they can do and that they are not too well informed about what intelligence really is, or for that matter, how it can be fostered in children so that their minds shine brightly throughout a lifetime.

Helping children become very intelligent first requires "know-how" from the immediate family environment. It requires intelligence in parenting as well as knowledge about how a person can achieve excellence in adapting to the environment and in contributing significantly to society. Such a parental knowledge base and "know how" require more than another self-help, "how-to" book crusade. Parents need to be informed about how intelligence develops from a scientific perspective. I say "scientific" to clarify that the approach to this book is based upon decades of research. You will learn that being intelligent is a lifelong process and not just the ability to score well on various tests during the school years. It is a process of learn-

Introduction

ing how to learn, learning how to deal with information and do... ative things with that information.

Why Parents Education is Important

My thesis is: If we now have clear evidence about how to foster... ate children's intelligence, many parents will want to know and use ...edge in raising their children. If (smart) parents are shown that they must have a sound understanding of mental development first before learning what they can do in practical terms, they will commit themselves to learning and will succeed at smarter parenting. Parents must understand why certain things they do routinely with their child make sense and where such things and activities lead to eventually.

Parents, who do not know what they are doing, are similar to someone who knows nothing about gardening tending a garden. A lot of potential is wasted. Well, this is exactly what happens with many children most of the time. The problem exists not because parents don't want to learn, or because they don't value the child's potential. Some (a very few) parents have mastered the art of gardening, but most parents simply lack the "know-how" to cultivate the child's developing intellect.

As a matter of fact, the lack of parental "know how" explains why it is currently so easy to excel on achievement exams (score above other children) given the current norms. It appears that society is still in the "pre-scientific" era when it comes to parenting. Many social problems stem from the unenlightened ways children are socialized. You are an exception. You are reading this book, you are recognizing the importance and implications of this issue, and you are trying to do well by your child. In contrast, other parents invest hours and weeks on their own hobbies which do not improve parenting skills and know-how. So what constitutes parental "know how" and what might be the long-term results of informed parenting? Parents must develop an "intuitive feel" for what is happening in their child's mind, for what kinds of information and experiences are needed by the child at a given moment. They need to know about the *child's readiness to master one small area* and to begin pondering about another. They need to respond strategically so that the child can "move on" in his development and mastery of that topic. This process is called "Strategic Assistance", which, if and when it becomes a pattern in your home, can lead to rapid advances in intelligence.

This book has been designed to help you to develop this "feel" and know how. But first, we need to define the big problem and decide where we are going once we have this know-how. In chapter II, two other components which help to define and develop intelligence will be discussed. The power of expectations and motivation is considered in detail. Children behave in very predictable ways. They usually go by what they think is expected of them. Expectations account for most of what children accomplish in life.

To get the most out of this book, parental expectations and the way they are communicated to the child are critical. The power of suggestion and positive feedback can promote 20-40% more growth for your child, 20-40% higher grades, and even more creative potential than using drill specific exercises. In the remainder of this book, the influence of fixed factors like parental marital status, socioeconomic status, birth order and such are considered in order to help parents avoid common errors.

It does not matter if you are a single parent, or poor, or if your concern is about a middle child who is not as "sharp" as the first born. You will learn how to activate key factors in the development of intelligence which can easily make up for difficult life circumstances. In fact, the less optimal your marital or economic situation is, the more you may profit from this book. In sum, MKS (Making Kids Smarter) integrates research and theories to provide a clear understanding of what is going on in the mind of developing children. It suggests what you can do, at different times, to match the ever changing needs and questions.

The Advantages of this Book

MKS is for all children, from infants to teenagers and even for yourself. We are already born as very creative and intelligent life forms. A common myth is that some children are more capable than others, from day one. This is silly, because as we will see, the concept of intelligence reflects on not only the child but also on you. (You are a big part of the child's intellectual environment.) In an associated myth, authors of how-to manuals tell you that their methods can increase your child's I.Q. score. Such statements show a total misunderstanding of the issue of intelligence. I.Q. or the intelligence quotient mainly tells you what the child has learned but not necessarily how intelligent a person he is. *Measured intelligence is not the same as intellectual development and potential, and great care is needed to use I.Q. data wisely.*

Some parts are for parents who are not familiar with human development theories. Other parts are aimed at more sophisticated readers. It is designed so that you are either prompted to think about important parenting practices which you may want to try or affirmed in your current parenting practices (that is that many of the things you are already doing are on the right track). So, get ready to see the big picture in intelligence making, but be patient. The key to making your child intelligent is to help you to become more informed, knowledgeable and consistent.

My goal is to develop your own understanding to fit better with your child's needs at different points in time, and to make you a better custodian of your child's innate talents. In the final chapters, the book tries to unravel for the reader those things that make a difference in children's development that are associated with social class, culture, sex differences and birth order and family status. You see,

Introduction

there is a long record of differences in measured I.Q. depending on the above factors.

This book shows why such differences occur and how these factors can be used to the child's advantage regardless of the child's financial circumstances. The key factors are free and simple but do depend upon you, the parent, becoming more educated and knowledgeable about parenting for intelligence.

Footnote:
The author, a university professor in educational psychology, has spent years reviewing, researching and synthesizing information relevant to what makes children smart, particularly in the family environment interactions. Much of the credit for what you will be able to do with your child's potential goes to the dozens of psychologists and educators who have taken the trouble to conduct studies before trying to change the world. The main ones appear in the bibliography. However, one thing that has been missing in all of this research is a synthesis or a way of putting the results together in a way that makes sense to you, the parent, so you can apply the understanding in relating to your children.

CHAPTER I

CULTIVATING YOUR CHILD'S SUPERB INTELLIGENCE

Are You A Knowledgeable Gardener?

Do you focus on certain key goals for your children; intelligence, self-esteem and motivation? If your children develop all three fully, you have succeeded, and they will adapt to society effectively. What's more, the world will be the better for it. What better feeling may a parent have than to know that his child is well equipped for life and that, regardless of the situation, the child has the smarts to deal with it?

To develop your kid's smarts, first you need to know how intelligence develops generally and then to add or to reduce some special events. Over time, the mind of the child is co-constructed intelligently. Parents are both stewards and gardeners, but they are often unaware of these roles. Therefore, they lack critical, important knowledge about how to best raise (or foster) different types of plants or talents.

A child's mind is not simply a plant that grows. A child's mind is a whole garden, full of plants (types of intelligence, for example). Think of these types, or areas, as the math plant, the reading or writing plant, the music or arts plant, and so on. To understand high level intelligence, it is crucial to understand the context that helps to develop and to define it.

Lesson One
To help you do one of the most important things in the world, increase your children's intelligence, you must increase your own. Do so particularly when it comes to the topic of parenting and child development. This means that the very activity which you are now undertaking, learning about cultivating your child's intelligence, is the first step in getting the job done well. Digest this book and keep your mind active by keeping up on your readings concerning this topic.

The Cultural Context Matters

Certain *contexts* and *situations* help the mind to grow. Typically and most importantly, such contexts can be seen in the patterns that characterize the family environment. For example, a child who is advanced in verbal skills or art is usually one who learns anew through informative and positive patterns of interaction at home.

Other Levels of Culture

Some contexts for intellectual development appear in the form of communications provided through cable TV or films. Other cultural settings for mental development are found in the neighborhood or the community. For example, a child who grows up to be talented in music is likely to have had a long record of support and encouragement from parents at home or significant others in settings that are open, like church or the environments of the child's peers. Opportunities might include a piano in the home or in the activities of a friend or a relative, who in turn models for the child.

Lesson Two
Understand your role as the key representative and teacher of human culture. Talent grows where there is an intelligent cultural context that provides <u>dynamic activities</u> in one or several areas. You need to make sure that, from now on, your child is "connected" with activities which directly foster certain talents or intelligences, on a regular basis.

A MODEL FOR UNDERSTANDING HIGHER LEVEL INTELLIGENCE:

$$\text{INTELLIGENCE} = [\,P \times E\,]\ T\ \times (+/-\ \textbf{SPECIAL EVENTS})$$

P= the person, and what this person *does* with what nature has provided
E= the environment
T= the time **P** has been *interacting* (=X) with **E**
(+/- **Special Positive or Negative Event**s) = the learning experiences which the child encounters overtime that nurture (above and beyond the *normal course of events*)

A good way to describe how intelligence is developed is by using a simple model or formula. The formula says that as your child or a person interacts with the environment, learning begins to be accumulated over time. This learning, which occurs naturally, leads to the development of a "record" in the mind of the child of those interactions or experiences that becomes permanent and useful. The child can then <u>act</u> with those experiences "in mind."

Now, this accumulated learning or product can be multiplied or reduced depending upon certain events in the child's life. For example, if parents punish a child often or simply give the child too much corrective feedback with few positive strokes, these events will actually reduce intelligence. A child must feel safe and well perceived by others (within his home or by primary care-givers) in order to have a good self-concept. Without a good self-concept, learning is interfered with, like static on a music tape.

Chapter 1: Cultivating Your Child's Superb Intelligence

A much better idea is to structure positive special events for your children. To do this, it is best to arrange for the child to expand into an area of interest that is already developing in his mind. For example, a special event that can further learning would be to have the child; travel, be exposed to different people, or even surf the internet for fun. In actuality, the advantage of possessing parents who know more about how to develop children's innate talents, as compared to the average parent, is also a <u>very</u> special event. Each event tends to influence the interactions of the child with the environment over time. What the child develops in the mind, as the result of these interactions and events, is intelligence. These intelligences or capabilities that are etched in the child's mind help him/her to adapt to the environment effectively and to make the environment respond to the child.

Normal refers to the average results most parents produce with their children. Intelligence is the sum product of the mental and affective assets which a child has developed. Intelligence is the sum total which the child possesses (and is on the way of developing) that is considered valuable in dealing with life. Since the people with power in the world generally decide what is valuable to teach in schools. Intelligence depends upon what different cultures value across different contexts.

Lesson Three
This is How the Mind Works. *As your child acts upon and responds to the environment over time, certain skills and knowledge systems are being developed in the brain. This etching in the brain leads to the gradual construction of what computer folks understand as microchips or what we refer to as concepts. So to understand children's development, note that they are always learning, regardless of what you may do. That is, they are constantly grasping or practicing concepts that exist "out there" and reconstructing them in some form in the brain. This means that you need to be selective. You also need to have a plan. The way to do this is to plan for short, medium and long-range goals, keeping in mind your child's talents. Then you must gradually weave these goals into your social interactions with the child on a routine basis. Other chapters will explain this lesson in more detail.*

Speech Is A Tool

Most people overlook the fact that: Certain uses of language in the course of daily activities actually make the mind more intelligent. As you will see, the process is more than just talking a lot to children although this helps early on. The key presented to you in this book is that you, as a parent, must learn how the use of language can forge the tools with which the child adapts to the environment. The mind is made up mainly of tools like know-how skills, strategies, concepts, beliefs, and expectations that are formed as the child interacts with other minds through language and a variety of activities. This process is the main way that intelligence is co-constructed. So you should focus on the development of these tools, rather than on just content, that is, focus on the vehicles through which the child "comes to know." Concepts are brought about by interaction with others. It is that simple. So the question for parents and teachers often lies in being selective with what *and with whom* the child interacts, and how he does so. For example, does the child look forward to those activities that promote concept learning?

Interactions involving social speech (also sign language for the deaf) are much more "powerful" than sensory or motor interaction alone. For example, a four year old learns from T. V. about the good/bad guy theme, or fighting with the bad forces in order to save friends, royalty or self. These themes become tools with which the child plays later, using toys to reenact, reconstruct dialogues. New words are employed. New schemes are attempted with the neighbor kids later. Eventually, what the child has acquired is quite different from the original input. The TV content served as a vehicle for development, including the social dialogues, the motives for action, and the like. Speech is a tool that speeds the development of thought, like an interactive educational video or a computer program, or like a dinner time conversation.

> ***Speech is crucial. What you talk about is what you think about. Now, how would this be important in developing your child's intelligence? Reflect for a moment. As the child enters elementary school and onward, what people are thinking and talking about around him is most relevant. So this means that you should consciously try to cultivate certain cultural themes, like the meaning of words, the history of things, the geographical location of others. Do it in a smooth, subtle fashion, and make this a part of your interaction style at home.***

Your child is able to perform certain functions, which demonstrate that connections among concepts and skills are present in the mind. A child performs a function when, for example, he asks if most cars have antennas, then, why don't they travel with remote control. Such a question shows an "expansion / elaboration" effort on the part of the child who knows about remote control cars, trucks and other concepts like "four-wheel drive." It may sound cute, and some will laugh at how naive the child appears to be at that point. The truth of the matter is that the smart parent realizes what is going on and uses these type of questions to expand the current systems of knowledge, which develop within the child.

The child's awareness about history, science, music, math etc., can begin to grow just as plants, which have their root system feeding from a particular field (or culture), grow. A lot depends upon how responsive the child's environment is and

Chapter 1: Cultivating Your Child's Superb Intelligence

how patient and intelligent. Parents comprise the most significant part of the child's intellectual environment. The sooner you begin, and the more consistent you are, the further the child will be able to go later in life. Are you with me thus far? (If not, read again).

Organizing Special Events

Now, some special events can be provided which can make one field more productive than another in terms of the types of plants that are nurtured and how well they are nurtured. For example, think of a given style of interaction between parents and children like one that is inconsistent or over-demanding, or one that is punitive. Now, compare those to events provided in a super-encouraging environment. You can easily appreciate what happens to the grade of plants that a child ends up with down the road given those events and family environments.

> *Lesson Four*
> *Children's mental development at first involves recreating inside the brain as much of the outside world as possible. This process is one basic working principle you need to be aware of constantly. Ask yourself regularly, what aspects of the world has my child explored and recreated in her mind lately? How can you tell? Focus on what your child is doing or talking about. Too much TV violence in your child's diet? Maybe you just think that sitting in front of the TV keeps the kid occupied, so that you can take care of household demands. Or maybe, you can't be bothered? If you are interested in your child's mental development, arrange, organize or pay for alternatives and support them emotionally: A child must gradually develop a picture of what the world consists of, how it is organized and all those interconnected facts. The first few years of life simply consist of absorbing and thus representing the culture around one and in refining those pictures through interaction with the environment. Do you allow the TV to be the main source of interaction for your child?*

The child also picks up on tools that make it easier to absorb culture like reading, music, art, writing, plays, etc. In addition, many tools evolve out of these and other activities. Besides tools, like reading or arithmetic which are part of the culture, the child develops other less obvious tools that help him act upon the world like problem finding/solving skills and mental strategies. Think about how tools like reading and language open up the world to the child's mind. A simple 5-minute conversation can open up the mind if it's on target, even more than 5 hours worth of class time. These tools are developed naturally in the course of interactions with the immediate family. Families have their own trademark. Some family contexts have patterns that promote development better than others, a fact which ties back to the idea of special events. But such exposure varies. One child may have 2 hours a day being actively guided by an adult, who responds to the child's natural thirst for knowledge, while another child may not (for whatever reason).

In effect, these subtle patterns form a mini-culture around the child, which determines to a large extent, how much of the big culture gets through. These patterns tend to accompany your child and set his paths of development. Think of different radio frequencies transmitting information to your child. Your child interprets and acts upon information that is available. Certain family routines serve to transmit better than others. So play smart games. Children will learn and develop anyway. They live in the little culture of the home and develop from it. The little culture they grow up with then becomes the foundation for bigger cultures like school. Although it is hard to goof as a parent, because children are so resilient and tough, there are many things parents can do to promote the development of their child beyond what the parent of the average child does. Parents can learn a lot about being better agents for their talented children so that a bigger and more precise picture of the world gets through on a regular basis. Just as some gardeners' work patterns result in better outcomes than others, some family interaction patterns are more conscious and effective than others. What makes the difference? A number of things, some of which you know and others with which you may not be familiar, like *zones of potential development* and *verbal regulation of complex learning*. (These come later in the book). Some parents tell their child, "go look it up in that reference set we bought you," while others take time out the first few occasions that something should be looked up and make it a joint and fun activity.

How well parents set up the conditions for children to develop, and how wisely they orient and assist their children make a big difference. It is not that children can't make it on their own, as they sometimes do. The point is that when parents assist, the child can develop further. Sometimes parents don't assist their children, because they do not want to or do not have time to. Some parents barely have time to provide for anything other than physical needs. However, a smart parent "keeps an eye out" for her child by ensuring that tutors and learning activities become part of the daily routine. The fact remains that parents who provide the "special events", enriched activities and encourage reflection have children who are more intellectually advanced.

Lesson Five
The Brain Is Like A Garden. A child is a whole garden, a complex, multidimensional system made up of various talents (plants) that may reach full development and others that may never get there. In a similar vein, you hear about humans having several intelligences. A child

Chapter 1: Cultivating Your Child's Superb Intelligence

can develop musical, artistic, mathematical or creative writing talents. Some folks believe that, since brain functions are located in different areas, there may be more than just one intelligence. Our theory explains that intelligence is understood to be not just in the head. These multiple intelligences are the result of you, the parent, providing for the excellent conditions for cultivating your child's various intellectual plants. So what have you done for the motivation plant lately? Good question to ask yourself on a regular basis. You see, any type of high level intelligence, whether it is related to a law of physics, or an application of a psychological principle like positive reinforcement, originates from outside of the mind or in the context you provide for the child in the immediate culture. Only later does the intelligence enter "inside" and become measurable. So if you provide for the cultivation of the motivation plant by giving genuine positive reinforcement, this context will eventually be internalized by your child.

An example: Think of science fiction notions such as exploring whether there is intelligent life on other planets. If on a particular planet, one were to find creatures playing the flute or drawing, they would be considered intelligent life forms. On the other hand, if one were to find creatures that were attacked by others, could not obtain food and did not survive for long, then what might be concluded? Such defenseless creatures would not be considered very intelligent. Intelligent then means having information and skills that allow for smooth adaptation. The funny thing is that we don't need to go to other planets to make the point. Maladaptation in society is happening all around us everyday. You need to understand that children are raised in different cultures which affect the development of mind and its many facets, to various degrees. For example, low income, or rich, inner city, suburban or rural families at one level of culture or how parents interact with children on a daily basis at another level, both are what I mean here. Circumstances such as family finances and locations and opportunity for parental interaction can set up the child's development to move away from certain other directions and possibly to follow certain directions. One child can become very intelligent in surviving out in nature, or in some neighborhoods, while another can survive easily in the world of computers, science or sports. You may call these different intelligences or plants, but the process of developing skills and talents all share the same roots.

In sum to help you to understand how to assist your child to develop a high degree of mastery (talent) in any area, we must first define what intelligence is in general and then show how it develops, especially when it seems to happen automatically in various areas.

Defining and explaining the development of intelligence will be our next topic. In this chapter, you have learned:

- **That intelligent parenting tends to occur when there is a guiding plan or model in mind.**

- **That parents provide a certain "trademark" style of interaction with children which may affect the course of development.**

- **That certain special events can be arranged for parents in order to maximize children's development.**

- **That parents need to have a plan in parenting, a way of organizing challenges for the child in daily routines.**

- **That the child's mind can be viewed as maturing very much as a garden is cultivated. Gardeners tend to their garden; do you tend to your child's intellectual and creative development?**

After reading the remaining chapters, try to summarize the main points you learned and reflect on what you can do differently when interacting with children.

Suggestions
Often we are busy with life and feel we have little time to teach our children. What to do parents? Well, make the time and also use the time you have to teach in fun ways. Do this everyday, make it a routine. What you invest in with your child now, pays off big later. Follow-up on your child's interests and provide for tutoring or activities connected with those interests (particularly in preschool.)

CHAPTER II

WHAT INTELLIGENCE IS:

Let's Define It Before Increasing It.

If you do not exactly know what it is that you are trying to develop, then parenting can become erratic. So next, let's try to develop our own theory of intelligence based on the facts. Let's map our strategy so we know what and when we need apply what is learned in this book.

We must have a theory that is valuable to not only scientists, but also to parents and teachers. In this book, we are talking about human intelligence, something that is our most precious commodity. That means that a good, practical theory can not only help your child but also the society in, which we all have to live. That's the big picture.

Such a theory already exists but is not well known to a certain extent. It is a theory that links culture, its tools and activities to development of the human mind. The theory is the foundation of this book. I know that for you to discover a new model of intelligence, it might take some time. You probably want to cut straight to the action and understand what needs to be done immediately. However, it is important that you take a few moments to consider the basis of intellectual development—the theory.

What is a good theory first of all? Mainly, a theory consists of a number of assumptions that can be tested outright and that explain what something is and how something works. It predicts how that something will work in the future under different circumstances. What are the implications of knowing how to make children smart? You may be already getting the picture... by thinking smart.

Intelligence is a term humans made up to describe how well someone adapts to a given environment or how successful a person is in society. After they described the term intelligence, humans developed questions to assess "it." By taking the number correct and dividing by age, "it" was given a score. "It" was measured by how well and how much people had learned about coping with the environment of a particular culture. (More on this later.)

Tool and Concepts

Intelligence depends upon having access to a variety of concepts/tools, and developing and using them in creative ways and in a variety of contexts. Tools are like concepts (e.g., female impersonator) that often lead to activity inside the head.

For example, when a child uses a concept like "brush," she associates it with paint (illustrate with drawings). The concept "snakes" triggers the idea of poison or death. The finer the tools a child has in mind, the more intelligent and creative she can be. Your child first learns basic things about numbers and quantities and things in the world, and in so doing, begins to see certain relations that help form tools for solving problems. How the child comes to know is the name of the game here. The tools are applied in formal and informal areas. For example, your 6-year-old encounters the problem of gravity one day when he hears someone ask, "why doesn't the moon fall down?" This episode may be one of the first events which the child encounters that deal with the formal area of science. Before the child can solve problems in this area, many concepts and discussions must first take place in interactions between P and E. (person and environment)

Science, like literature, history and all the other areas (plants) that we hold dear, may serve to develop tools for thought. We say a person is intelligent, for instance, if a person has mastered enough of a field to be proficient, as in learning several languages. But it is not the field or plant per se that is important in considering intelligence. Such a field represents an opportunity in which formal and informal skills can be invited, learned and mastered.

In helping parents become intelligent guides so that the child can be considered very intelligent and creative, we must define the fields that are going to be used for developing the tools and personal strategies of information processing. These areas will lead to faster and better learning, day in and day out over the formative years. Often, parental interests serve as a basis for such interactions. However, just because dad is into sports, the child should not be pushed towards sports only. That is, parents should think about what areas seem to motivate the child intrinsically after providing for a variety of experiences. The home can offer a variety of fields, areas, zones or cultures (however you want to think about it) that are expanded (sequentially or spirally) as the child develops.

Learning is sequential. Math learning is sequential, mastery at one level is necessary before mastering the next level. The child is always ready to learn, but sometimes learning can be designed so that the more basic skills are mastered first. Don't hesitate to involve your children in a lot of activities where knowledge is discovered and used repeatedly, but try to change the level from time to time.

Some homes are said to contain "hidden curricula", which means that there is a lot of support for one or more fields of development like a second language, science or history. For examples, family friends speak two and three languages to their children from birth. The children are on their way to being perfect tri-linguals.

Chapter 2: What Intelligence Is

My neighbor Karen is a music teacher and she provides piano and singing lessons. Her kids are well ahead of most in the performing arts.

How does the hidden curriculum work? Very simply. A parent may travel a lot and tell the spouse over dinner table conversations about the history and geography of various places and peoples. The child listens, gets reinforced for participating at times and slowly develops notions or schemes that later make formal learning in school more easy. Some kids have music and art going on around them, and sometimes they are taught key things about each area.

As you will learn, parents' best bet in guiding development is through the verbal interaction channel, mixed with lots of illustrative activities, praise and encouragement. Why the verbal interaction emphasis? Read on and learn about the theory of the making of mind by filtering aspects of culture, like the internet, the classics, science, history, math through various routines in the home environment. Speech is not the only symbolic system, nor is it employed just to communicate. We think through speech which reflects on prior experiences and interactions.

Social activity and speech help you think. Parental speech gets internalized by children, they hear it in their minds, and this speech guides their behavior. Some activities, you see, involve thinking or reflecting within oneself. Verbalized speech is parent's main tool. So watch how you talk to your children, because you are programming their computers (minds) whether you are aware of it or not.

Have you ever wondered why many of us, when we encounter a difficult problem, begin to talk aloud? We need this help, because we cannot think very far without speech. In fact, thought is mostly verbal. When we think, we are acting stuff out with speech symbols and manipulating the environment in the head. Our behavior is a function of the speech which regulates our thought. As you are probably aware, when children play or work they often "tell themselves" what should be done next or before. This is how children learn a lot of complex skills. Such a process is usually based upon prior social interactions, in which something was said or explained that is "on target" with the child's level of development.

In any one individual, an area of the brain may be more developed in artistic, mathematical or other ways than another's, so that a person may be said to be more intelligent in some things and not others. Here the term intelligent means that one has developed expertise in an area and as a result becomes more sensitive, and understands more about that area. One thing is for sure, for various types of intelligences or skills to develop fully inside your child's mind, you've got to have the external tools, the outside verbal guidance and encouragement, and the strokes for the right things. You need to provide plenty of recognition for efforts that involve your child's mastery of reading, logic or memory skills, which in and of themselves are considered tools to be used in the future. Other tools which prove helpful for the child's mental development are resource materials, games that have educational value, intelligent tutors, informative siblings and activities that provide practice and expansion. Even love and a loving environment can serve as tools for intellectual development.

Children need lots of time being loved even when they are ready to learn and work at something. The use of time becomes a tool when parents block it out for learning. By doing this, parents provide structure for the child so that learning takes place in a given area. A smart parent needs to target a particular area of interest for the child in which intelligence can be developed. For example, playing chess can be used to develop anticipation, logic and self-esteem with proper guidance. Not only those, but timing and sequencing are crucial, for the child must feel some need to stick to a given area. And, parents also need to provide a varied context.

Any skill or degree of intelligence your child has now developed can be traced to some prior activity between your child and a source, a context, a more advanced person who showed how or helped. This usually happens through social interaction. Patterns of social interaction that are informative, challenging, in which children account for what has already been learned in order to learn something new, and in which there are plenty of strokes for the child, need to be established in the home. Your child may be more turned in to one type of intelligence than another. This may be because there is a "model" the child likes who does or knows about a particular area. He may want to go further in a given area or microculture (jazz, chess, computers, anthropology) such that his mind becomes more intelligent with respect to it. Your job, as parent, is to build a natural bridge between his mind and that external field or culture. Taking kids to a museum and to ballet lessons are examples.

But that is not enough. Taking them to see the best zoo in the world, talking to zoologists about what they do, and talking about it at home or elsewhere is helpful for developing the mind towards a natural science. If you want your child more oriented towards a performing art like music or ballet, a different pattern of activities is necessary to maintain the child's interest. Live and fictional models are needed.

Take for example a social interaction in a swimming pool during the summer. You do a pH test of the water with a kit, five drops turn the pool water to a given color and all that stuff, now think, how can you use that event to build a bridge? You could start the interactions from a "what happens when the pH *is off*" question and move on to chemical reactions and chemistry. Don't get used to leaving the child at a concrete, basic level, even if you have to stage a strange chemical reaction to arouse interest. Help him discover the concept "*off-balance*" at some level.

Chapter 2: What Intelligence Is

But what if your child is not interested in anything? What if he changes his mind from one field to another? These are questions dealing with motivation and mind "sets" that are discussed in other sections of this book.

The family is a brokerage house of culture. Have you ever noticed how some children become interested in stocks and bonds at an early age, while others seem interested in other countries through stamp collection? Any one of these activities serves as nutrients for some plants or talents to develop more fully, a bridge to future areas of expertise, some of which are more valued than others. Suppose in a particular home environment, classical music has been played throughout the childhood years, and perhaps the child is even witness to a parent who pretends to direct a concert. We would say that this particular home culture serves as an incubator for the child to develop in that direction. A **set** or attitude is being built, assuming that there is a good relationship between parent and child. These examples serve to show how parents select certain aspects of the world and interact with them in ways that help children to develop a positive attitude towards them as well as some knowledge. This process is called a set. Parents set up the child to travel along certain roads simply by what they allow to be incorporated into daily family life. Such a circumstance represents a more direct channel for mental development as compared to television for a number of reasons. For example, some parents allow for quality educational time by engaging the child regularly in some topic area, like science or literature. They ask the child to describe a plot in a story, or the parent may describe it inaccurately to jolt the child. While other parents are keener on viewing the evening's TV programs and do not want to be bothered with setting up educational opportunities. They say "later" or "not now" to the child thus setting up a negative pattern, a minus under the special events part of the intelligence formula. Opportunity for mental development suffers. While some parents value education, others focus on making money or having leisure time. These are values that impact the child's learning sets later on.

What Is A Learning Set?

Sets are predispositions or attitudes in approaching things. Sue might have a negative set when it comes to math, Joey might have a positive set related to jazz or computers. A set is like a habit or a bias that is learned in a very subtle way over time.

Hannah may have received lots of strokes while traveling in a car with Dad. Perhaps dad used to ask her to figure out how many miles to here and there and to see if there were shortcuts on the way. What kind of set do you think was being developed?
A) Science B) Math C) Art D) All of the above.

Now think about this parent showing the child how to use triangles and to figure their sides' length in miles, then stressing that miles can also be converted to kilometers. Hannah is being primed for a math-oriented set, and the process was carried out in a playful way through open-ended question, positive strokes for curiosity, and examples. Learning sets make a big difference in determining what areas of intelligence are most advanced. They can affect a child's mental development about learning as a whole. If parents know how to influence sets, it will be much easier to expand their child's mind in any area, for example science or history. You can see in this example that a particular technique is not the key to the game, but rather it is in knowing how to develop your own methods.

(By the way, if you expect to see the "right" answer to the above multiple choice item, forget it. I have a "set" by which I do not give answers to everything. This makes students think, and they learn more by it).

You need to sense when your child is ready to learn. A six-month-old is said to have only a 20-second attention span. Actually that depends, because at some points during the day when physical needs are met, it can be much longer. With older children, the attention span can be much longer, but often it is not. It is well worth building this span on a day to day basis by working with your child in a positive manner. This span is part of a learning set, that is, how a child goes about the business of learning. Avoid a negative set. Do not try to induce one. Avoid forcing the child into it. They can learn to hate what you want them to be good at. The key is the use of positive reinforcement when the child moves closer and closer to an area that is worth developing. Another key for success is in creating and providing the conditions for the child to become interested and active in a given area and in making sure that fun, nice things become associated with that activity.

Two Questions Parents Should Ask

In trying to advance your child's intelligence, you need to consider at least two paths or approaches. First, what talents are most likely to flow naturally from your child? And in what areas would you like your child to be intelligent which may also be of great interest to her? What is the best match between what "the child is already turned on to" and what "society values?" Here, parents need to think about how to facilitate the growth of intelligence in practical areas (while letting the child play at it). Such areas are likely to pay off later in life by providing educational and professional opportunities. You may want to pay little attention to things having to do with car racing or wrestling but come out energetically if the child is "into" pollution or the workings of a catalytic converter. That is because the latter, you figure, can be stretched into *a set* about scientific knowledge and conservation of nature. Again, values are important.

Secondly, you may be most concerned about the development of intelligence just for its own sake. You may not want to position your child to have an edge, rather you may want him to develop more fully as a person. In this instance, the parent figures that an intelligent child will surely find his way in the world, since that is what intelligence is all about. You figure that having certain talents, skills and tools in the head will make adapting to life an easy, positive experience. Of course, this adaptation requires that a child be motivated, to want to use what is learned, to want to learn more about certain areas, and to have a positive self-image and self-confidence in his ability to learn. Of course, these two paths can dovetail and do not rule each other out. However, in order for this to happen, you must take a different approach in selecting what is to be presented and valued in the home. The first path suggests that you should select an area or two and consistently reinforce and nourish them over time. Here, the practical parent may observe the areas that the child enjoys and focus on providing special conditions for developing them formally in regard to a special intelligence or talent that will pay off later. The second path suggests that it doesn't much matter what talent is selected as long as it is cultivated in ways that advance the child's mental development. Here, the parent allows the child to set the agenda and provides ideal conditions for areas that are tied to intelligence (without a specific target, like having the child score in the 97th percentile of a standardized test).

In either case, remember that you, as a parent, are mediating or brokering culture (much like a commodities broker). You stand between your child and all that there is in our human history and civilization. You are the bridge-maker, the contact. However, you may not always remain the teacher. Parents of gifted and talented children usually know when to resort to obtaining a more sophisticated teacher. They make it feasible for the child to get expert guidance.

Your child's mind is a product of the portion of the world that is around him, and the way you guide and cultivate it. If you want a child who goes about an intellectual task methodically and carefully, at least one of the parents needs to be methodical in everyday activities, approving and creative. Why use activities? What people do day in and day out ends up shaping their minds and their outlooks on life. If you are raised in a culture which the people sail a lot or explore the seas and navigate, you will find the development of certain skills that are not found in a farming community culture. For example, children from Kentucky draw horses and jockeys frequently for State Fair exhibits. These artistic subjects represent an activity of the culture. Culture has many levels, national or local or even among teachers or adolescents, there are specific cultures.

Children of teachers will tend to use reference materials a lot, if that is an activity pattern in the home. If your child is into soccer or basketball, then you are most likely aware of how development in those areas is advanced. The implication here is that you provide a context outside school in which the child's favorite areas of intellectual development are activated on a regular basis. By the way, do not ever rely on school exclusively to develop your child's intelligence, there is only so much schoolteachers can do. That is, given the number of students they are expected to teach and varying levels of parental support, teachers are limited.

All of these social contexts or cultures, in which the mind is slowly made, are useful. Some cultures don't do much for the mind, like the culture of poverty for instance. In this culture, parents do not generally speak and teach their children as much as in those with more educated parents. Educated parents, like well-to-do parents, tend to invest in their children, but in different ways.

The principle is akin to the saying: you are what you eat. Your mind is made up of representations of activities in which you engage routinely. The key for parents is then to have routine activities and patterns of social interaction that advance learning above and beyond school. Such processes can be effective even if they occur over short periods of time.

In this situation, it is as if your mind is intelligent in areas in which you are active, and it doesn't matter whether your channel of absorbing culture is reading, after dinner conversations, or sailing. After all, reading, after dinner conversation, and sailing can all lead to learning about astronomy. The question for you, then, is how many minutes a week do you spend interacting or having someone interact with your child intelligently in some area of interest?

Activities Shape the Mind

The child learns about the world all the time and through all kinds of seemingly useless activities. I'm not going to tell you "make sure your child gets into these certain types of activities and not others." Yet, I want to help you to see how different types of activities can be exploited to yield useful knowledge and to help develop the child's mind to ever-higher levels. And yes, there are times when activities seem hard to use constructively. After all, sometimes children misbehave. Do not fight them, but do not reinforce them either (like aggressive or inconsiderate behaviors, king of the hill stuff, etc.). Let's take a look at one of these activities. When reading a book with a child of 3, 4, or 5 years (age doesn't matter) and the child tries to tell you about something seemingly unimportant, the fact is that the point of the story may not be as important as the activity of expressing thought and perceptions through words. Storytelling is an art, parents can work with children to have them practice new techniques, to avoid the redundant, all in a positive context that is not associated with criticism or overly demanding parental expectations. You will notice in the bibliography some books with suggested exercises for developing children's intelligence. You can use some of these as supplements or games, but don't be fooled into thinking that these exercises alone will do it. Rather, you can use any learning tool wisely with the model of development you will know very well after reading this book.

Chapter 2: What Intelligence Is

The most important thing for me is to help you the reader to become intelligent about parenting, and to help you to understand your child's development. I do not intend to force techniques on you that leave you saying to your neighbor "well, the book says to do X and Y". Rather, I want you to understand that intelligence is defined by one's developed and developing potential in various areas, which makes adaptation and actions on the environment easier.

This thing called intelligence is a serious matter and must be defined clearly. If the reader is not shown clearly or does not agree, then the rest of the reading is a waste of time. The mental development of children is something that must first be presented to parents in order that they can become more aware, more intelligent, forever. Under the influence of the reading, some parents will do things differently, while others will be reinforced to continue to take the time to schedule what they are already doing. In this way, the book makes parents more conscious about the kinds of special events that can be created to foster the child's mental growth. I intend to show you how to increase your children's intelligence by increasing your own. As the old proverb goes, the secret is to teach you how to fish rather than giving you a fish. And the book shows you how the formula can be developed for different types of children.

Later you will learn why it is important to travel with your child. For now, let me say that at as early as 12 months, children's concept development profits from the regular connections provided by daily walks. Later, further travel that provides for audio, visual and tactile experiences helps the brain to become a sharper tool. The child may babble during the travel experience. Baby talk is not intelligent, but don't talk down to your child, as if he/she were not capable of understanding. Give the child a chance and be patient. Invite and answer every question or request. Acknowledge the child's efforts to communicate at every level and be responsive. Intelligent parenting involves following the child as much as guiding him/her, since the child will let you know what interests and abilities need attention.

What Intelligence Was Believed To Be

Some people believe intelligence is what tests measure, and that it is fixed for the most part. If your child achieves a score of 135 (I.Q.), for example, special classes for the gifted are usually made available that can help to maintain that mysterious mass we call intelligence.

Most experts today agree that intelligence is not a fixed characteristic like hair color or height. Intelligence refers to a person's ability (capacity) to adapt to the environment or society. A child's behavior shows to some extent the degree to which that ability is present. Sometimes, parents are amazed by the insight and clever behavior (also verbally expressed ideas) of a child. They rush to the nearest psychological assessment center to find out what they have. Is my child gifted? Is he/she overly talented and creative? What do we do now? When parents are fortunate enough to have children like these, they tend to underestimate themselves, as we will see in later chapters.

An intelligent child is one who learns quickly, but can also be one who has learned much under special conditions. In the past, intelligence has been misunderstood. It is more than a score. It is more complex than responding quickly, relative to others. You see, getting higher scores and getting them fast reflects on the intelligence associated with development early on, and parent's own capacity to be guardians of creative thought and self-esteem. Children are born intelligent. The question is: How intelligent has been the environment over time?

Intelligence Explained

A child is said to be intelligent when he has learned much, and hence, scored very high on an I.Q. (intelligence quotient) test when compared to other children his age. The way it works in practice is that you take the number of correct answers on a test, divide them by the child's chronological age and then multiply this by 100. The average intelligence score is 100. What this really means is that most children have average, mediocre environments. Children are not average, nor mediocre, but they can become so if the culture around them is that way. It is not difficult to raise an above average child. The longer they are in a mediocre or substandard environment, the harder it is to break out of a barely average level of development, especially after age two to three. Mental development occurs most intensely during this time, and those patterns that influence intelligence get pretty much set. Does "set" ring a bell? Yes, the way parents interact with their children tends to be set early on.

Remember, by age 4, most of your kid's intelligence is said to have been developed under normal conditions. What this means is that by age four, the intelligence of a child's immediate context can pretty well be said to be set or established. A child who learns quickly is sure to have a pattern or system of acquiring knowledge. This pattern develops early. By having certain conditions ready in the home that match the child's needs, you then produce above average intelligence.

You can tell how much the child is likely to receive from a given family context by how much stimulation it has provided around this age. Some of these conditions concern set, motivation, practice, role models, activity and speech patterns which are discussed later.

It is relatively easy to have your child score high on these I.Q. tests once you have certain patterns of interaction in the home. Once this happens, it is easy to get the child placed into an advantaged setting in school (special classes) so that some of these patterns can be maintained, although often they are not maintained very well. However, this is still better than having a bright kid stuck in an average class.

Special advanced classes are necessary but not sufficient. Schools cannot be expected to take care of developing intelligence(s) where your child is concerned. Special classes are not enough to support the intelligence "in the making" of a child whose home environment has set him on the fast track of development. Parents need to bring together other special events, to orchestrate activities that support the superior development track they have devised.

Children Are Driven

Intelligent children enjoy achieving mastery. They like getting the gratification of understanding things around them and how they work. Parents need to supplement school once they have placed their child into the best, most advantageous conditions possible.

All children have a drive to achieve mastery, but only some are allowed to keep it going. All children are born creative and with a positive self-concept, only some stay that way past elementary school. It seems that there is a conspiracy of ignorance. Golden learning opportunities are wasted by both parents and teachers, thus indicating why children use only a small part of their mental capacity. When children gain mastery over certain key aspects of the environment (that we adults consider useful in getting the most out of life) we then judge them to be intelligent. For example, a four-year-old child who guesses that the concept "double" means taking an original amount and "multiplying" or making another equal amount side by side, regardless of size, is said to be intelligent if no direct teaching was present.

If Sandy figures out that sent is a past tense form of send based on what someone said, and that bent then would be a past tense of bend, she then would be considered smart if little or no direct instruction took place. Parents who are available to reinforce these little miracles of learning, these "*ah-ha!*" experiences tend to help maximize intelligence.

Recognize that the response is not as important as the process of discovering a rule or concept. When parents learn to pay attention to what is really going on inside the child's little head and to rejoice when little steps are made, they evidence a pattern of parent-child interaction that is extremely important. Intelligence inside the child's mind depends upon intelligence existing outside it in a dynamic, stable way.

Intelligence, then, is a combination of having a sound background in the types of knowledge as well as an established knack of making use of this knowledge across different tasks (especially those we prize). Intelligence is also defined by special contexts, like that of music, science or foreign language mastery which bring out the child's interests and skills. When there is a match between what we believe is useful and what the child is able and willing to do, then there is a case of above average intelligence. What is believed to be useful? What exactly is considered to be adapting to one's environment? To be considered intelligent (above average), a child must not only have learned lots of different things but also have learned those that are deemed important in school.

Similarly, when a child develops skills in thinking or a knack for figuring things, in order to be considered intelligent, these habits need to be in areas that are considered helpful in doing well in school. Why? Because school is the environment in which we expect children to adapt most intelligently. Kids who excel in school are those who have

an "edge" outside school. Here are several questions that you, the reader, should be wondering about:

a) Can a child be intelligent without necessarily being tops in school?
b) What about kids who just seem to have a lot of stuff memorized, who are able to answer teacher's questions correctly, but who are not all that insightful and creative?
c) What about those who do not do well on formal tests, yet show that they are very keen in day to day things?
d) What then makes up or defines a real intelligent kid? (The answers to the above are given as we move on).

Zones Of Intelligence To Be Developed

The process we are examining is just like working on a project, building a house, making a dress, or even writing a book. Although the work is not finished, it is in the process of being mastered. During this process, the individual can benefit from outside help, this includes somebody who is more advanced because of having access to books and videos. A child developing a new skill or system of knowledge is just like one of the above projects, especially when the skill is being attempted or approximated for the first few times. The learner goes through a lot of trial-and-error, or discovery learning and can benefit immensely from outside guidance with examples and encouragement, which is usually accomplished by social or symbolic interaction that hits the target.

The process we are examining is just like working on a project, building a house, making a dress, or even writing a book. Although the work is not finished, it is in the process of being mastered. During this process, the individual can benefit from outside help, this includes somebody who is more advanced because of having access to books and videos. A child developing a new skill or system of knowledge

Chapter 2: What Intelligence Is

is just like one of the above projects, especially when the skill is being attempted or approximated for the first few times. The learner goes through a lot of trial-and-error, or discovery learning, and can benefit immensely from outside guidance with examples and encouragement, which is usually accomplished by social or *symbolic interaction* that hits the target.

After the approximation of the task with help, the result is acceleration and enrichment of intelligence-related information and skills. Whenever this match between learner and outside help occurs, a **zone of proximal development** (ZPD) is being established and advanced to a higher, more complex level. When this match occurs regularly (and becomes a pattern), that is, when outside guidance and encouragement are provided in a timely and positive fashion, then one can expect high levels of intelligence and creativity. This is basically what acceleration in mental development is all about.

Facts about Intelligence

By age 4, remember, 64% of your child's intelligence appears to be already fixed under normal circumstances. That is, a child whose I.Q. is 130 at age four is likely to have a similar I.Q. at age 17. It is not necessarily that the child's intelligence is fixed in the head. It means that the environment in the home is generally fixed in terms of patterns of social interaction that will surround the child over time. In other words, 2/3 of a child's intelligence can be predicted before entering school, because the home environment's patterns are becoming established.

What develops in the head before age 2, often referred to as infant intelligence, does not predict how smart the child will be later. Trying to rush your child is not intelligent, but responding to children's readiness is. Intelligence tests measure at least two kinds of abilities. One is based on what's important for school learning, which is called ***formal intelligence***. The other kind is not taught directly and seems to come about more naturally, like noticing key details or getting the big picture quickly. This is called ***fluid or informal intelligence.***

You can increase intelligence in the preschool years by providing a special environment in which to cultivate certain skills and areas of knowledge. But, if you take away those special conditions, the intelligence that is measured and shown by the child later is lowered. In fact, if you do not maintain those conditions, there is very little to gain from providing special conditions for just a couple of years during preschool.

It is known that general intelligence requires different types of abilities and information. A main one is the ability to verbally express oneself. Another one is the ability to perform tasks using visual, audio and motor skills. For example, an intelligence test requires a child to verbalize the number of weeks in a year, seasons, presidents and capitals of the world. Such knowledge is factual and learned directly. The ability to memorize information, or numbers, or to say what is appropriate, responsible behavior in social situations are other tests. Other parts of intelligence tests require children to identify what is missing in a picture, to put puzzles together and to be quick in memorizing symbols. Some skills are harder to teach directly, such as figuring the abstract meaning behind "Shallow Brooks are Noisy", (which suggests parents need to pose and find problems in interactions with their child).

Intelligence Defined

Recall the earlier definition: "Intelligence is one's developed and developing potential in various areas which make adaptation and utilization of the environment easy." A very important question in relation to the definition of intelligence is not only figuring out what it is exactly, but also determining how many types of intelligence there are. Even after decades of research, psychologists argue much about whether there are three, seven, or only one intelligence in our heads. The argument is silly, as you will see from our theory, because the mind will be as intelligent as the culture around it. The child then decides what to do with that cultural menu of choices. That is, if in a given culture you find only math and art, to a large extent, that will determine the types of intelligence in the minds of the members. But, if a member develops music, and the culture responds well to it, then there will be math, art and music as areas of intelligence that can be developed.

As stated earlier, it is well known that general intelligence requires different types of abilities and information. A main one is the ability to express oneself verbally. Another is the ability to perform tasks using visual, motor, memory or audio skills. For example, an intelligence test may require a child to recall number strings both forward and backward, remember the number of weeks in a year, and even the names of some presidents or capitals of the world. (Is that intelligence or a question of what the child has been exposed to and learned?) Of course such information is just factual knowledge and can be learned directly. Other parts of these tests tend to evaluate more indirect learning, for example, what may be required in a social situation, like a fire in a theater. What else is measured by these tests as evidence of intelligence? Identification of what is missing in a picture, represents evidence that the child is alert. Also, if the child can put a puzzle together quickly or memorize a new set of number symbols, that is regarded as intelligence. In fact, you can teach these skills to your kid, and the test administrators will tell you that you have a genius for a child. But stumping I.Q. testers is not the point. Right now, I'm just trying to demonstrate to you that intelligence is not what most people think it is.

Let's go on with another example of what is in these "so called" tests of intelligence. They may ask your child (say at age 11) for the meaning of a proverb like "strike while the iron is hot." The correct response requires that a person answer at a symbolic or abstract level. In this case, an answer that is too concrete and simple, like "you have to wait for the iron to get very hot before forging it," is not as sophisticated as a response like "do it when you get a chance." Or as another example: "How is a circus like a zoo?" Here, the child needs to find a common element like animals. Those children who do well in these tests also do well in school. The inference here is that current explanations of intelligence are *circular* and not convincing. That is, if test makers take skills that are important in school and put them in a test, of course they can predict that the test will identify who will do well in school. In a similar manner, if they take stuff that is learned in school and put it in these tests, of course they will be able to tell who is doing well in school. In both cases, we are looking at adaptation to the same context (that of school) from a "means to an end" perspective. The "means to" skills refer to informal or fluid intelligence which leads to outcomes or "ends" that are learned in school.

In any case, experts suggest that there are two types of intelligence:
- formal (crystallized)
- informal (fluid).

So what does this mean for the parent?

If you know what areas are tapped by intelligence and standard tests ahead of time, then you need to provide a not so "hidden curriculum" for each area from early on. These lessons may not be early from your point of view, but they are if you consider the child's level of readiness. Such lessons need not be strenuous endeavors. The creative use of various daily activities by parents holds the key to developing both types of intelligence. The intelligent parent realizes that helping the child to read early, or to know about concepts in several areas, or whatever, is not just important in giving the child an edge in school.

Rather, this is not nearly as important as giving the child confidence and familiarity with the learning process itself. When a child has a "hook" on which to hang new information, mental development is advanced. When these hooks are connected with each other, they form systems of information that are well organized. Such mental organization allows for intelligent behavior which is then likely to be reinforced under more and more varied conditions. So the bottom line is that you are setting the child up for success, which in turn helps to establish a cycle or system of advantage that runs upon itself. Still later on, you have less and less to do with it, and your input needs to be very well thought out to be helpful.

By the time your child is an adolescent, the processes that define intelligence are pretty much set and begin to show their worth. This is not to say that it is too late to make an effort to further your child's mental development. It is never too late. In fact, when conditions in the home are not that ideal, kids can go a long way with what some teachers offer in school. Yet, the child needs to have both home and school settings operating well in order to be competitive down the road, when intelligence becomes actualized or fulfilled.

Not all children who are intelligent do well in school, nor are children who do extremely well in school the most intelligent. The explanation is that there are at least two ways of defining intelligence. (See Fluid Intelligence)

The same holds true for creativity. The most intelligent may not be the most creative and vice versa. Often, you see talents bloom later in life, after the child has had only a slightly above average school record.

Children who are born blind have a tougher time developing intelligence as compared to those who become blind later in childhood. Children who are deprived when young are set for a "slow down" in mental growth. The longer they are deprived, abused or neglected, the harder it becomes to bring out their intelligence. Their socio-emotional development has been compromised which is after all the foundation from which intelligence develops.

The level of intelligence of the child depends upon the intelligence of the immediate environment which accompanies the child over time. Intelligence is said to peak around ages 4-6, but that is because the environment tends to show its own level of intelligence early on and has a tendency to stay that way. If the environment's intelligence level (as defined mainly by family patterns of interaction and activities) does not keep up with the child's mental development, the child's intelligence has a difficult time breaking through. Other environments can help to meet the challenge, as when an extremely good teacher makes a difference. Children's creativity tends to be stifled by society, particularly in school and also by not-so-intelligent parents. (See section on Creativity).

Birth Order and Intelligence

Are first born children always more intelligent than middle children? Not necessarily, but there are good reasons for why first born children tend to succeed. Yet, once you know why, it is easy to give all of your children that same edge.

Be aware of the powerful influence that the structure of a family has on learning and thus on intelligence. The position of the child in the family, the spacing between siblings and their sex are all associated with measured intelligence (I.Q.) because of predictable patterns of behavior. That is, most families tend to treat each child fairly consistently depending on both his novelty and the number of children in the household. Novelty: First born children typically score higher in I.Q. than middle born children. They also get a lot of high quality adult interaction. Number: Children in large families score lower on I.Q. tests than those in smaller families. Twins tend to score a bit lower than single born children. Why? The novelty wears off after a while, and there is more competition for a limited amount of quality interaction

Chapter 2: What Intelligence Is

time with adults. The number and spacing of siblings, then, can lower the quality of activities, reduce opportunities for matching adult input to the child's zones of development that are "in process", and so on. It does not have to be that way, but it tends to be so. With the first born, parents are often not sure when it is safe to leave the child alone, so they demonstrate a tendency to give a lot of attention. By the time the others come along, parents figure they "can get away with" giving a lot less attention, also they often can't seem to make the time.

True, siblings can interact with each other. Peer interaction is good for the mind's development but not as good as interaction with tutors or intelligent parents. The child can use both to fertilize areas of development. Tutors, parents and mentors guide and create zones of development, while peers and siblings provide for practice and consolidation, which is reinforcement of knowledge.

First and last born children are usually considered the most intelligent. Can you see why? The first one gets the quality interaction and gets to practice stuff with the siblings. This has the effect of: "You learn stuff real well when you verbalize it or have to teach it." The last born gets fairly good interactions from older siblings. Such interactions during the early stages of development do not need to be that complex. Later, as older siblings leave the nest, the younger kids get more quality interactions from parents, when they need it most. Parents, also by that time, are a bit wiser as well. So the timing here can be an advantage. The "baby" is now more ready to profit from quality interaction from adults, as long as these adults are intelligent and good mentors.

The more children in the family, and the closer the spacing between siblings, the lower the measured intelligence tends to be. The limitations placed on parents to "deliver" learning situations when there is a lot of stress and also many kids to attend, are the main reasons for this fact. Yet, it does not necessarily have to be this way.

Often, in large families, there may be 2 or more sibships or "litters," if I may use this term. The first three kids form a group or cohort, with an older, middle and last child. Then a spacing of five years comes along, and another first and second born appear. Finally, another third shows up within a short period of time, and these form another cohort. Psychologically, what you would predict is that the first born in each group would do better in school, and that the second born would tend to be hard pressed to find an area in which to shine. Without enough support, middle children have a tough time getting their talents served, or their plants cultivated.

Often these children become good at something the first born has not yet taken over. In actuality, sibling rivalry can influence the development of mind quite a bit. Each child must be respected and tended to as a first born or a last born. It is important to motivate middle children. They need special treatment, perhaps much more than you think.

Parents may assume that they are providing what is needed for middle children, but typically they are not when the interactions are examined minute by minute and day by day. The problem is based upon another big misconception: Parents believe that their children all have the same environment, simply because they are raised in the same house. They think that their first born, Rob, is more intelligent than Paul, a middle child, simply because they were born that way. Obviously, the parents claim, both kids have had the same environment. Of course they may note "Paul is more artistic, or athletic" (meaning non-intellectual). WRONG.

The environment was not the same for Paul and Robert. They each met with different sets and inputs, when they were going through different developmental stages. For those few cases in which the first born does not take over being the smart one in school, another sibling will soon rise to the occasion. First born children are usually under pressure, and they fear being dethroned.

So note here something critical: It is called ***the process of differentiation.*** Each child demands his own individuality. If you say to Bonnie, "I never had that problem with your older sister," then you are introducing the needless baggage of sibling rivalry and derogatory messages. It is not intelligent parenting to say: "Your brother used to zip right past these math problems at your age." The damage you may induce here is emotional and motivational, the very base upon which intelligence builds. If this message gets through, all the activities and special tutors won't work to undo it.

If you want your children to have special talents, then every child is special and needs to be treated very specially. The power of your suggestions and expectations count much more than any specific intelligence related techniques.

Ideas to Keep in Mind For Parenting Intelligently

Children who are outstanding in one area tend also to be quite good at others. The idea that a child who excels in school is not going to fit in socially later on in life is a myth. A child usually does not excel in order to compensate for a weakness in a given area. Rather, the child who is doing very well in science or music is probably quite capable in languages and math, relative to other children. Children's abilities tend to go together, and smart children tend to be socially adept. While it is true that some school environments put pressure on children not to do really well, and in these settings the peer group may actually require poor school performance as a prerequisite for belonging, when the school environment fosters mediocrity and peers apply pressure against developing the mind, parents do have choices. One is to remove their child from that context and to place him in an environment in which value is placed upon the development of mind. Another is to try to change the context at the school while supplementing it at home or through other special events.

Chapter 2: What Intelligence Is

How to Use Test Scores

Let's assume that your child is doing quite well in school, but in one or two areas of the year's end achievement test there is a drop. Let's say that abstract skills, which are involved in the formation of concepts is one such area. What are your options? You may just accept this feedback as part of Joey being Joey. Perhaps he is just not that intelligent in that area. Or, you may ask yourself what kinds of supports have been presented to him over time to foster growth in that area. You may want to structure experiences for each test area that seems low and to build into them patterns of social interaction that are supportive at home. Do not worry about the score but use it as feedback about the context of that intelligence. *Don't be fooled into thinking that this is the way your child is.* He is that way for very good reasons, some of which you will begin to see more and more clearly. Remember what the child has or does not have in the head is a function of what is or is not in the environment that interacts with your child over time. This means that as a parent, you need to see yourself first as a designer and then as a gardener.

What you, the parent, need to realize is that a child learns all of the skills which make up intelligence. The more children learn, the better they learn how to learn. It's like the "rich getting richer" saying. Intelligence is made up of a number of skills that we value and that relate to doing well in school. Obviously if you do well in school, you usually do well in society, and that process is called adapting to the environment. People who adapt are usually very productive, make money and occasionally contribute to society in very significant ways. It's curious how some people are judged to be very smart according to these tests, and yet they are not really well adapted. Although, such a situation represents the exception, there are some persons whose intellectual development is great, but their socio-emotional needs are not well met, thus creating an imbalance that makes really smart people act dumb. For example, recall the part that Dustin Hoffman took in the movie "Rain Man." Have you ever heard of an idiot savant? Savant is French/Latin for being wise or a whiz, exceptional talents can exist even when other key areas have not been developed, but unbalanced skills are not part of being intelligent.

If you discover a cure for AIDS but you have a drug dependency problem, then are you really intelligent. You may be intelligent about AIDS related science, but if you are harming your own body or others, having a high I.Q. score does not make you intelligent.

WHAT INTELLIGENCE IS REALLY ABOUT.

Intelligence is a process, not a number on an I.Q. test. It is a process that occurs between child and environment. The child is already intelligent but he requires an intelligent environment or context in order to develop his potential and to manifest it through performance. If the environment in the home over the years is responsive and intelligent (in helping the child to adapt and to learn about the world), then the child's mental growth is advanced, and is considered to be accelerated relative to children's mental growth when raised in average or poor environments of other family contexts.

The average level of intelligence is much less than half of what it could be if the ideal conditions were provided by parents. This is why helping your child to become superior is not that difficult. When parents are sensitive to the child's interests and current level of development in any one area, they can match experiences to that level.

They can provide guidance that is attuned to zones of development (ZPD's) that the child is about to reach. When this match happens a lot, day in and day out, it accelerates the child's intelligence relative to other environments that may not. Hence the key is working with the child at the "cutting edge" of his knowledge. If your guidance is not matched to this cutting edge, it is like missing a wave in surfing. You may think that you are doing a very thorough job of showing the child how a concept like gravity works, but if the help is too far back or too far ahead of the child's developing concepts, little progress is made. But if your input matches the child's unsure notions about what something is, or how something works and sheds some strategic light on the subject, acceleration occurs. The child catches the wave. The wave is one of many in the sea of science or political science. The more waves the child catches, the greater the expertise. The parent helps launch the surfboard, which is the child's mind. The distance traveled is how much is learned and how many connections are made. The child returns next time more ready and motivated and with a sharper mind. If you routinely miss the magic moments when the child is ready to understand further in any one area, then days, weeks and months can go by before certain relationships are discovered. When the general patterns of interaction in the home make for frequent "matches," the child's mental development rides the wave and acceleration and enrichment occur. This means that the child has clearer notions about the world and can adapt to it better, as in school or on tests.

When the parent's inputs and responses coincide then with the child's "almost there" concepts and skills, a pattern of intelligence, or a field of intelligence, is created between the two. This field of intelligence, if maintained, leads to genius or what is considered exceptional. It matters not how old the child is, nor what is learned. What matters is how learning opportunities are formed day in and out. What proof is there to support this view? All research on the home environment and intelligence support this view in different respects.

The Child-Parent Interaction Study

Let's take a study with elementary grade kids and their mothers who were asked to work on some problems together. *This study was designed by the author to*

Chapter 2: What Intelligence Is

examine how high and low achievers differed in their interaction style with their parents. Some parents had a style which was distant and removed from the child. They just let the child go to it. Others seemed similarly distant but helped the child when asked. While still others seemed to sense how much their children knew and mostly helped out when they felt the children needed certain inputs.

Other parents interacted with the child a lot and tried to do the problems themselves, while showing the child. Finally, some parents interacted a lot but were not able to show the child that much. Which of these are you most like? Which of these parental strategies was most helpful? According to the study, mothers who had the highest achieving children most where those who:

a) held back, studied what the problem required,
b) understood what their children knew already, what they were currently learning, and what they did not know.
c) selected a strategy which focused on what the children were learning that was relevant and the things that they needed to know to solve the problem.
d) used praise a lot and let the children try to figure things out.
e) were not judgmental or uptight if the children could not respond right.

These parents interacted with children intelligently. Their interaction style in the study was close to what it had been at home over time. As a result, they tended to have the brightest children. They connected with their children precisely in the area between what the children already knew and what they were in the process of learning. (In theory, this area is called the zone of proximal development (ZPD)). They prompted the children to recall or to pay attention to certain details. They asked open and closed ended questions, that is questions that stimulate thinking that guide children's strategy and that may have more than one answer or a simple yes or no response, so that the children could think along with them. Humor was prevalent. (An example of an open ended question would be as simple as "What is missing in this picture?" and an example of a closed ended question would be "Isn't that right?").

Certain styles or patterns of interaction or communication which are on the cutting edge or ZPD lead these children, over time, to learn and to develop more fully than others. When ever parents guide and regulate their children's minds (a computer that it is) intelligently, targeting that zone of development (rather than harping on the obvious or expecting the unlikely), you find smart kids.

The Maternal Verbal Guidance Factor

I should also note that high ability children and their parents had a good relationship. They did not argue or fight over the task presented. The mother expressed confidence in the child and left him alone until help was needed. Unlike other parents who tended to take over, these parents of sharp kids knew when to back off and when to provide cues. These results suggest that the child feels secure and has a positive self-image going into the school related tasks. The mother guides by monitoring closely the child's responses. She also provides lots of encouragement and reinforcement.

In short, it is quite easy to tell from the way parents interact with children how well they are doing in school and how well these children are developing their intelligence. Parents who can establish a common psychological space with the child and who anticipate what the child might need next are the most successful. This process requires practice and intelligence on the parents' side, something which you are doing now by becoming informed and intelligent.

Divorce and Intelligence

At present, we know that sometimes divorce causes children to get depressed, and to lose interest in school. If they lose interest or their will to learn, a lot of the prior investments in mental development can be endangered. Certain conditions need to be changed for the child's intelligence to continue to grow. The main one is to reduce parental conflict at all costs. Even if you can't stand your ex, cooperate and do it well for the sake of the children. Use your ex for your child's sake. The second point which goes along with this admonition, is that the child needs to maintain thecognitive support system which ultimately depends upon emotional support.If your ex did not provide much in the cognitive domain (such as challenging the abilities of the child and guiding him), then find other channels. The biggest challenge for the single parent is to fill the void of emotional support. To do this, the single parent needs help. Get it and use any and every resource to keep delivering to the children the emotional or affective "supplies" needed to maintain motivation. In some cases, children perform just as well in school after a divorce, and they can even find constructive ways to deal with stress. These children are intelligent and resilient, meaning that they have the coping skills needed to survive in life. Typically, this means that you have been doing a very intelligent job of parenting all along, which involved being rational and logical with the child.

Why is it that some children of divorce do less well in terms of intellectual achievement and grades, while others do extremely well? This is often the case because school represents the only stable, positive aspect in their lives which is not undergoing disruption and parental conflict. To understand the relation between divorce and intelligence one simply needs to consider the child's stage of development, his socioemotional needs and the kind of family atmosphere around him. If parents fail to resolve issues for long, extended periods and do not stabilize their personal lives, then the children are at risk. At risk because they are learning incidentally from parents about problem solving. More importantly, if a child's socioemotional needs are not adequately met, these needs can and will interfere

Chapter 2: What Intelligence Is

with learning. Learning is the engine of intelligence and development. Yet, the child won't be able to learn well if his self-esteem is threatened, or if he feels insecure.

Parental conflict and animosity tear up children and usually teach them poor problem solving skills. Yet, parents who handle such difficult situations with reason and consistency teach children effective skills. Divorcing parents need to attend to children's stages of development and not get caught up in their own melodrama. An eight-year-old child of divorce needs to be handled differently from a thirteen-year-old. How differently? Here are some guidelines.

Before adolescence, children need to feel capable in undertaking little projects. They need support in constructing and arranging things such as, in producing and interpreting music and shows. They need to be actively engaged in projects that support their sense of mastery, as opposed to feeling inferior or useless. Once they feel good about things, they can do well. Their self-concept begins to change during puberty. As they mature physically, sexually and mentally, they need to depend less and less upon parents and to move on to peers for figuring out who they are.

Early adolescence is marked by concerns about one's identity and the transition of shifting one's focus from parents to peers. So peers help the divorce process at this stage, since it is a natural and normal transition to define oneself in terms of peer feedback. This is why divorce is tougher on younger children, as they have fewer coping skills and opportunities for intimate support.

Children are not satisfied by parent's definitions as to who they are. They need to break away from parents' definitions, and this is why many rebel. They rely on the peer group temporarily to "borrow" an identity, marked by clothes, music, speech and other props. Parents tend to misunderstand and antagonize their teens which means they cannot continue cultivating their child's intelligence as well as they might if they still had a good relationship.

Understanding intelligence

As we have seen in the previous section, intelligence is made up of different abilities that come together in adapting to today's world. Some of these abilities are heavily influenced by verbal skills, others are advanced more through exposure with problem solving activities that require coordination of verbal, perceptual and motor skills. Yet, every aspect of intelligence is enhanced by certain types of social interaction that teach, directly or indirectly, new things to a less advanced, younger person. (Age quotient).

The child, of course, will discover and learn considerably on her own but perhaps not enough or quickly enough to stand out. Smart children have smart environments where there are ample opportunities and routines to develop existing skills into higher levels across ability areas.

We need to understand that intelligence is a dynamic entity that is in a state of flux, processing various kinds of information and forming specific skills for new learning. (If all parents were to understand and act upon this principle, new tests would have to developed).

Two Types Of Intelligence
There is a zone around each child's intelligence that is different from any one else's. The zone is not only made up of what has already been learned but rather of new concepts and skills that have not yet been quite fully developed. The child is always ready for new kinds of experiences and outside guidance to be delivered from the environment in these zones.

When this match occurs, it is usually through parental verbal directions, questions and interaction that are focused on the child's ever changing needs. Sometimes older or more advanced peers can be helpful. Yet, what is required is not an off and on, hit or miss, occasional match between the child's zone and the outside verbal guidance, but a consistant pattern of interactions.

Parents of smart kids are constantly and vigilantly attuned or sensitive to the child's current zone of development and continually serve as facilitators (or as go-between) for the child and the culture. They regulate the child from too much television and active in other activities, and keep them from aggressive or pampered company.

As we see, the issue here is not one of what should I teach directly to make my child very intelligent. It is one of learning how intelligence can be expanded by targeting, promoting, motivating, and engaging the child in conversations and activities that are relevant to where he is developmentally. This match can occur in math, science, music, history, art and many other informal areas. Below are some examples for children at different stages in different content areas.

Michelle is an average 3-year-old. Things that 2 year- olds know about this time are about 200 to 800 word meanings that stand for objects, perhaps scores of verbs that relate words to each other, and a few adjectives and prepositions. These tools help form concepts and make the world meaningful to the child. Most of what the child has learned came about indirectly, gradually and with little effort. The more Michelle knows about the world and words, the easier it is to understand what others talk about. Michelle may only understand 10% of what Mom and her older brother are talking about and she's forming guesses and hunches about what is going on and what will happen later. Her brother is asking for his allowance to go to the circus where there are these neat creatures like tigers, lions, cats, monkeys, elephants, and giraffes. Michelle's interest is aroused because the word cat and tiger are familiar. She now interrupts and rambles on about wanting to see cats with her brother. Mom says she's too young to go to the 'circus' with her brother etc... Now

Chapter 2: What Intelligence Is

Mom says she is not to go to the "seechus", (Michelle thinks it sounds like that) and Michelle insists, while not really knowing the definition of the term, " I want the seechus", or some term like that which is becoming meaningful. There are two levels of meaning going on here. One is that which parents attend to usually in terms of dealing with what can be or cannot be done, etc. The other is one that. Mom has just approximated, a new concept. The social interaction led to the making of a guess within a request and learning is taking place. A new concept is being introduced into Michelle's mind, and it has to do with animals, later it will include others attributes or things. Parents miss many of these golden opportunities and fail to see that the important thing is to reinforce that indirect learning process. The issue of going to a place or not is not exactly what is most important in this interaction. This is why harsh disciplinary practices like "get out of my hair" or "hush now" or even ignoring or changing the subject are not helpful for developing intelligence. Taking a little time and noticing the child's new attempts to come to terms with new ideas is important.

You could respond playfully like "OK, Mich, what are you going to see at the circus?" It is not difficult to help the child out with some feedback, especially with a positive tone and some strokes like, "That is very good". You are so smart in figuring out what a circus is. It's a place where... We will go sometime soon because you are so smart." The main thing is not to turn off any one learning opportunity, even if it means hassling with not developing a "spoiled kid." That is a different issue and there are effective ways of dealing with such problems. However, what is being suggested here is that the child be spoiled when it comes to knowledge acquisition, filling gaps in existing domains and using these every day opportunities to elaborate and bring out new gaps and matches in the child. The child's brain craves information, and new curiosities arise from stimulation. Learning at this age proceeds quickly. There are many gaps to fill. Verbal interactions bring these curiosities out, and children instinctively want some understanding and mastery over their world. Never deny the child the opportunity to become competent in a given endeavor, regardless of how insignificant or useless it seems. It is the process of knowledge acquisition, the habits that are formed, and the strategies that are developed which outweigh the content or outcome, (that part we often get hung up on.) The above general example is a micro process, so small and so routine that psychologists and educators have ignored such processes in their macro experiments. Micro processes are so simple that they are difficult to measure. So how do we know one home environment is more effective than another, or that one style of interaction is less stimulating than another? It is premature to say what is "the best" way to bring about super-learning. Yet, we know a lot about:

a) what not to do in parenting,

b) what parents of smart, talented and creative children tend to do. Below is a checklist that summarizes most of this information.

WHAT NOT TO DO
1. Do not hit, *spank or shake* your child. If you do, it should be directly related to a situation that is life-threatening and in which previous reasoning and milder measures have not been effective. Do not make a habit of spanking or scolding. If parents rely on punitive measures regularly, it shows mainly that parents are inept, and children's development is not seriously being considered.
2. Do not use imperatives that are harsh, especially when the child is trying to learn something. Statements like "hush up", "shut up", "go to your room or else", etc., as reactions to a child's question or request for information hinder learning. When a child asks "Why can't we do X or Y?", an explanation should be given that a child can understand. This is an educational process. Never use "don't be stupid",or "you're slow", or such other negative statements.Your tone needs to be kind not harsh.
3. Do not belittle or compare your child.
4. Do not threaten to withdraw your love if your child does not do what you want. Love is to be given unconditionally. On the negative side of some of the above parent behaviors show, we can see that some parents simply are not aware of how the mind of the child develops, how there is a need to make time for mental reflection based on trust.

Many learning problems stem from having children become impulsive. Other learning problems can stem from disorder in the family environment or lack of consistency. Children's computers cannot tolerate inconsistencies for long, particularly when these cannot be resolved. Children need to feel like they have some control or say in their lives. If you take away a child's initiative, his attempts to resolve inconsistent stuff become futile, and watch out. You are not being an intelligent teacher when you allow this. Think of the consequences.

PATTERNS OF INTERACTION HOLD THE KEY TO GENIUS
Certain patterns of interaction can be very powerful in developing your child's mind to the point that most would agree that it is exceptional. Patterns of parent child interaction are probably the most critical in establishing a mode or avenue whereby the child can access knowledge at any time or be shown how to get it. Such micro-environments of learning and learning-how-to-learn can advance the zones of proximal development (ZPD) very rapidly. When this happens on a regular basis, through a pattern of interaction in which the child participates, you will find exceptional children.

Chapter 2: What Intelligence Is

But exceptional or smart in what regard you might ask. Well, children become intelligent in whatever hunk of culture in which they are actively involved, like sports, science, crime, or art. If your child becomes active and likes a given mini culture, he can develop in it and internalize a lot from it. Music is one such example, as are reading and math, composed of a set of symbols and communication.

Avoid Having a Hyperactive Unbalanced Child

Don't try to get your young child's attention away when he is focusing on something. Avoid constant stimulation when the infant is observing something. Allow for touch and tracking whenever possible, be a facilitator. Later during the next couple of years, do not impose your agenda on the child, especially when the child is attending to some aspect of the environment. Do not yell at the child or over respond with a lot of verbiage. Play with the child.

Early on, children become very keen on tracking stuff, particularly after 6 months. They try to get into every thing and often parents try to call off their focusing. They will call her name, make noises, stamp their feet, anything to get the child's attention precisely when the child may be contemplating something. Relax and observe the wonder of the computer at work. Intervene when you have thought about what information the computer might want or need.

In sum, one of the best ways to start thinking about raising your child intelligently is by paying attention to the above key points, as these become expanded throughout the book. A good way to see how this works and how to develop your child's intelligence in a particular field is to look at the family histories of very intelligent folks. I will summarize some of these later on.

What Intelligence Is Not.

Intelligence is not a score. It is not fixed at birth or at conception. It is not like other physical traits that are inherited. It is not remembering a lot of facts. It is not reading at an early age. For speed in reaching milestones is often deceiving, unless the general pattern of family interaction that got the child there in the first place is observed. Intelligence is not just doing well on tests, that is, it is not always applied in the real world the way we know to measure it on tests. What is measured is just the tip of the iceberg. There are many skills and concepts that children already have mastered or are just about to master, that are not included in intelligence tests.

Children's intelligence can be grossly underestimated by not asking the "right" questions. There are certain areas that intelligence is applied to, like math, science, music or art. These areas are not intelligences, as some claim, that already exist in some DNA or genes in the brain. Rather, these are areas towards which a set of information processing skills can be applied.

Notice how I just substituted intelligence for the processing of information. That is, doing something with information gathered. To be considered superior, intelligence wise, you need not excel at everything. Einstein excelled at some things but not others, like organic chemistry. This means that intelligence exists within given fields or areas of activities that interact vigorously with the person. An individual is considered superior according to how she uses certain tools or skills in a field that poses problems or opportunities for new solutions.

So before going on, let's define the fields upon which intelligence can be applied in our late 20th century context. Intelligence is not found alone. It is based on patterns of thinking about things, of interpreting and learning from one's environment. Something as simple as understanding difference between 3:30 and 3:50, or understanding what is one half of seven minutes when cooking a frozen dinner, is noteworthy. Even as you encounter the word noteworthy, you may say inside of you " what is this word, I never use it and I don't see it much." Yet, your intelligence comes back and says to you (the operator) "look, you know a and b, so guess at what c is and see if it fits." This is an example of adapting to your environment, and the whole interaction is in your head. Yet, as a parent, remember that anything important that your child learns is due to an interaction between what is known and what is about to be learned. You play a key role in presenting what is to be learned at every minute and hour that you interact with your child. You can structure the learning environment, but this takes more than just buying an encyclopedia. What counts is what you do with it. How you use the tools that make one's intelligence.

Your speech has an impact on the child's thought and perceptions. This does not mean that you have to push or cram stuff into your child's head. Do it naturally, when the child is receptive, ready or motivated. Yes, often a child will let you know when it is time to master a new skill, word or concept. To parent intelligently, the better question may be "Are you ready?" Do it with ease, for there are plenty of opportunities once you establish an intelligent style of interaction at home. Think of these interactions as play.

Your child will set the tone. Your child will present the menu, and it is up to you to use it, to stretch it creatively. The key is whether you can see the menu. Can you read the signs? Sometimes the communication is non-verbal as when the child gets "fuzzy" because she is bored.

There are times when your child wants to play and learn and other times when she does not. Just like you and me, we are more ready at some points than others. This is called the Law of Readiness. There are different types of readiness as for reading, writing, and math problems.

FRIENDLY ADVICE

Watch for these teachable moments; when 2 minutes count for 2 days' worth of teaching. When your child is ready and you are too, take the opportunity to pick

Chapter 2: What Intelligence Is

up on what is of interest to the child. Think about how you can orient him so that a rapid advance in the development and mastery of a concept or skill can occur. So, what can you do? Spend time with your child co-discovering the world. Find out what typical books "Say" is happening at this time for your child, but do not take it too seriously. Notice what these books list as skills which should occur before and after your child's actual age, and try to see this activity as the tip of the iceberg. Your child is capable of what these cookbooks say, but also much more. The books are useful such that you can get a general idea about the direction that your child's development is headed.

Focus on those abilities your child has gained in the last 10 months and the ones that are about to be mastered. Get a sense of those abilities your child will have a year from now. If you want to focus on one content area more than others, go ahead. That is smart too. Show your child a lot of attention when important areas can be approached, discussed and advanced. Lose interest when they are not that important (such as baseball trivia). The child soon learns to think according to certain rules or guidelines. The child gets "the hang of" asking key questions, finding resources for a project (reference skills), or reading a map or set of instructions. Once he does this in one area or context, he becomes more confident when encountering other similar situations.

Yet, even trivia can be used to take the child further in a given field of knowledge, if you know how to make the connection. Be careful in your judgment. Remember for a long time to come, your child's intelligence will be a function of the intelligence in the home environment. Fortunately, children go out into the world, and they can surpass the home level under certain conditions. You can help create such conditions by working on yourself and learning more, just as you are doing now. You may be sensing about now that you need more input on how to teach or interact with your child intelligently. You are right. There are certain fundamentals that apply regardless of the child's age level. These are found in Chapter Five.

Formal and Informal Zones of Intelligence & Development

1. School is an environment to which the child must adapt. If the child adapts very well, then she is considered very intelligent. Right? So, being intelligent means that the child is advanced enough in formal zones or content areas so that adaptation is easy. The author's suggestion is that parents need to beef up these zones more than the informal ones, so the child gets the most benefit from teachers. School is another culture which requires development of certain areas or zones like the 3 R's, history, science and a bunch of other areas that form what we refer to as Literacy. To be literate, you need to know how to use certain symbol systems or tools. You know the main ones. Now there is even computer

literacy, as well as second languages in the curriculum. There are others, but most definitions and tests of intelligence are based upon these formal zones or areas of intelligence. Each one of these has zillions of details and can lead to very complex levels, the process resembles the layering of onion skins. We call the above zones: formal disciplines like logic, science, literature, history, music, art and many others.

The reason why they are called disciplines reflects back to the old days when the mind was thought of as unruly and primitive. Schools had the mission of "disciplining" it, so that the mind could develop further and further, (which is a negative way of looking at it). Children's minds are brilliant to begin with and programmed by nature to develop fully. Back in those old days, for example, education insisted on teaching Latin and Greek languages in order to discipline the mind. Such disciplines, it was hoped, could be transferred and science, math and other subjects would be learned more easily. That view has not proven productive. Of course, in your role as parent, you want to help in your child's mental development. You, the parent, need to be on the alert so that your social interactions support the child's development. After all, it is a competitive society. Giving your child an edge helps to qualify her for better classes, more advanced teaching, scholarships and a pattern that is helpful in meeting her potential.

2. School also represents a means of adaptation to the larger context. A child needs to master what schools offer so that they can improve and contribute to society in their own right. Since children are the future, we must realize that what our culture is able to do today is related to how formal knowledge was shared and used in the past. By enabling children through the sharing of all mankind's knowledge base, they can invent and solve problems that are beyond us today. Yes. Intelligence is also time relative. What was a genial accomplishment last decade is only a mediocre accomplishment a decade later. Figuring how to use the low lands for cultivation in Holland today is not genial anymore, but at one point in history, it was considered intelligent. The dike system led to new resources and surpluses, which in turn, made that culture more able to educate its population, thereby raising the quality of life for all. Formal education or schooling includes areas of mental development valued by the society. While informal education refers to areas that are not valued as much by society. For example, you can help to develop a very intelligent child who is multi-talented but does not specialize in any one area. However, this may not get her scholarships, as the knowledge is informal.

Chapter 2: What Intelligence Is

On the other hand, a child who, with very few resources, develops well in a number of areas may be considered intelligent, even if some skills are not recognized formally.

The bottom line concerns what the child does with her intelligence later in life, in adapting to different life situations and in contributing to society. Often, people who are considered geniuses because of what they have accomplished are those who have mastered several areas, both formal and informal, and who later, have brought them to bear upon a current problem. They think in creative, unusual ways when they discover brilliant solutions. Interestingly, these folks were seldom considered the most bright when young.

For example, d'Arsonval found a century ago that power can be generated by using the ocean's waters which have different temperatures. As vapor expands, it turns a turbine that produces kilowatts. Imagine the creative genius of this mind functioning in the 1880's when few knew about such a discovery much less had electricity. As parents, we must recognize these two forms of knowledge (formal and informal) and help children to make choices between them. Parents must also insure that children's innate love of learning does not get ruined by formal school based knowledge alone. On the other hand, parents can steer the child from things that are merely of interest but are not connected to formal knowledge. Perhaps helping children to discover connections between the formal and informal knowledge structures and to capitalize upon those connections would be parents' greatest feat.

For example, a child may be interested in catching butterflies. What could you do with this in order to apply what we are saying? When he comes to you bragging about his exploits, how can you respond wisely? Currently your child is quite concrete or nonintellectual with this activity, but, if you can show him just a couple of formal things, (like what a larva is, or explain metamorphosis), your 5-year-old may really turn on to a more scientific approach in play. You can help him classify things under formal categories. For example, by playing with an expression like "a snake is a reptile just like an alligator," you relate two examples of one class (superordinate category) and help the child to realize that it is not the other way around, that is a reptile is an alligator. You can also help your child to establish and to use knowledge seeking patterns (reference books, observation skills, questioning patterns) that might come in handy for other areas later on.

Intelligences Depend upon Cultures

By now, you have read and tried to interpret the term culture in dozens of ways. Sometimes it makes more sense than in others, but the point is, you are getting the hang of it, just like children construct meaning out of what you expose them too. This is precisely how you can gradually lead your child to different types and levels of learning. Notice that I am using the term culture, as if it were a yogurt culture, a germ culture where stuff multiplies and grows. Culture is not just a static entity, like the Latin culture or the German or Mayan culture. Such an entity is too big or *macro*. What I want you to see is how, even in a macro culture, there are a lot of smaller micro cultures, like the home, the neighborhood and the pre-schools. These microcultures, like the school that your child is actively involved in, soak up the larger culture. To put it differently, the macro culture is like an onion, with skin after skin representing various levels of culture. A recognized genius such as Einstein had cultures like these around him in which he interacted. He was raised with certain patterns that allowed and encouraged his mind to grow and become very informed (intelligent) about certain aspects of the world (fields, zones, etc.) He applied it in such a way that his intelligence became well known. He probably had a pattern set that made him see things through, a stick-to-it-ness that eventually transformed the world of science. Others are equally intelligent but do not demonstrate their knowledge due to the cultural niches which surround them. So, you see, it takes a certain coincidence between what is needed outside and what the person is intelligent about.

Intelligence resides in culture. That is, what is considered intelligence is one's ability to have and use skills and knowledge that are based on what mankind has discovered and achieved over time. That ability of the person to harness what is out there and to use it in novel ways is considered creative intelligence. It is only on the basis of what culture provides that new inventions and advancements can be made. Culture also has a lot to do with how a child learns to acquire knowledge.

Different Kinds of Intelligence

A lot depends upon how the person learns about what there is out there. There are different types of cultures which relate directly to what previous literature has considered different types of intelligence. For instance, there is a culture for music, a foreign language, science or art which serve to inoculate and incubate the developing intellect. Within each of these cultures, there are levels which range from the simple to the complex that actually develop parallel areas in the brain.

As the person masters each level, he is enabled to become more intelligent about a particular field. His brain structures become more complex to reflect the complexity in the outside world. You see, there is a parallel between what is in the external world of culture and what happens inside the mind of the person.

Many researchers in psychology believe there are three, or seven or many more intelligences in the brain. In reality, there are as many intelligences in the head as there are in society's cultures. The individual must first come to grasp what the external culture has preserved before she can make unique contributions and be considered intelligent. If a culture is intelligent in nine areas, then a child has nine types of intelligence to develop.

Getting Intelligence, Creativity and Giftedness Straight

The above terms often confuse parents. Some believe that a high I.Q. score is the definition of high intelligence, while others view motivation and the possession of a hard-work ethic as necessary for success in life. The word talent also enters into this confusion of terms. What is important for you to know is that these terms are all social constructions, and they involve the basic idea of being exceptional in some ways that are "good." Take for example a current definition of what is a gifted child: It is when intelligence, effort and creativity intersect in the person. This very popular definition is in a way a contradiction in terms, since popular belief is that one of the nice things about being intelligent is not having to work so hard as to become uncomfortable. Creative people are expected to not to have to expend great efforts to do well. However, creative people do often work intensely on something which may appear to the rest of us to be hard work. In actuality the creative person does not see this as hard work. Rather, it is interesting work and part of a disciplined pattern of self regulation which is rewarding to the person. In this book, rearing children in an intelligent way so that they can become talented includes some of these aspects: learning to motivate and to train work habits that lead to intrinsic motivation as well as cultivating creativity and intelligence which are defined as operating at high levels in a variety of areas like music, science, math or literature. Another popular tactic for defining intelligence is to examine a child's score on a test of intelligence or school achievement. A child who scores in the top 5% is designated intelligent. As you will see, this definition is also problematic. While this book will help get your child get into that top 5 percent, that is not how we define a child's intelligence.

The Problem with Other Books

I want to back track at this point and reiterate that other books emphasize the I.Q. approach to children's intelligence and give you a cookbook formula to upgrade their scoring on tests. These books lack a clearly articulated theory. Certainly there are books which provide guides to what your child should be doing at certain ages. But there is also a great deal of flexibility so far as even these guidelines are concerned. As you will learn later, how well your child performs intellectually is only one of two indicators about development. When you ignore the second type of development of your child, a lot of well meaning efforts miss the mark, and you can even 'turn-off' your child. Some books are written for gifted children. Parents are given suggestions as to what they can do for their special child but are not told how the child became that way. What these folks don't realize is that kids are already gifted to start with. Some children have the conditions that favor rapid development, others do not. This book has the intention of explaining how intelligence is developed from a well-grounded theory. In order to help our children learn, we should first be informed as to what type of learning is involved and what objective or goal it is serving. Complex learning depends upon language development and other symbol systems.

In sum, intelligence is not just a trait that your child has fixed in the head, but rather it is a process (in which you play a major role) that gradually becomes part of your child. Your child is already most intelligent. The key is allowing this mental development to reach its full potential by parenting intelligently. The patterns of interaction in the family and in the subculture that the child is born into influence the development of intelligence of various types. Social intelligence can be as important as book-type intelligence, for example. Some children respond better to one type of mini culture (e.g. mathematical) than another (e.g. musical). When parents respond and cultivate what the child is interested in, that is when intelligence can be seen as a process. The more intelligent the process between the child and you, the more likely it is that you will have a talented child.

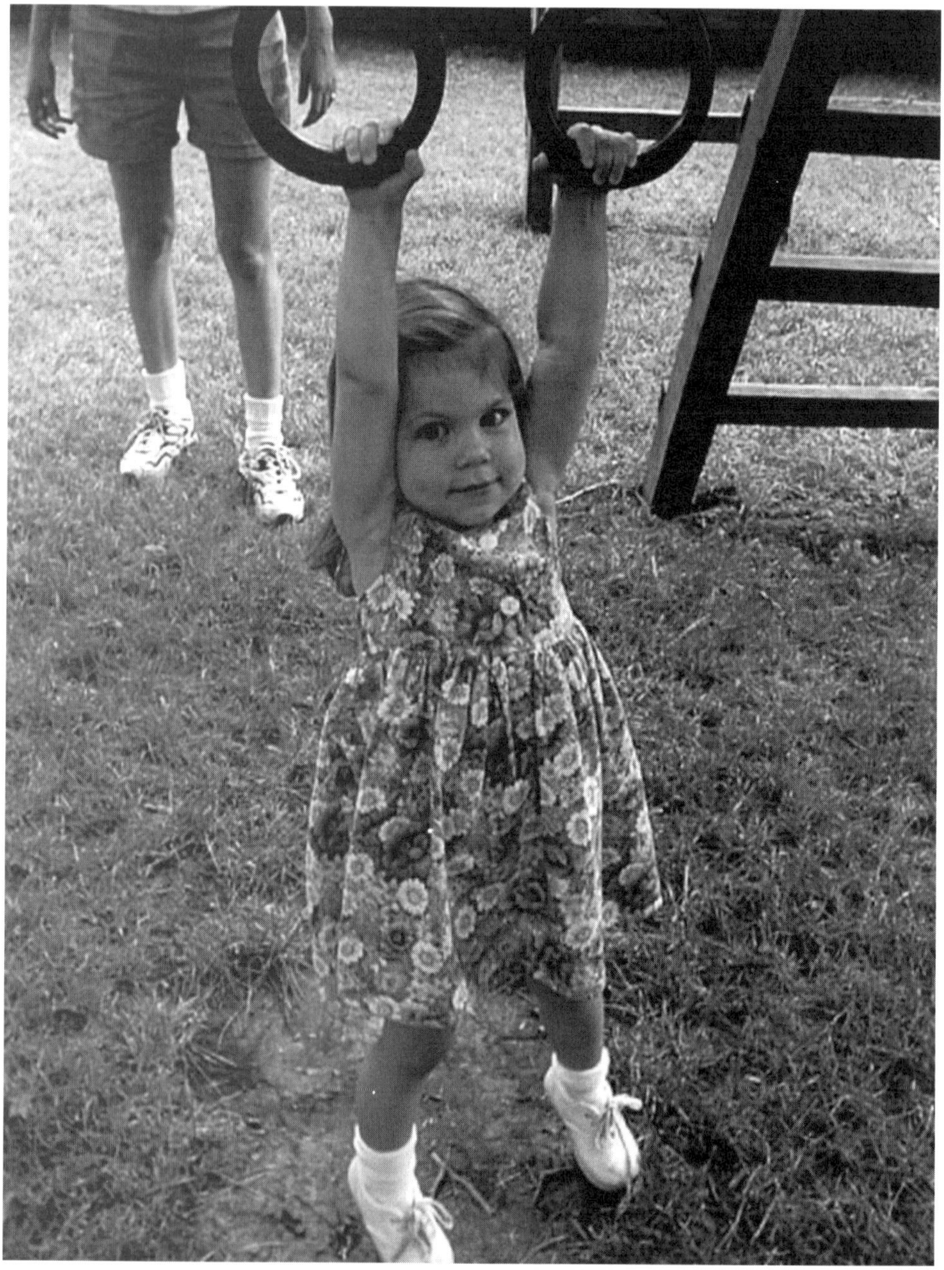

CHAPTER III

THE EARLY YEARS

"Development of the mind unfolds at the rate at which it is Started"

When that baby comes, your life is changed and you can't imagine or know how much. It is at this time that the parent's own intelligence is tried and tested, as well as demonstrated for the first time in the area of parenting. The odd thing is that, on the whole, parents have not been specifically trained to foster children's mental and social development. Without this training, it is easy to lose wonderful opportunities to make possible the full development of your child.

Parenting is a new area which is beginning to be recognized in the world's literature. Yes, it's finally being recognized as a legitimate area in academia. Unfortunately, the field is in its infancy and has not yet produced a comprehensive account of what works best in developing intellectual talents in the child (until now). Parents have never been prepared in the past to know the relations among language, social development, and intellectual development. Nor has the study of parenting produced a straightforward model that can account for simple things like: "How long should you let the baby cry?" or "How well are you picking up on the baby's signals?" For you see, even infants have a signal system which they use to connect with you.

It is essential for you to understand how to establish intelligent ways of interacting with your child and how to begin preparing an intelligent context for the coming years. After all, that is where intelligence comes from. Intelligence is "stationed" and acquired in dynamic, changing social spheres as well as within the child.

Each baby is different in the way she wants to establish a routine that parents can cope with. The baby goes for the maximum stimulation that can be handled, and she's often ready to interchange with you at some level. You need to engage your child to the greatest extent with which you both feel comfortable. It is not a question of "Gee, if I let him cry or stay away, he won't get the stimulation for his intelligence to develop". Wrong. The more you play and engage your infant child docsn't mean necessarily that she will be smarter. The important consideration is how well you learn to match your input to the child's desires. Such learning may begin when the infant cries and you figure out that movement helps soothe her. But, you get tired of holding and carrying her weight around the house. So you discover that, when this fussiness happens and you need to get her to sleep, putting her inside the stroller in the house and moving it over small bumps is a definite help. This simple adjustment, or one like usually keeping the visual field interesting, is an example of a pattern that parents use to establish synchrony with the child.

> ***This learning process of matching your input to the child's level may continue, as you detect special times when your child is most receptive to learning and you provide her with strategic guidance. Later, it becomes critical to provide for intelligent interactions with your child on a regular basis, particularly after age three. But your child is primed for maximum intellectual development only if the first three years have been full of love, and your child feels trust and security, and a sense of mastery and joy.***

Your baby's first drive, when awareness begins, is proximity, meaning that responsive folks need to be around. Without enough being near to caretakers, the child's basic security may be threatened, impacting upon certain personality traits, such as self-assurance which matters in developing intelligence. A fearful child doesn't stand to learn as much as a secure, confident child.

The above are examples of parenting styles that surely vary much over time. The important question is how well a home environment maintains intelligent styles over the years. In the long run, what counts is how well you engage the child, allowing her to participate with the world and to process certain kinds of information. The food of the brain is information, and how you use your interactions to cultivate key areas of development is very important, particularly in the preschool period. Some kinds of food (or concepts) are more useful than others perhaps, but how parents and tutors *relate* to what the child is interested in, and how they respond are most important. For example, the child might be asking about something that may not be considered useful. In this case, you have a child demonstrating a curiosity drive that can serve as a diving board to more useful concept formation and skill acquisition. What to do?

Remember, how you interact or say something is more important than what you say. Even with an infant, how you play with your baby is more important than what you play with. For example, during the first few months of life, your baby is not aware of how a tool like a bottle is related to feeling full and happy, yet soon he learns this. If you know when your baby is developing a type of concept like "bottle", you may play in ways that help connect the bottle with feeding, and so you facilitate development. Before three months, your baby feeds from a bottle but doesn't know what it is, that it is the instrument which provides milk. You know this because you can present her with a bottle at feeding time, and there is no attempt by her to focus on it. There is no reaction. When you take the bottle away, the baby does not cry.

Chapter 3: The Early Years

Only after the infant senses that it is not producing a sensation (that is sensory intelligence), and that the mouth has nothing to suck (motor intelligence), does the child begin to protest and cry. When you present the bottle visually at this age, crying goes on. Only when you put it in the mouth, back into the sensorimotor channel, does crying stop. Through such a process you can tell what is developing mentally and what is not.

How is it that the baby goes from not knowing that *bottle* is what provides that full belly, to the point at which she gets excited about simply seeing the bottle, because nourishment is about to come? The answer is developmental. Again, simple examples like the bottle one, can be used to demonstrate some points of infant development. First, the knowledgeable gardener knows that the baby is about to enter the stage in which grabbing stuff is made possible by physical maturation. By seven months, your baby is pointing to stuff to let you know he is already recognizing objects (which means memory functions are shaping up). As soon as the baby starts grabbing, then the connection between bottle and food can be made. Physically touching helps the child to develop a "pre-concept" of what a bottle is at a very basic level. She grabs the bottle, and into her mouth it goes (like so many other things). A stimulus-response bond is created. Then the baby notices that milk comes from that response. That response led to a reinforcement, so the child's mental computer makes a note: "Some things (that look like, taste like feel like) lead to nourishment and others do not."

A tree grows with an increasing number of branches over time, just like the human mind. Trees of knowledge form in the child's mental structure which serves much like a note pad. Branches of data get connected and expanded and drawn out on the note pad, as new things are discovered.

Also, a new strategy with which to interact with the world is born. Now the baby can go around testing and collecting data for her mental computer with the new strategy (or game or scheme if you like). Parents who play by allowing their children to self-feed and to see and to touch the bottle and to make the connection explicit have children who differ from those of parents who take full control of handling the bottle themselves, but in what way? One child's mental development gets to the concept of bottle a bit quicker. Yes. But, that doesn't necessarily make one child smarter than the other. The important consideration is to look at the pattern of interaction, and to project what it may lead to, if continued over time. Two years later, the first child is being allowed to experiment and to play with all kinds of things around parents who are patient. The parents routinely take the opportunity to add to the child's interaction with first one thing and then another (or what is known collectively as the world). The other child tries but has parents who handle it differently. They make it less easy for the child to input data into his brain because they tend to say: "Leave that alone," or "Come over here," or "Your brother doesn't do that." All this represents the parents' efforts to maintain control rather than to turn it over to the child. Descriptions of this type help to explain why intelligence seems to be fixed early on. Patterns get established very early through parenting styles, and they determine how much of the world or culture is delivered or mediated to the child.

By age three, the child from the first environment knows about plants, birds and earthquakes... and the child from the second family environment knows half as much. Such knowledge can be tested and expressed as I.Q. scores. And you know what? These scores become predictive of the next test scores two or four years later. Yet, you should notice that what was is measured really is not the kid's intelligence but, rather, the kind of garden in which the child is being raised. That is, intelligence at this point is best found outside and around the child, and this mental development depends on family context. The knowledgeable parent notices that the child's mental growth around 6 months is such that the baby won't search for the bottle when it is out of view. Yet at eight to ten months, the baby will search for things that the parent has hidden before the child's very eyes. "Glee. There it is again." "Let's peek-a-boo some more," thinks the infant as skills are mastered. What does this imply for parents?

Why do babies delight in peek-a-boo games? The answer is that they are making a transition during which they go from inferring that "This only exists if I see or sense it" to "This can exist, go away, and a new but similar one comes back, wow." They delight in this magic. They are amazed. It is as if they saw a Martian appear and reappear time and again. Their minds are slowly getting the picture that things exist outside them, but within the reach of their senses. So you can provide games in which the baby sees a pacifier (a binky or a nuky) in the process of being covered by a diaper and partially within his reach. First, it is mostly uncovered, then more and more covered until it is hidden. Through the progression of lots of games like this, you will help to establish the teaching relationship and style needed for your child's future mental development.

Infant Intelligence?

> **Some books try to get you to accelerate and to press your baby into doing drill-like routines and exercises which supposedly will accelerate a number of school related skills. Some books suggest that parents should follow the steps of a strict program in which one year olds are taught math concepts, for example. Most basic skills in the first two years come naturally with age and common sense anyway. The point is: why bother with investing your time in low-pay-off activities when you could be doing better things, like learning how to avoid the criticism trap or how to encourage motivation.**

Chapter 3: The Early Years

Infant "intelligence" is a misnomer, and refers to a set of sensory motor abilities that are largely fixed by biological and pre-natal conditions. No need to push this type of development, simply love and be there for the child.

Many books advocate concrete formula devices to make babies intelligent. The idea is that the sooner children are exposed to and respond to certain test situations, the smarter they are and will be later. Such an approach is problematic because "infant intelligence" actually refers to a baby's sensory-motor responses and biological machinery. It implies that the hardware of the brain computer is in a functional, operational state. This is not intelligence, according to this author, because intelligence has not been born yet. Rather, the brain computer demonstrates sensorimotor reflexes and activity levels that form the basis for intelligence later on in development. This so-called intelligence is based upon abilities like tracking an object visually, reflexes like crawling, expressing emotions, or turning the head and opening the mouth when something brushes the cheek (rooting reflex), making a connection between a response and a consequence, and many other examples. These abilities are "givens" with normal infants, and, except for gross differences due to organic defects, like Down's Syndrome, Tay-Sachs disease, Sickle Cell disease or other problems causing brain abnormalities (such as drugs or injury), do not have a direct relation to later intelligence. Babies' activities come from raw bundles of nerves which require time for maturation before actual concepts of the world are developed in the mind.

During the first few months, parents can use the few built-in schemes babies have to focus the child on building sensorimotor connections like the grabbing of a bottle example from above. Through such activities, the child's attention span and response patterns can be tapped into, thus making the child's learning pleasant.

Learning to learn at this stage is more important than what is learned. Drilling children with letters and numbers or colors is of little use, especially if the child is not too keen on it. However, the pattern of interaction used daily may help the baby to respond sharply, to focus attention and to be alert. These are basic elements in developing the intelligent mind's information processing capacities. Without interaction, and synchronized communication, many skills which would lead to intelligence stay underground or begin to develop only to wilt later. Yet, the speed in reacting to external stimulation and the sheer quantity of stimulus-response activities are by no means a determinant of later intelligence, although both help.

What matters is how well the quality of interaction is maintained and attuned to the particular needs of this maturing child. Infant intelligence, as measured by reaction time and sensorimotor response patterns, is not related at all to later intelligence. What is predictive is the kind of mental supports the child has down the road of development. You, as a parent, are one such support. This means that a child who has lots of positive, loving interaction most of the time develops a better, more fertile garden to develop the mind than one who has not as much.

The First Year

The baby needs to be responded to actively and consistently. Perhaps the reason why some children seem slower is because they are taught to be passive. Parents who fail to respond to infant behaviors regularly, or who deal with crying by ignoring or restraining the child too much, or even by tranquilizing the child through medication, may engender a passive learning style later. If you get used to sending a message to your child that "you are not that important," "you don't deserve to have that," ...etc, then you won't most likely have an intelligent child. Because you are not meeting the basic conditions that are required for intellectual development. Some parents worry about other types of problems that might affect intelligence.

What about slight birth defects that can pass for being in the normal range? For example, what if the baby required resuscitation after birth because oxygen was cut off for a very short time? Or what about the use of drugs during delivery which afterwards caused the baby to be slow resulting in the use of other drugs to counter the effects of the first drug used? Couldn't these problems cause a child to seem dull, although he may still function within an accepted norm? Unless the above problems were extreme, the answer is that a child is probably not harmed mentally by these occurrences in the long run. Unless the damage impacts upon the brain's basic functions and/or it stays with the baby over time, like malnutrition or hunger, there is no strong evidence that these slight birthing problems cause significant intellectual damage. There is a lot of evidence which suggests that children are so resilient that they can make a great comeback, even after a bad start in the first year. As the child grows, however, it is not easy to bounce back unless the environment changes for the better and stays that way. This requires good parenting. For instance, Joey was premature, needed oxygen at birth and was incubated. During the first year, development was a bit slow and so was learning. However, after age two or so, Joey caught up. Both parents spent lots of fun playtime and talked a lot to Joey. In first grade, his performance was excellent. But by 4th grade, the parents were fighting continually and divorced shortly thereafter. This family disruption of parent-child interaction interfered with the excellent pattern of mental development that was going on and placed the child on a different track or level. His former parent-child interaction was in the top 10%, but afterward Joey was placed in a "very unproductive garden." In this new place, few plants were tended, and his potential for being exceptionally smart was stunted by inconsistency and irregularity in the interaction patterns that defined the cognitive environment.

The divorce did not cause this problem per se, rather it was how the parents handled it. Joey's mental development could have gone the other way, if only the parents had known what were the key things that influence the child's intelligence. Even in intact homes some parents do not expect much intelligence or talent, for whatever reasons, and they devalue the context... ruin the garden... lower the "yield" of the garden which represents the child's potential talents.

Are Nurseries bad for your child?

Since the 1950's, parents have been concerned about the effects that leaving their children in nurseries or day care may have on development. Of course most parents have to work and leave their young ones with someone else. What every parent fears is leaving a child with 10-15 other children and only a couple of adults. When these other adults are not that knowledgeable about our topic, the potential for problems is great. One-on-one interaction is not as likely to occur, and when it does happen, that interaction may be of a less strategic type as compared with that which involves an informed parent at home. What matters is not so much how many adults to how many children, as what actually goes on or does not go on. After all, some children do not have that much more at home than they get in a nursery. What you, as a parent, need to look at is how much is being delivered, when and how. Psychologists are only beginning to understand the minds of infants. For example, infants and toddlers have one main concern besides food and sleep, that is, they want to be close to you. They will smile and act cute so that you will stick around and help them to survive, and so that you will show them stuff to learn. Children are built for social interaction, to discover new things and to respond joyfully. Yes, this means that if you have to err, do so by being lenient. It is far better to spoil the child than to have one who is shy and afraid of constant and loud "no's."

Up to age 2, the child has yet to develop the foundations on which learning from a rich environment can make a huge difference. Concept and language development must still intersect fully. So as long as the nursery, extended family, or parents provide for warmth, love, and active stimulation, there is little to worry about. Young children will thrive, because they are born gifted. The rate at which things are presented to the child and the style in which stimulation is provided in sensitive ways and matched to where the child's mind "is at" are the factors that most matter. But after age 2, the child can profit even more from social interaction from sensitive care-givers. That is because the brain is now more ready to learn new "stuff," if it is there to be learned. The infant can be presented with a lot of interaction, and the child can only profit so much from it. With maturity, the child is ready for more, and the style of interaction becomes increasingly important. In the final analysis, most nurseries provide about as much as typical or uninformed parents would in the home. Neither context operates very well for children in general. The reason is that neither context is informed enough about child development. These settings have instituted a pattern that is not well designed for the development of intelligence. Sure, these contexts work, and so we have average contexts producing average kids, but this consideration is relative. It is not average in terms of the potential that is locked out. Don't settle for what there is. So as a parent, go for it. Design a more intelligent context or garden for your babe, and she'll be glad you did. Most likely, you are probably doing about 20% of what you could in this area. This is why most of us are only using that much of our mental capacity. If you know what the child's mind is like, it is more important to provide prime time social interaction after age two than before.

For example, at age 1, the memory capacity of the child is not yet developed, he knows about the world but mostly through what is being sensed. Sensation comes before perception and then comes thinking. Children before age two do not think much. Thinking requires language, and language has to develop in it's own right. Language has it's own sequence which is universal. Together, both thinking and language form the mind into developing channels, or mechanisms with which to pick up intelligence "out there" and to represent it in the head. We must remember that intelligence is defined as a composite or combination of information-processing abilities and knowledge which allows for full adaptation and utilization of the environment. During this period, intelligence is being developed so that it can absorb complex data, and in so doing, it becomes transformed by what it encounters. In short, intelligence isn't yet, rather it is in the process of becoming.

What then Should Parents Do in the 1st Year?

Relax and concentrate upon the emotional well being of the child. Make him feel loved and secure, and play. Don't push or try to give your child an "edge" by over-stimulating him. The child's main task is to establish trust in you regarding meeting basic needs. With that under control, the child can prepare his brain for higher level learning a little bit each day. Parents should relax and revel in the joy of having a brilliant being, who is just beginning to develop talents. Be responsive and consistent, but there is little advantage to cultivating the mind, for the mind is not yet ready for you. The seeds are barely sprouting future talents. Provide security and also a sense of trust, so that the child feels in control and good about himself. The best you can do is to work on yourself. Read, discuss and learn so that you are more intelligent yourself about parenting. Work on knowing how to provide an interesting environment for your child. Concentrate on finding and developing resources for when it counts most, starting in the second year when language and you, through language, begin to activate the mind. Intelligence interacts with language which allows for expansion of the brain. Thus, the most malleable period for intelligence is after the first couple of years when language "kicks in" biologically. Through this breakthrough, which is part of our human endowment, the child becomes exposed to culture. Only then does intelligence begin to develop. Until then, the development of the brain is programmed biologically for the most part. The type of garden or context you'll provide (that makes most of the difference) is not programmed so.

The infant requires a normal amount of stimulation and nutrition at first. Speeding up development during this period does not mean that a child's intelligence later will be higher. In short, infant intelligence does not predict later intelligence. In psychology's way of defining and measuring intelligence, we do not speak in terms of something which implies or predicts something else. However, how parents behave early in their child's development does predict how they will act later on and how much their child's mind will be developed. Parental behavior early on tends to perpetuate itself, and this behavior pattern affects the type of garden which the parents provide.

Establishing a Parenting Style

The author's point, as noted earlier, is that the term infant intelligence is misleading, since it does not really mean intelligence, but rather sensorimotor "normality" of a limited number of functions. For example, a four-month-old cries when hungry. He is presented a bottle most of the time. Still, he can't connect the bottle with feeding. He looks at it without realizing that bottle is what gives the full tummy feeling. The brain of an infant is immature and can only process 1% of what there is, since the tools for processing have not yet been made available. So what happens is that reflexes like smiling, grasping and sucking are randomly connected with all sorts of things. Most of these connections are forgotten, for memory hasn't yet developed. But a child's sense of security and trust is being shaped. Don't neglect or abandon your babe. This does not mean parents are helpless or incapable of preparing for an intelligent child. On the contrary, they can do a lot. Not to the baby, but to themselves and to the environment which they are building. The home environment is like a launching pad which directs and propels development. Parental focus should not be solely on preparing for physical types of conveniences like toys, but rather on focusing informational and affective supplies which means becoming and preparing a responsive, intelligent environment for the child. For example, parents can learn how to use different games regularly to support their child's development. Consider the patterns you will use as the child seeks intelligence about this world. Your child is born with the will and potential for mastering what there is in a short time, if you help. In the first couple of years, the child is getting the equipment ready for higher intelligence to develop. During this period, the baby is achieving rapidly what it took humankind to develop over many, many centuries at the sensorial and motor level using very simple, animal-like intelligence.

Once language develops, and other symbol systems, the development of higher intelligence takes off rapidly. However, to stress the point once again, the foundation of the prenatal and infancy years is very important. The infant needs to feel capable of exerting control over the environment by getting your attention or getting fed. You would think that this competency seems natural and automatic, yet some children learn to be helpless instead, because parents don't allow for this simple behavior pattern.

Later, parents who have provided for this exerting control competency can use it to orient the child towards learning. For example, in one strategy, the child is allowed to exert control when learning is taking place but not in other settings. So for the first year, start communicating with the child. Remember, you, as a parent, have the time to learn more about encouraging and teaching, because the child's development is on automatic. Just don't interfere with the child's need for security by having conflicts at home or by giving too much or too little stimulation. Be responsive, happy and enjoy the gift for now. Provide lots of approval but make the child be active too. The trick is to turn over ownership for learning to the child, responding to child initiated behavior is caring and informative ways. Remember, information is what the child thrives on below the surface. The child wants to know why, when and why not. Know that you have their attention, play and add to the information banks...

Common Sense Stimulation

Provide mobiles so that the child can regularly track stuff moving. Talk to you child while in the kitchen or the bathroom. Haul the baby to where you are so that he can watch you. He needs to pursue sensory objects and people over and over again, until a trace is developed in his head, and then to move on to another item. The infant starts by recognizing the mother or whoever has been tracked the most. Start varying the toys you use. Let the baby play alone when possible.

Encourage independence and time alone, to track stuff visually, as well as contact time with others the baby can also learn to trust and recognize. Recognition means to think again about X out there, because it has been experienced before and coded inside the mind. Repetition is crucial at this stage. When infants seem to recognize you and derive joy, the process of mastery in representing the world in the head is beginning. Recognition means that the baby has finally etched a symbol or a concept in the head and smiles or wants it. This means that a simple skill, like that of putting things that exist out there in the world inside the mind, is finally taking place. The implications are awesome. The tough part comes later, when the child acts with and manipulates these etchings mentally. This skill comes about usually by the end of the second year. Play is very important for the development of intelligence and self-esteem. It provides a bridge for practicing what is learned and for consolidating new learning. Make sure to try these games, if you are not already doing so.

Chapter 3: The Early Years

The early months:

<u>1-2 Months</u>: Rattle games for baby's eye and ear, senses, like mobiles, crib or playpen gyms, or colorful pictures that promote baby's tracking ability.

<u>3-6 Months</u>: Tastes and chews to discover; supply toys or safe household items such as measuring spoons, plastic utensils & cups.

<u>5-9 Months</u>: Lap games for sitting such as pat-a-cake, the itsy-bitsy spider, etc… Games that engage your baby in hand and finger play; also start placing objects just beyond baby's grasp so she begins to reach out for them; and most important, provide a mirror for your baby's endless moments of enjoyment.

<u>6 Months and On</u>: Use language: talk in complete sentences, change speed and tone.

<u>7-9 Months</u>: Baby know-how: place a toy or other object on a blanket or towel and let your baby pull it close. Play peek-a-boo, hide-n-seek, and cover & discover games.

<u>8-13 Months</u>: The Creeper - Crawler: Play fetch games to encourage crawling; "fill'er up" games to teach space, volume; searching games with boxes; and provide baby with blocks.

<u>The "Stander" & Toddler</u>: Open jar with objects inside; let your baby/toddler play with old magazines to promote reading readiness.

<u>The Toddler (older perhaps)</u>: Guess which hand games; (hide) old shell game; quiet time language activity, reading with pictures, begin teaching body parts; provide container with many different shaped objects; play catch.

The Second Year

    From now on, you need to ask yourself some of the following questions: Do I know what my child is now capable of doing? Do I know what is going on inside her computer? What is coming up next? Do this now and every so often as a rule. To some extent, I'll show you how during your child's second year. Rule number one - there are no set standards for every year of your child's life. No one can tell you that "by age six, your child is supposed to be able to do a, b, and c, which he could not do at age five." Yes, there are some minimum levels early on, but these are biologically "wired-in" or automatic like walking. These are called milestones or developmental markers, for example, when your child learns to speak or walk. Yet, it is helpful to know what the norm is for a given age and what the child is able to do.

A general guideline is as follows: The child can learn a lot more than you think or can teach him. The best strategy is to think of parenting as engineering the launching pad, or as building a smart, responsive, informed context. What does this take? A lot of learning about parenting, how learning works, and teaching effectively. Parents need to understand how we learn, what we learn, to what extent and when we learn, and then to apply this knowledge and other aspects like motivation to the rearing of a child. Some do it almost accidentally. Sounds tough? Not really, it is actually a fun experience, because the funny thing is that you want to learn just as your child does.

Some say that all this parenting is not needed, that children grow anyway and always have, and that all this psychology stuff is not worth much. Well, that is just exactly the attitude we have had about children until just recently, and this approach has led to a lack of cultivation of children's intellects.

It is important that parents learn to become good teachers, although most teachers do not know much more than parents about how intelligence is developed. (Most teachers are not cognizant of this new learning theory. Rather they use behaviorism. I'll address this issue in a later chapter.) So back to age two. A very important development takes place. The child now has a mental representation of a lot of objects and processes things in the environment. She knows that the people around are stable, that the house pet is Rover, etc…

All that visual tracking your baby has done was mainly for the purpose of finding that objects are permanent. They do not and you do not disappear from the planet, when you are not there. A mental representation is left in the brain, but it has no name. It is a concept based on sensory or physical interaction. Children develop about 200 of these before they connect them with verbal labels from their particular culture. Also, by the end of this year they "know" that there are cause-effect relations such as: "This bottle will result in a full tummy," or "The dog barking means someone is coming here." This is why peek-a-boo games are so fascinating for little children. Infants begin to see the relation between their actions and outcomes. Later, they can think about what they have seen over and over again. Language now begins to help the child's mind to expand. Communication now is more economic and effective. So talk to her lots and respond to what she is trying to label. Guide her actions verbally. The child is transforming all that has been explored into more economic mental traces with which she can interact inside the head, not just out there. These traces are basic associations, for example, high chair - food, telephone-talk, or TV box -picture and sounds.

Chapter 4: The Preschool Years

Towards The Third Year

Your child's intelligence about the world now centers around those 200 concepts which the child knows about and that are in the head. Through lots of sensorimotor, stimulus response trials, the child has formed a representation of people, animal and things like the TV, bottle, water. These also include happy and crazy grandmas who go ape over the baby and, whom the toddler looks at and thinks: "Here is that adult who wants to eat me." (If you have ever watched the morning cartoon 'Bobby's World', you have a good idea as to the visuals young children can conjure up in their heads). The child also learns action-subject bits like "adults-talk, ball-moves." Now, he can't tell you that he knows these concepts and action verbs. But he spends the next six months matching the concepts to your language, and this process goes on and on for life. So you ask, should I confirm and reinforce these concept-matching efforts constantly, even when the child is only trying to get my attention? More on that later in the next chapter.

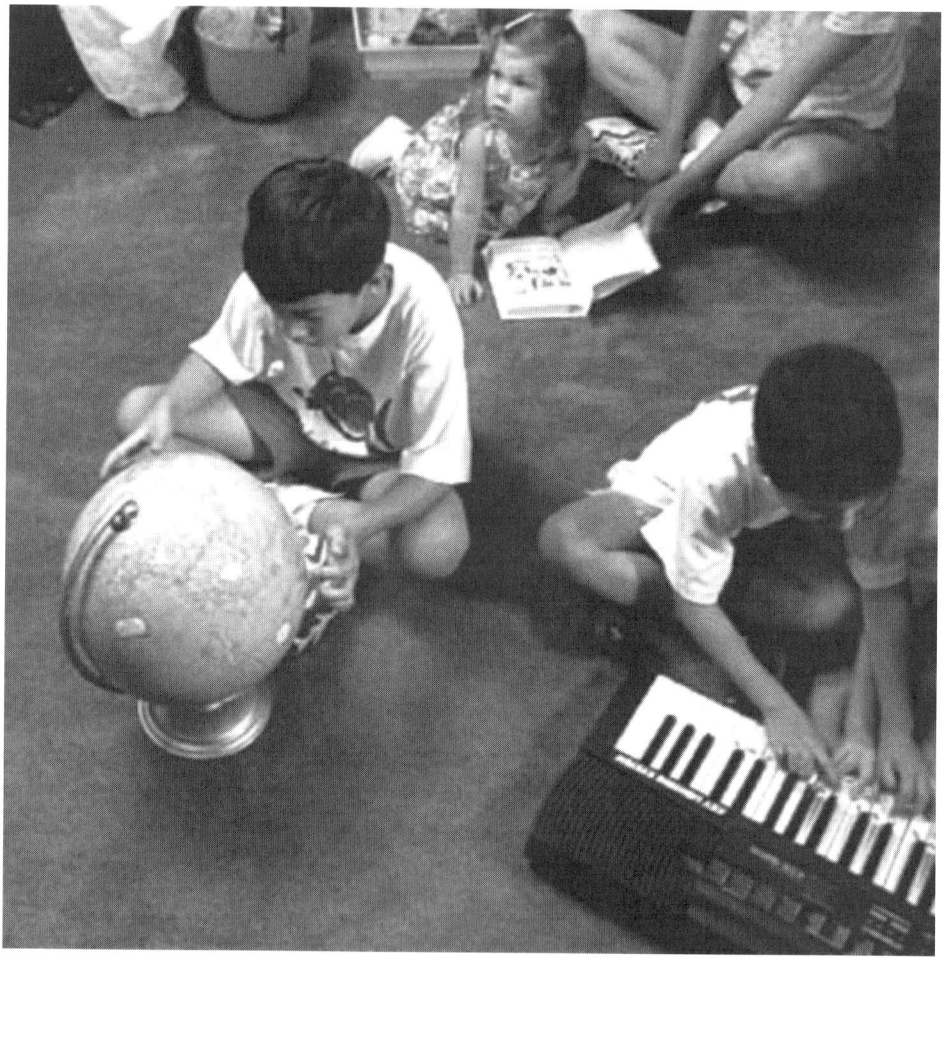

CHAPTER IV

THE PRESCHOOL YEARS

"The child's mind is like magic in action, unfettered by rules and limits. It is at this stage that intelligence explodes, and that which you have done as a parent establishes how well your child will adapt to the world".

THE PRESCHOOL YEARS: INTELLIGENCE IS BORN.

Certain concepts are important for parents to understand well during the formative years of intelligence. In this next section, more of these are discussed.

One concept which parents need to know about is habituation. Habituation means that a stimulus has become "old hat" for your child. You can tell that a child has stored and coded a new object by noting at what point the child gets used to the new entry (a kitty in the house for example) and no longer keeps responding to it. Infants spend the first year tracking new entries in their brain and slowly develop a mental representation of each and every object and action which they encounter. The new entry exists only when it is in contact with the child, who is busy collecting data. Eventually, the brain says enough and the child moves on to something else.

As the brain begins processing information, it directs and organizes the knowledge into various sectors, much as a computer assigns sectors on a computer diskette. The brain grows rapidly, and at first, you are well advised to foster it but not to overload it. Simply vary and reinforce new connections or associations in general so that the infant is attuned to them and finds fun. Once again ramming more and more knowledge into the computer (your child's brain) at this stage does not predict or guarantee that the child will be smart later on, especially in light of the larger sense of the concept of intelligence previously discussed.

During the first couple of years, respondent, social and stimulus-response learning occur all at the same time, the implication here is for parents to understand how the computer in the head of the child learns and develops new connections over time. An upcoming chapter (Chapter VII) will cover the four ways that children learn all they know. Be sure to read this carefully.

For now I will say that it is rewarding to follow how a child, through discrimination of two or more objects, develops a new concept of the world. For example, a three-year-old may think that "tall and big" are roughly the same thing. After the child sees 12 ounces of cola go into a tall, thin container and also the same amount is put into a short, wide one, he may be asked which of these containers holds the most cola. Most likely, at this age, the child will choose one container or the other. Only later, through discrimination, will each concept, tall and big, emerge separately. At this later point in maturation, when asked about which of the containers has more liquid, he will state that they are both the same.

Eventually, the child comes to understand that tall does not mean that there is more liquid. The amount of liquid in a big, shallow container is the same as that in the tall one. The child has been forced to adjust meanings mentally. Through your feedback, the child can make such transitions more easily. The type of intelligence which is more complex and capable of being accelerated is that which can be represented verbally. Once children begin to talk and to label objects and to incorporate these sounds into actions or sentences, then they can really move 3 to 5 times faster in developing higher order concepts. A 3-year-old child who can sound off a label in a communication with another person, as opposed to one who simply points to the objects or grunts any old sound, is a lot more likely to develop higher level ideas about the world.

Hence, verbal children tend to appear more intelligent when tested, for they show what they have etched in their mind or represented symbolically with words more easily than other children.

Once the child is ready, then make sure that labels are verbalized routinely. Don't settle for shy signals. Parents who emphasize discovery activities with verbal terms in everyday situations, thus, tend to have children in the upper tails of the intelligence curve. This performance helps to qualify them for typically more challenging educational opportunities which then allow for faster and more complete learning and a sense of confidence (special classes, e.g. gifted education).

Speech Codes

An English sociologist found something quite interesting concerning how parents talk to children and how this conversation impacts upon children's intelligence. Parents of slow learners use a style of verbal interaction that is curt, bossy and even abbreviated. Parents of high ability children employ a more wordy, elaborate code, using explanation and reasoning. This wordy style gives children more information per minute, per hour and per day. Children who can express themselves freely and who are told why they can or cannot do stuff clearly learn more. Those who learn more this way on a regular basis eventually learn faster. Children who are around 18-24 months have, in brief, developed not only behavior patterns (like tracking objects) that help to gather and to process information, but also a permanent register or memory of actions and objects in their immediate contexts, as well as notions about cause-effect relations. When the child's kitten, Bertha Motriz, disappears at night, the child still is aware that the kitten can exist without being next to the cat. By having sighted the cat, heard its sounds and felt the fur, the child now has a sensory-motor bond or connection literally etched in the brain. Seeing the mother cat leads to an expectation of seeing Bertha near by.

Learning is a physiological reality, when learning occurs, the brain changes, and even weighs more. Learning comes from the transformation of real, concrete activities into mental codes. When these are formed via the sensors of sight, sound, smell, taste and touch, they are connected with various external events and objects. Such concepts stay in mind over time and reflect basic intelligence (which at this age is simply a wide number and variety of coded information bits and the know how of affecting the environment to obtain stimulation). Verbal communication leads to real intelligence. Sensory motor intelligence is like that of smart animals which learn a lot from sensing and moving about (*motor*). A seven-year-old German Shepherd is smarter than a one-year-old in many ways. Yet, the child's capacity of understanding, emitting and developing speech is much more important in the real realm of intelligence.

The basic building blocks that are formed through sensory and motor experiences form what we call lower level intelligence. They define the first communication system of humans which is very basic. By gesturing, pointing or acting out ideas, we signal and receive simple information.

The second and most important aspect of intelligence involves the second communication system that is symbolic, verbally mediated and complex. Speech is not only to express thought or simply to communicate. Speech has other functions, including the role of helping guide thought and hence action. Through speech, the child can learn a lot faster and better than it is possible with only the first system. Notice that a dog can respond to a verbal command, but you can't teach it to do anything using words. In fact, the dog doesn't respond to the meaning of speech but only to the sound it has learned to discriminate and to associate with reinforcement. It is precisely this human second system of meaningful speech communication that allows parents to expand their child's intelligence once they understand it better.

Concept Matching

At first when a child is learning to speak, we can see how concepts are learned through their sensing and moving about the immediate environment. For example, the house pet, Sam, eventually gets "matched" with the appropriate sound in a given language. This makes a lot of people think that thought (the notion of a live furry organism that smells like X and makes sounds Y, Z etc... that the child "knows" is a pet or interesting type of creature), comes first, and then it gets a verbal label. From this view, language comes only after the concept of dog or pet has been formed mentally, that is, language serves thought and just reflects thought. In this view, the two year old child might know around 200 different concepts and thousands of percepts, and indeed he later learns to associate various labels to them after he learned them through the first communication system. However, later on the child doesn't just use speech to express itself, rather speech plays a critical role in the development of higher order intelligence.

Concept Formation - Part I

As the child grows, he can learn a new set of ideas and form a concept about events and objects mostly through verbal references that are only later associated with a concrete experience. A child can form a new concept such as fish simply by being told about Jaws or friendly dolphins and talking about them, even when he has not had any first system experience. Naturally, it helps to provide children with stories and pictures and first hand experiences, yet the point is: Speech transforms the mind, it causes thoughts about the world. Once a child masters the second communication system, we see that intelligence tests do begin to predict later intelligence. Reading and writing are also second system activities that transform the mind, as is learning a second or third language.

> *It is critical that parents realize the power of speech in the development of thought and hence of intelligence. In the beginning was the word. It is the most important aspect that differentiates us from other living forms. How one uses speech is critical but how so? Do you know that when a 4 year old relates a story, and parents clarify and ask questions about what happened, the child incorporates these inputs when he tells the story again to someone else? Parents' speech guides and helps to organize thought for the child. This is a subtle but very important fact. The point here is that it is not only a question of how "much" one talks, but "how" speech is used, elicited, sequenced, and modeled that helps to foster intelligence.*

Learning in the Preschool Years

When parents explain things in simple straight forward ways, children not only get the ideas or message but also learn about causes and effects in a more sophisticated form than before. Parents who are short in explaining things or who are bothered by many questions limit the development of intelligence. They shortchange their children in more than one way. Not only do they provide largely incomplete information, but they also lessen the opportunities that a child needs to understand what things are, how they function and which can be connected with what they already knew before (in their Mental Structure). Parents who are unaware of the role of language in the development of their child's intelligence tend to use patterns that are not optimal.

Chapter 4: The Preschool Years

When new information is connected with old information through verbal interaction, things often seem to "fall in place," like the "*ah-ha!*" experience that helps to solidify and to retain new knowledge. The light bulb goes on. This is the type of learning that parents want to see most. Why? Because when a child discovers a new relationship with a little guidance, the "*ah-ha!*" experience motivates him to learn more and makes him feel competent. The child develops intrinsic motivation. The point here is that it does not matter that much how many different varieties of animals or plants a child can classify at age 4, knowing a dozen more does not make one child smarter than another. What does matter is *how* the child comes to have that knowledge and what kinds of daily routines are present in the family that favor discovery and direct learning. The response patterns of parents, insofar as their encouragement and subtle prompting is concerned, can make a difference over time. The kind of daily routines parents establish make a difference in terms of how powerful a mind the child will have, like the horsepower in an automobile engine. Some engines have four cylinders with 760 cubic centimeters (cc), while others have eight cylinders with 3,000 cc's.

Take for example the routine of reading or classifying new objects according to one or more characteristics (e.g., wings, beaks, fur, color, shapes, etc...). If a parent spends time with a young, illiterate child and reads to him regularly at age 2, new associations in the brain as well as new hypotheses and ideas are being constructed which can be called schemes. The child gets closer and closer to being totally ready for reading by learning to sit still, decode and verbalize.

With the three little pigs story, the child visualizes different types of house construction and learns, at a basic level, how buildings with different characteristics respond to the wolf. Not only is the wolf the bad guy, but anticipation is being learned as well as cause-effect sequences. The young mind delights at hearing the same story over and over because, each time, comprehension improves, and different images are developed and remembered. Familiarity is something that attracts humans. Children enjoy knowing something about what comes out of this written story text. Their hypotheses are tested and new ones are formed. The parent who routinely asks questions which challenge the child, or who explains what something is, or why, is guiding and programming the child's computer. Not only is the parent explaining or testing, but teaching the child intellectual strategies. The parent is teaching the child to ask himself questions, to get information from others, and to analyze the why's and wherefore's of things. Whatever the parent notes becomes part of the child's mental real estate. What happens with a parent who hardly gets into these routines, and who does not interact energetically with the child over time? The brain is not exercised or stimulated as much. And, since the more the brain is used the more it grows, the more it wants to know, and the more ready it is to go on to the next level, then if you <u>don't use it, you lose it</u>.

Dr. Pedro R. Portes Ph.D.

Parents who want to have smart children need to structure or design a learning environment consciously which permits two-way communication and the modeling of new things that the mind can do. Don't get hung up on doing it "right." What matters is that you try to construct such an environment and try to improve what is being done. With reading-related activities, the child also learns something that is even more important than the story itself. She learns that stories come out of books, that letters stand for things and actions, and what is more, she now wants to read too. Children learn in fact, an attitude, that can be positive towards expanding many areas of the brain. How reading activities are structured makes a difference. These have to be fun. The child will let you know. The same applies to painting and writing. You can get your child to like school long before he enters it. We call this school readiness which can make all the difference in the world as far as intelligence is concerned. Avoid forcing the child into dull drills.

Parents are constantly shaping their child's curiosity, creativity and talents, yet they rarely know what they are doing or how to do it better. That is why it is important to understand the upcoming section concerning the four ways that we all learn, so that learning becomes intentional, not an accidental process. *Home environments vary not only according to how much education and income parents have, but more importantly, in how they make their children literate or knowledgeable about different fields that our culture finds useful. That's the key to genius, doing it consciously.*

A parent can ask himself "What am I doing so that my child is aware about how people live and think in other cultures?" (Anthropology), or "How to say I love you in Greek and Latin?" (Bilingualism), or "How to distinguish between more and bigger?" (Math), or any other topic such as natural science, music, drama etc... All of these areas are "literacies" or intelligences that can be developed to *some* level in the early years. So what can parents do? For one thing, make sure that you provide different special learning environments for the different capabilities to be developed. Each capability requires a special environment, but some are interrelated like language and culture, or math and physics. Parents are engineers who design what fields the child is likely to like or dislike or to be neutral and detached about due to lack of exposure. During the early years, it helps to provide some continuity and stability in several areas, while just giving some basic exposure in others which are more difficult to obtain and maintain. Some tips about design:

1. Cover the basics better than most other folks, a little each week adds up. As noted elsewhere, it is important to make sure that in the process of developing your child's interests, you include those areas that are traditionally covered in school tests and that are used by some to assign your child to later learning environments. (This is called tracking.)

Chapter 4: The Preschool Years

2. Reading readiness includes getting your child to feel motivated about receiving information through the second communication system, sitting still, taking turns listening and trying out new words, finding their meanings, making guesses and receiving feedback and reinforcement. Some children do not have this *set* and prefer constant motor sensory experiences. The latter are fine, but they should not limit the child's intake of information about the world. Readiness in arithmetic includes knowing concepts such as less than, adding to and making simple associations between number symbols and actual physical objects.

The concept of equality (=) is a major milestone in this field. The closer you can get your child to discriminate between a set of four glasses and a set of six and employ the word more, the further along that developmental function comes to completion. Such progress then allows for a number of advantages:

a). Less frustration because the child feels that what the teacher is doing is something he is familiar with. The child has a structure in mind to absorb the information that you have presented. What parents have taught in the preceding years then becomes like the building of a bridge (or a "schema") that prevents the child from feeling totally lost in a school situation. In fact, the child feels good about knowing stuff inside, and this satisfaction becomes intrinsically reinforcing.

b). Given that a child who has a more advanced developmental function in reading or math feels less stress or pressure about learning, she is also more likely to get reinforcement from the teacher and more direct guidance. Teachers are human and prefer children who pick up on new learning quickly and often ignore those who fall behind. This ability to learn easily is a second advantage that carries its own reinforcement.

c). The child feels rewarded and her self-esteem grows as a result of what she brings with her into the class situation. Motivation is more likely to be maintained in this case as opposed to one in which the child feels inadequate or dumb in comparison with others. Parents of school age children, if smart, will prepare the minds and not just the lunch pail.

Children without the school readiness set may not be as comfortable when questions are asked, because the parents haven't familiarized the child with the set or they haven't played school enough. These children are less likely to seek information, because they haven't had the practice and the coaching at home in the art of asking questions. When they do not understand something and need help, these children may not know how to get the necessary help, because at home, the parents were not usually on the look out for such situations.

3. Try selecting fields based upon family strengths and resources. If your family has a member who sings, paints, computes or cooks, then learning in these areas can be specially designed so that school readiness is increased. A mother who cooks with a 3 year old can talk out loud and explain what she is doing on a regular basis. The child learns the name and definition of various things, realizes how things are mixed, transformed as well as measurements and proportions. All the parent has to do is engage the child, make cooking a fun game, and involve the child. In cooking for example, the parent can start by stating what she is going to do, then ask the child something he may know and then ask about a related topic. The parent then could verbalize the differences and similarities between the topics, say milk and butter. After this, she could start talking about the animals involved, what they produce, and how these products get to the market and then to the table. All the parent has to do is to share information and to invite participation. The parent merely openly verbalizes what she is thinking and checks regularly for the child's comprehension. Open-ended questions and positive strokes help.

The parent elaborates on concepts that the child probably does not know and explains them in simple, honest ways. What is the parent accomplishing here? Parents are seldom aware of it, but they are actually programming the child's computer, not only in terms of providing information but more importantly in use of speech to guide actions. Mixing ingredients can be related later to chemistry lab activities, if you know how to guide the child in a fun way. Thinking strategies are taught this way, and they serve to discover and to solve problems. The child will use a lot of what was earlier grounds for play. Play allows for the growth of intelligence.

4. The daily routine is important. Some parents wonder what is the point of actively   engaging the child when he hardly understands much at age two or three. Yet, if routines, such as the one above, are repeated over time, the child moves from 5 to 10, 30, 50, to even 90% comprehension. What is more, it does not much matter if the child learns specific bits, or comes up with "ridiculous answers and questions." What is most important is the process. Listening and paying attention play a big part. The child is learning how to learn. She gets the idea that questions sometimes lead to answers which make more or less sense. She learns that it is O.K. to ask or make observations, or to confirm the messages from mom which have been received.

Chapter 4: The Preschool Years

Remember that the child's computer is always hungry. Try to keep the child with you during daily activities and turn these into social dialogues in which information is processed in different ways. The child's mind is a sponge and can absorb a lot more than you think. Forget about daily lesson plans with specific objectives and tests. These may even spoil the natural disposition to learn and to feel competent. Do not interfere with your child's motivation to feel competent and do not allow others to belittle your child or to make him feel like he cannot master something. On the contrary, make sure that the child is provided with lots of encouragement and small doses of guidance.

5. Follow the child's strengths and motivation. Complement and do not impose your agenda. In a learning situation, *make sure that positive strokes outnumber blatant corrections*. Look for things which the child can do and acknowledge them while new turf is being introduced. A child may not want to be drilled in math or vocabulary, but if asked, she may want to learn about the stars or about something more relevant at the moment. As long as they have or can be used for some educational value, follow the child's wishes. In this way, you are helping him to become autonomous. An autonomous child is self-motivated and independent. However, there is a balance. Your child can become spoiled or conceited, and these interfere with learning. There are ways to overcome the problem. One strategy is to make her work a bit harder on something before you give in. Besides overcoming the problem of overindulgence, this teaches perseverance. During the first 5 years, learning opportunities abound, and a smart parent can always introduce or expand a new skill in a creative way that is not regarded as a chore.

You see, every home has a hidden curriculum in which children are most definitely taught some content. In some homes, the curriculum is such that little of the content will help the child to succeed in society. The idea behind this book is to make the curriculum less hidden to parents and to emphasize that the home curriculum must contain lots of the right stuff, or what we define as that which is practical for creativity, school and the mind. For example, take the following learning situation which is hidden in play interaction between a parent and a 6 year old child:

P - Suzie. Do you remember E.T.?
S - Yeah.
P - Do you know the neighborhood E.T. comes from?
S - Nope.
P - That's O.K., few people know that. Do you want to see it?
S - Yeah.

P - All right. I'll show you, First close your eyes and take some long deep breaths. Try to wipe out all pictures from your mind and relax cause I want the back of your mind to be a blank screen O.K.? Is it blank yet?

S - Yeah.

P - On the blank screen I want you to imagine yourself coming upon this beautiful green meadow. It is a beautiful, sunny day, and then you notice, all of a sudden, this very pretty lady and her name is Venus. As you come up to her, you see this wonderful, beautiful red shiny car drive up and the name of the car is Mercury. Mercury says to you and Venus: "Say, want to go for a ride around the universe? Get in." So Venus gets into the car Mercury, and just as she sits down, she notices a candy bar by the name of Mars under her fanny. Venus says oops: "I'm sorry Mr. Mars." And, she puts him on her lap, and they go for a ride to look for E.T.

The above represents a creative play scenario in which the parent can begin expanding the child's intelligence about astronomy. Later, the story can be told so that different planets can be included in the order in which they are located with respect to the sun. I know of a former school "master" who did this with first graders, and in twenty minutes, he taught all the planets of the solar system and their relative positions from the sun.

6. Structure recitation, review, maintenance and expansions regularly. This can be done beautifully with daily recitations of nursery rhymes and later short poems. Eventually you can build up to the child doing detailed story telling and reciting longer poems. Have you ever tried to hurry through reading your child a story before bedtime? You soon learn that by trying to skip a couple of pages to quickly get to the end your child catches you red handed and says, "hey, that's not how it goes." You have discovered two things here. One that your child knows the story and secondly, and most important, you are witnessing that your child has memorized the sequence of events and has perceived your deviation of them.

Developmental Principle

Development proceeds at approximately the same rate at which it is started. This developmental principle is simple, yet one of the most important for parents to bear in mind if they want to make their children smart. Although it does not always have to be true, children who are helped to develop their intelligence in early childhood, tend to stay ahead of their peers later in life. The main thing for parents to realize is that, due to several related reasons, it pays to invest in setting up and maintaining the "cognitive" supports early in the life of a child. The first reason

Chapter 4: The Preschool Years

why it is important to give your child this head start has to do with studies of intelligent and creative persons. These persons had much support and stimulation early in life which were maintained over time. In other words, smart parents provide environments which help their child's intelligence to take off, and which tend to continue being beneficial years later. Secondly, if their intellectual curiosity and desire to learn is reinforced early on, children learn to motivate themselves. In the section dealing with instrumental learning, you will see how intrinsic motivation works and how the parent can help establish the pattern early in life. If children have confidence in their learning capacity and hence, a high level of self-esteem, what do you think happens once they enter the primary grades?

These children tend to outperform others for years to come. If the parents get the child started "right," it becomes much easier and less time consuming for the child to become smarter later on. Why? Because a lot of what children learn early on, and especially how they learn early on, enable them to have what are more complete cognitive or mental structures. Here cognitive means activity in the head. Structure means how much and the way in which knowledge is stored in the brain concerning a given area, similar to a map or a record, or a blackboard diagram. This mental capacity is what we call intelligence from which new learning becomes easier.

There are countless cognitive structures or maps in the brain that result from experience, observation and interaction with others. To the extent that a child has been exposed early on in a positive manner to lots of different types of learning, she is going to catch on that much faster, better and appear more intelligent later in school. Smart parents recognize the importance of this pattern or early intervention and launch their child into intellectual pursuits at a higher level. They realize that a little effort early on pays off tenfold later. With sensitivity they come to know how to do it, when and in what areas. Once again, how learning is encouraged and structured in the home is far more important than the learning of specific things. Other parents who are busy with job demands may try to hire others to structure and support their child's early learning.

So how does a parent promote this development? Well, one thing to remember is that, fortunately, children arrive on this earth already motivated. They come wanting to learn about most things. Remember, never turn down the child when she is trying to learn about something, even if that something does not appear important to you. If you're tired, too bad. Don't lose the moment, as the child's interest may not be there later. Rather than save time by giving her the answer, if you sense that the child already knows or is close to knowing the answer, challenge her to discover the answer. If it happens, great. Reinforce her ability and perseverance and creativity. If not, help her to reason through what is required, to recall what she knows and the different ways to apply this knowledge. Praise everything without focusing on the *right* answer. It is far more important to learn how to learn than to learn specific answers.

Children want to engage their parents at any and every level. The child finds being close to you physically a lot of fun as well as satisfying with regard to emotional needs for affection. As a parent, you can choose when you will be engaged. You can choose primarily situations in which certain types of learning occur for the child.

A parent may refuse to be occupied or "dragged into" other situations in which the issue is something like eating or not eating the food on the plate or getting ready to go out. The smart parent discriminates a learning situation from one that is not, and responds accordingly. Not only is this parent aware of what the child thinks she's after, but also knows what she needs emotionally and intellectually. This is one way you avoid being at the mercy of a spoiled child. However, to promote intellectual development you must set aside certain times and situations during which the child knows that you are available. She learns to discriminate these situations from others.

Remember, the more a child knows, the more he wants to know, if in past experiences learning has been associated with warmth, praise and confirmation. The child is attracted to situations in which he receives positive attention and in which effort and application of past learning is reinforced, in sum, where the affective needs are satisfied. Your job is to connect these positive moments with the development of various intelligences. The smart parent assures that these emotional needs to a large extent are satisfied, involving the types of learning situations in which verbal communication and discussion, as well as modeling of new "stuff," occur. Whether these occur around a science, math, language or other curriculum is up to you.

Planning these sorts of activities makes you a good intellectual designer and a smart gardener as well as an architect of learning environments. The sooner these procedures are planned and started, the better. Once the rate and type of delivery of information and information-processing skills are built into patterns of everyday activities, the rate of development has also been set. Hence, intellectual development continues at the rate at which it has started. There is nothing magical about it. All that this says is that some environments continue being intelligent and relevant to the child over time. Other family environments start out good then become mediocre. Others begin and stay mediocre. The environments of those parents who, at the beginning, do not facilitate their child's development of intelligence and other areas at the beginning, are not likely to improve that much later on. This explains why there is a high correlation (association) between a child's intelligence at age 4 and at age 17. Those children who were intelligent at 4 are also at 17, and vice versa. The child's environment for intellectual development tends to stay about the same, unless something radical occurs. For example, a poor child from an unstable home is adopted into a smarter, richer environment. In such cases, a "slow" child is provided with a sharp and intelligent context. The child's mind actually increases in intelligence.

If your Child is Older, is it Too Late?

Let's be realistic, parents have less and less influence as children grow older. But let's be smart, it is never too later to begin interacting more intelligently with your child, even as a teenager. When a child matures and is finishing adolescence, intellectual growth is going to depend more and more upon him but also on parents and other adults. This is not to say that an average teen cannot become quite smart. It is possible, but unlikely in most cases. Parents have already cast the mold for different types of abilities. It is true that college and certain types of jobs help the person to continue to grow intellectually, especially if the person becomes motivated and activated by an intelligent context.

The point here is, start where the child is at and go from there. It may be somewhat difficult for some, but it is never too late. A lot of children are late bloomers. The good news is that when children become adolescents, they are ready to learn in more effective ways and if you have a good relationship, a lot can be accomplished. Keep in mind this and other principles of development and relate them to different areas of intellectual development like creativity, art, music, languages, literature, and science. Finally, recall what was covered under Critical Periods and note that these time lines represent a relative concept. It is never too late for development to occur, since this follows an orderly sequence that can always be supported from the outside.

During adolescence, an average child may become interested in science or art and begin a rapid pattern of development in that area, thus becoming intelligent in such a field. What parents should look for is not whether there is a critical period for the child, but rather whether there is a critical period for parents to begin being smart in their parenting. However, it is much harder to help this child to become intelligent in general, at this point, compared to another whose intelligences were cultivated from the start.

Concept Formation - Part II

There is another and more important process which your child begins to use in order to learn about the world that surrounds her. For example, the child might hear you or someone else say "godmother," when he doesn't know what is meant. The child begins to search his memory banks and uses what little word attack skills he has to figure out "why is this godmother deal so important..." So he says to you: "Mom, you godmother?" And, you say: "No. Barbara, your aunt, is." Later on, the child hears the godmother herself say the word and so on until the child figures that this term means something like a special aunt who gives you more attention than the others. The child is forming a mini fuzzy concept that falls under family relations but remains unclear for some time.

The process is called "accommodation," which means that the child needs to make room in the head for some concept, and he is not sure exactly where to put it. You see, the child's mind is made of these maps or menus of different kinds of concepts which are related in some kind of order, depending upon age, culture and learning experiences. He still doesn't understand the full meaning of the concept until a series of other events occur first. In the godmother example, the child must first figure out the terminology for all the other family titles and interrelations. A four-year-old has trouble figuring that he is the cousin of your husband's sister's son. He has trouble figuring that reptile is different from snake and turtle. Although reptile represents a bigger category, all three terms are always mentioned together. Children learn the first rule of thumb as: if a goes with b, then a is b, or a makes b appear, or something like that.

Toddlers aren't very precise or particular. They are happy just to know a little bit about all kinds of stuff. This is especially true for pre-schoolers and for most kindergarten and 1st grade children around the world. Children of these ages are still developing these mental maps or shelves, and often they don't have a spot or category in which to put the new word. From about ages two and to past seven, the child tries to organize thousands of experiences into sets of organized, interrelated bits. Each bit is a mental representation. It is a "directory of concepts" arranged in some order. Through interactions with the culture, these directories begin to resemble those of the culture and become similar in the order that they are arranged (e.g. cardinal goes under bird).

Before schooling begins, children are dealing with a limited number of mental directories. What they cannot fit in, goes into a "to be sorted" directory which is in the process of being organized and developed fully. Some call this stage "preoperational," meaning that the brain still doesn't have certain logical operations or thinking skills, and knowledge. As a result, these children usually cannot solve certain basic problems. But this term "preoperational" is not accurate. In fact, it is misleading. Children are using logic, which is based upon what has been learned thus far. Take for example, when a child hears that an alligator is a reptile, the child assumes then that a reptile is (typically) an alligator.

What is a bit? A **bit** *is a set of organized concepts* like fruit or tool. These can be sorted in different ways under a more powerful concept.

Chapter 4: The Preschool Years

Figure 1.   BIT

```
        (1)                                    (2)
       FRUIT                                  TOOL

Apple Melon Grape Tomato?              Ax Saw Knife Drill Miter
       seeds,                                          factory
          skin                                 metal, wood, electric
             \ verbal concepts          and labels,- connectors /
              texture size, color        s sound, smell, shape
                    \ attributes or  basic sorters /
```

We must remember that children's brains are very logical. They feed on data and produce rules and strategies in a very intelligent fashion, as long as favorable conditions are met. Many bits are developed in children's minds that also contain associations with contexts of activity. How many verbal concepts does your child almost know this week? Find out and play.

    The intelligence of the child is often reflected by how well organized the child is in using and mastering her verbal concepts and strategies. For example, not only is a bear added to the "bit", animal - wild - big - dangerous, but also to the context of Yellowstone National Park and to the activity of a picnic when one was encountered suddenly. This is where you come in, if you want a sharp child, put in the time to meet the conditions of learning bits or concepts. They will call you permissive, so what. You can spoil the child, as long as the child wants to learn particularly in key fields. By meeting these conditions for stimulating the brain's capacity over time in a field, you develop giftedness in that field. The main condition is your child's motivation, which you can help to establish through unconditional love and acceptance. The others come later under "Conditions of Learning."

    Let's stop here and review. Take a deep breath, close your eyes and imagine placing three of the ideas we have just discussed. 1.___ 2.___ 3.___. Close the book. If you can't, try again. Reread to find three only. Now elaborate. Explain the ideas to an empty chair. Make up your own map, a bit, the conditions, whatever. Ask yourself, what is this term related to? How so? By doing this, the ideas will stay with you.

    A mental map or bit can be as simple or as complex as the periodic table in chemistry. Now play with your child then and again, and help her to interact with what she has learned. Overtime, this pattern helps out a lot.

Another strategy is to ask the child to summarize the key things learned every week or day. Remember that the stage the child is in does not prevent you from building the base for complex skills gradually. Once the base is built, development speeds up. This process explains why children reach a higher skill level and appear to be gifted. So you see, being gifted depends upon having patterns in the home which foster (rapid) development. The child will learn to conserve mass, liquid and other concepts when his menus or maps are ready.

Since conservation is an important step in development, let me spell this out for you. To test your child's ability conserve liquid, pour a can of soda into a long, tall glass and another can into a deep, wide dish. Ask the child which of the two containers has more soda. If he realizes that both vessels are holding a can of liquid, that is, if he reverses what you did mentally and says "Of course they are both the same in quantity of liquid," he has "conserved" liquid mentally and logically in his head. The rule he used says "If a (soda) added to b (tall glass) = what a (soda) is added to c (deep dish) then b=c.

Another rule you could test is what goes up, must come down, (low level physics). There is gravity here, and out there in space there's no gravity. The lumping of concepts into general rules gives the child even more power over information as compared to concept maps. Reptiles lay eggs. Mammals have live babies. Both of these are rules. Children need to have learning experiences in order to figure out logically what is what by paying attention to details. You can help children to develop in many such areas. Allow your child to experience the maturation of frog's eggs over time until tadpoles develop. The sooner the child gets the big picture of how the world is organized, the smarter he will seem to teachers, and the more he will get out of them.

But as this discussion began, to say that preschool children are "pre-operational" is misleading. Of course they are operational, but until the mental maps or bits develop fully, the bases of rules and logical operations cannot emerge. However this does not mean that a 6 year old who solves the liquid problem is smarter than one who cannot. If one child can do it, then it is because he has an intelligent culture for mutual interaction which makes him more ready to learn in that field. Of course, if a pattern exists that gives this support for the child in many fields, you bet the child will be more intelligent about many more things as compared to a child who does not have that pattern in the immediate culture. This will show up in tests.

As the child matures, he learns that **a** (newspaper) and **b** (radio) belong under **c** (communication system), that **a** is **c** and **b** is **c**, but that **a** is not **b**. Such conceptual elaborations are taught by parents giving a response to each of these cases over and over, in interactions that vary in frequency and content, as well as response style from outside. That is why family patterns of interaction are so important. So, with the beginning of language development, your child's mental growth takes off like a

Chapter 4: The Preschool Years

jet. Language transforms the mind because speech mimics and mirrors outward actions (but in words familiar to the mind).

Language is like a fishing pole, a tool to bring nourishment to the mind. Most folks think language is mostly for communication. They don't realize that speech enables you to think. It leads to new concepts and strategies.

Once a child's mental bits or maps of the world get indexed by verbal labels, the mind explodes with internal mental activity mixed with physical activity. Watch children in any preschool and see how they talk out loud. Now look at only the 2 year olds who do not possess much language. What do you see?

Children's intelligence before the age of two is measured by what they can do, that is, their activities that are observed. With language development rapidly advancing, these activities go undercover and are regulated more and more by speech. The child's speech, even at first, mediates her interactions with those around. The child's speech is at first social in nature and then becomes internalized or inner speech. At this point, you will notice that the child is very self-centered, as if she was not interested in communicating with others. She is using speech for oneself apparently. During this time, speech begins to be interrelated with thought. The point here is that, at about age 2, you see two lines of development (language and thought) interconnect and create a marvelous reaction in the brain.

Language Development Makes the Mind

Language exercises the mind, allowing thought to become possible. It allows more and more distance between the world and the mind, without having to rely on sensory and physical inputs. As a parent, you should know about language development, if only to appreciate this marvel of nature. Language develops in an fairly exact sequence. My four-month-old is practicing sounds now cooing, making consonant and vowel sound. He even says "dada" and "yeah" without realizing it. But he will probably be 8 months before making the first intelligent use of language. He might say dog as the family Scotty comes marching in. He might say "paper" as Mom picks up the paper. At 8 months, he has a clear concept of who Mom and Dad are, but this concept is not yet verbal. It is physical. Suddenly, baby puts the right name with a physical object. Hallelujah. The baby labeled something. He knows what we call things on this planet. However, not until about age 2 years does the baby have enough concept stability of the world in his head to use more complex language.

Teach Language Very Early

At 8-9 months, your baby knows who you are. He doesn't know that you are Mommy. He doesn't know how to say Mommy yet either, because he's not biologically mature to do so.

Can you teach him that you are Mommy? Sure. Have dad carry him away from you into another room. Now dad asks Mommy's whereabouts (with eye contact). Dad then takes him to where Mom is in the other room and says with excitement Mommy. Play this game for awhile, and the association is learned between the physical form (Mom) and the label (Mommy). Gradually, the label brings the physical image to mind. The word elicits part of the physical world. The baby will make a sound that stands for X. The correct sound will come later, but the parents' environment of providing for the teaching of language needs to be there. Remember, social learning is a way that typically produces efficient learning even when the baby does not respond right away. Such learning may take months, but it filters in. The brain grows in spurts. A building period takes place before the mind erupts and gets re-organized. Language develops in a predictable pattern which you can monitor and enhance, but it cannot be accelerated early on. Have you ever noticed a seven-month-old making a strong primitive sound for a whole breath, like exerting power, and varying pitch?

Sounds cute but what is really happening is that the baby is connecting the variations in sounds which are being produced to his brain. She is becoming conscious that such sounds can be directed mentally. She says to herself, "Let's try this sound/pitch," then she is amazed that the sound was controlled by her will. She feels competent. She makes the first word with meaning (morpheme). After this, she will sound special words called holophrases which can mean different things. Baby says "shoe" at age one, and she is just letting you know that she knows her stuff (label). Yet, she says "shoe" later meaning: "Hey, look at that shoe. Ain't that something." And, you go "um-huh." Then she can say "Shoe" again, and she means: "Look Mom, my shoe. It needs to be tied." Or she says it again, and this time the deep meaning is: "It is sticky," Then later, she says shoe and means "There is this stuff, I don't know what you all call it (gum), stuck on my shoe. Could we get it off?" All of these complex ideas are expressed with only one word, shoe.

This stage of language development, like others, is a universal which occurs in the same sequence with all children all over the world. The brain is biologically ready to permit the child to acquire language, the main tool of a culture, in a fixed sequence.

Chapter 4: The Preschool Years

Precursors to Language: **Cooing and Gurgling, then Babbling**

2-3 Months on up: The child Practices a whole range of sounds through cooing and gurgling, then babbling.

Three months: Markedly less crying than at eight weeks; when talked to and nodded at, smiles; followed by squealing-gurgling sounds, usually called cooing, which is vowel like in character and pitch-modulated; sustains cooing for fifteen to twenty seconds.

Four months: Responds to human sounds more definitely; turns head; eyes seem to search for speaker; occasionally some chuckling sounds.

Five months: The vowel-like cooing sounds begin to be interspersed with more consonantal sounds; acoustically, all vocalizations are very different from the sounds of the mature language of the environment.

Six months: Cooing changes into babbling resembling one-syllable utterances; neither vowels nor consonants have very fixed recurrences; most common utterances sound somewhat like "ma, mu, da, de."

Eight months: Reduplication (or more continuous repetition) becomes frequent; intonation patterns become distinct; utterances can signal emphasis and emotions.

Ten months: Vocalizations are mixed with sound-play such as gurgling or bubble-blowing: appears to wish to imitate sounds, but the imitations are never quite successful; beginning to differentiate between words heard by making differential adjustments.

Twelve months: Identical sound sequences are replicated with higher relative frequency of occurrences and words (mamma or dada) are emerging; definite signs of understanding some words and simple phrases.

Eighteen months: Has a definite repertoire of words - more than three, but fewer than fifty; still much babbling but now of several syllables with intricate intonation patterns; no attempt at communicating information and no frustration for not being understood; words may include items such as "thank you" or "come here," but there is little ability to join any of the lexical items into spontaneous two-item phrases; understanding is progressing rapidly.

Twenty-four months: Vocabulary of more than fifty items (some children seem to be able to name everything in the environment); begins spontaneously to join vocabulary items into two-word phrases; all phrases appear to be own creations; definite increase in communicative behavior and interest in language.

Thirty months: Fastest increase in vocabulary with many new additions every day; no babbling at all; utterances have communicative intent; frustrated if not understood by adults; utterances consist of at least two words, many have three or even five words; sentences and phrases have characteristic child grammar; that is, they are rarely verbatim repetitions of an adult utterance; intelligibility is not very good yet, though there is great variation among children; seems to understand everything that is said to him. In sum, this is what happens with language at first: The 1st <u>Morpheme</u>: 8-9 Months on up, first meaningful sound, like "bah" (ball) or "mih" (milk)

<u>Holophrases</u> - Telegraphic Speech: 10-11 Months on up, single word utterance (a morpheme) is the earliest form of a whole sentence, accompanied by pointing, gestures like "puh" means "Look, there is an apple." Telegraphic means that the child speaks in a code that is mostly understandable to the parents only.

<u>Pivot Words/Two Word Sentences</u>: 2-3 years, full use of small vocabulary is used to form new sentences like "Go Daddy," "Go kitty," "My toy," "My Mom"; Go and my are pivots that precede the new word meaning that is being assimilated in the mind. Children of this age will also try putting the pivot after the new word concept, as in doggie-here, mess- here or cookie here. Before 18 months, your child knows less than 50 words, understands rapidly but is not frustrated by not being understood. By age 2, more than 500 words can be joined into numerous original creations, and there is much interest in language. By 30 months, a fast spurt leads up to about 300 word meanings, and there is no babbling. The child's vocabulary is a good index of how well you are parenting or interacting with the child. Frustration is noted when communication fails. Parents need to be very encouraging and respect the child's efforts to master language. Utterances now increase from 2 to 4 and 5 words. This means that before this time, you speak in simple but complete sentences. You are the model here who works with the biological unfolding of language.

<u>Complex language/Subject-Verb-Object</u>: 3-5 Years for example, "Daddy give book" is incomplete but serves as the new base for elaboration of speech like "Look, My pretty doll". From ages five to ten, children put the finishing touches on language. By age eleven, their accent in a given language is almost fixed for life. Mothers' language to children, or "motherese" as it is called, is very indicative of how well mothers understand the way to adjust to children's level naturally. Mothers omit pronouns when talking to infants. Mothers don't say: "He ate it," but rather: "Did your brother Alex eat it?" Is this bad? No, there is a good reason. Mom knows that the child must first learn subjects and people as nouns before he learns pronouns. "Look. Where are Mommy's hands?" Mothers also extend the child's speech, and they do not just simply correct it. The child says "Kitty there." The mother says "The kitty is playing there on the sofa (place)." In turn, mothers who expand and use language well have children who are more advanced, than those of mothers who simply provide extensions of the child's speech. For instance, the child says: "Get ball," and the day care worker typically responds "Uh hum, you get ball." But if the

parent says, "Sure, Mommy will get you the ball," then the correct expansion will lead to better development. Children are expert linguists by nature. They can discover very quickly the structure and rules of one or several languages. Bilingual parents should speak their native language to the child, but only one should do so (the more fluent one at that). The other parent should speak in the second language all the time so that the child can easily construct two parallel systems. This process will actually serve to develop certain cognitive skills. Any skill your child learns to apply on her own, any mental strategy that she has, is first learned in interaction with you or other parts of the environment. This means that social interaction is not just something people do to meet emotional needs. It is the main avenue for mental growth. Parents who take the time to explain, to show, and to quiz, have children who can, on their own, explain, show and quiz themselves and others. This is more and more true as they master language. So help the child to attain mastery.

The Fast Track
WHAT TO DO IN YOU CHILD'S FIRST TWO YEARS?

Love, enjoy, activate, reinforce and play with language. Establish a loving relationship. Do not punish or neglect the child. Be a willing host of this guest, show him/her different angles. You will find that young children will prefer adults who stimulate, and who provide variation in the visual field at the right times. Remember the child is building a mini replica of the world in the brain. The more complete this replica becomes, the more powerful the computer will be, and the more intelligent the adaptive behavior will become. I want to "give psychology away" in this book for the benefit of your parenting skills. Mothers can interact in different ways with children, and typically speaking, these ways are equally good in helping children to develop language skills. I say typically because some ways of interacting with children (and of not interacting) are definitely bad. You want to avoid anxiety and fear in the learning process. Avoid negative reinforcement and belittling. Be positive. Also, it does not matter if the infant is full term or premature for language development to occur within normal ranges in the first few years.

It turns out that even "premies" (premature babies) are not at a disadvantage in developing their intelligence. How much money or education parents have does not matter much either during this early period (2 years). Why? Smart, informed parents realize that certain aspects of development are under biological maturation controls during the initial growth period. We call this canalization, meaning roughly that the development of language in the young child flows within a canal that is set by what is inherited biologically. Children are said to be resilient (tough), because it is really hard to mess up this process and other wired-in types of development given a normal set of parents. But parents are not to simply sit back and wait for development to unfold. You need to encourage the child to learn and to use new words all the time, because the more morphemes a child uses by age 18-28 months, the faster the overall development of language and mental skills later on. Parents need to use full sentences when guiding the child, and the also need to explain why children cannot do certain things instead of using brief commands. As long as the brain is not defective due to inherited diseases or blows from the environment, the unfolding is "wired-in." You simply create favorable conditions for certain functions to sprout. (An example of a function would be learning to sort stuff by size or importance.) Parents will usually feed and interact verbally and physically with their baby, so that the basics for further development are well in place. Unless the child is severely deprived, neglected or malnourished, infant tests of "intelligence" will not be able to predict later intelligence as is noted elsewhere. Where we begin to see important differences in intelligence that do predict later intelligence is after 3 years of age. At this age, when the child can express herself and act upon her environment more fully, interaction processes in the family begin to show their effects.

Remember, what is being measured is what the child can do and what has been learned. Such learning depends largely upon parental interactions, that is, how they interacted and what they interact with and about, prior to the time that the child is tested. What is being measured is not only the "intelligence" of the child but also what you and your family environment have delivered and how it has been delivered to the child. These tests are measuring how intelligent your patterns of interaction have been on a regular basis.

These tests are not very good for measuring intelligence in the terms of the culture around the child's mind but they are all we have for now. Since culture is what actually makes the mind intelligent, I.Q. scores are early indicators and need to be re-interpreted. When you see an I.Q. score, wonder not about the "how intelligent is this child" question, but rather ask "how much has been delivered to the child's mind." So culture is what the mind lives in. There is yet another level of the immediate family culture. This is the <u>Culture</u>, which is partly the social, educational, and economic background of the child's and the parent's collective history. The I.Q. tests were constructed without a good theory or understanding of intelligence in terms of its interdependence upon mental and emotional environments surrounding and accompanying the child. In fact, people who write about how to increase your child's I.Q. by x number of points, or who believe that intelligence is what is measured by these tests are not very intelligent, particularly about learning and developmental theory.

In sum, in this chapter you have learned how children learn to represent the world in their minds, through concepts. You have also learned how language development accelerates concept development, particularly how external verbal patterns impact on the child's mind. If your child is at this stage, reread this chapter.

Dr. Pedro R. Portes Ph.D.

Chapter 5: Strategies for Parenting Intelligently

CHAPTER V

STRATEGIES FOR PARENTING INTELLIGENTLY

"A parent who goes about parenting intelligently sets in motion many of the child's future talents or types of intelligence by cultivating their development by the daily routine in the home."

As you may have already noted, the message which is most important in this book is that parents need to interact intelligently with children at all times. This includes engaging the child in activities that gradually and consistently produce a more accurate picture of the world. To interact intelligently means that you frequently "squeeze" the most out of situations, which come up daily to teach or to build concepts with your child. You do so mainly by telling stories and playing games. Of course, parents tend to do this anyway. The trick is how you do it. Your child becomes intelligent in general, by becoming knowledgeable or skillful in a variety of areas. Your job, essentially, lies in helping the child connect these "natural" areas with those that are valued in society. Your job is also to make the areas of knowledge valued by society seem natural to your child. The latter will take much practice and patience from you. It takes parents who have a smart attitude about the whole business of raising intelligent children intelligently. This attitude is one which causes you to say to yourself: "We are just going to try to build upon certain concepts a little bit at a time in ways that also meet our child's need for attention, approval and self-confidence." Parents need to use whatever children are doing, turning these activities into ways that nurture the mind. It sounds as if life has to be totally child centered. Surely limits have to be set, but always remember, children have rights to have feelings even if certain behaviors are disapproved.

You have already informed yourself in this book about ways by which you can establish patterns that foster development in various fertile fields of talent, competence and expertise in your child's brain.

Let's review our model briefly. The child has the capacity to be a genius from the start. You don't make the child intelligent, the child is already intelligent.Her brain is equipped with the necessary systems to represent the world, and to transform it. In fact, children spend the first two years of life learning to represent the world through their senses and motor activities, just as an animal does. The brain needs to record the basic building blocks like memory for previous experience, how else is the baby going to learn something new each day? The child's mind feeds upon information. It cannot live without it. In fact, if you limit visual stimulation, you retard the child's development in the early years. The same goes for language usage. The child is naturally motivated to learn and to become competent. Parenting intelligently and creatively means to not obstruct the natural process of development, but rather, to enhance it in smart ways. It also means helping the child's second, and most important, type of development which involves a second communication system that is symbolic, cultural, and learned. Developing the child's literacy is the critical and most essential responsibility of parents.

The child's mind or brain automatically knows where and how to process language, numbers, spatial relations, and cause-effect experiences that occur frequently. The mind is superior in man because it can transform and generate information through symbols. Primates can use symbols, but they cannot create and transform them. Animals only have the natural development process available to them, children have both the natural and cultural courses. Reading this book, listening to a story, writing, or drawing, are all symbols used for communication. This level of communication then is the key to intelligence.

In sum, language and other similar symbols are the keys, which open the doors to many forms of creativity and intelligence. If as a parent you know that the child has the task before her of representing more and more aspects of the world in the head, it is clear that expert assistance from you would be helpful. The child alone can only develop at an average rate which is fine if you do not want anything extraordinary. But if you develop intelligent patterns of daily interaction, then these will serve as vehicles to advance your child's mental development.

As was noted earlier, some parents introduce special events into the daily routine, for example music lessons. The child is then encouraged to become an active apprentice. She will develop talent in this particular area. However, parents are busy and often rely too heavily on TV and teachers to transmit culture to their child. Some teachers (like some TV shows) serve in worthwhile ways to aid the development of the child in particular ways. But, teachers' help is not enough. Parents must plan how they can use available opportunities for mental development, for example the local museum. Parents often fail to invite the child's natural interests and to connect them with cultural interests.

Many children go all their lives without parents providing special events. Considering that what the parent puts into the child's mind, is often what the child gets out of life, these children are doomed to a fate of being average or less than average. The point to be made here is that there is this parallel between activities on the outside of the child's mind and the mental skill on the inside of that mind. This simple principle of development goes unharnessed too often by parents. Special ways of parenting typically lead to children with special talents. If there are creative

Chapter 5: Strategies for Parenting Intelligently

activities between the child and the outside world with its players, then creative activities tend to develop inside the mind. The process is not simply a matter of knowledge or talents being recorded in the mind of the child. The child does much more than simply copy skills or talents. Rather, he transforms the talent and skills observed on the outside into self-directed activities or operations which we then refer to as intelligence, creativity or talents. These talents, in turn, help the acquisition of a lasting, positive self-concept.

Building A Positive Self-concept

Success breeds success. Parental expectations can help to either advance or slow the child's development. Because of this fact, you must dedicate your time con- scientiously to meeting your child's needs. You teach and support through your own example. Remember, your child knows innately when to go from feeling sufficiently secure and loved to risky experimentation and "trying himself out" socially. Once social and emotional development needs are met or "safeguarded," the child's intellectual curiosity is ready to go any number of ways. Based upon the exposure that the child is receiving, the child's mind captures the image, but then it also goes beyond. How far beyond often defines what we refer to as creative talent. Just as Mozart or Frank Lloyd Wright improvised on form and won acclaim, we should celebrate our children when they go beyond the ordinary.

As your child grows up in your home, he is exposed to some aspects of culture more than to others, like music or nature. Some areas are more accentuated than others and the child will likely develop talents in those areas. But, children are not cultural sponges. Often, children connect exposures from one area with those of another, and transform them into new concoctions that parents may not even like.

What does this imply as far as your strategies are concerned? You do need to have a plan of what you want to have in your garden. Parents can arrange to have some desired talents surface regularly in the child's experience. You also need to think of ways to provide exposure to areas that may not be your family's strengths. What parents choose to select and put in the garden is very important in raising smart children. But, parents also need to be open and flexible and to consider themselves learners. Parents may just learn from their children's interests. Parents are best advised to negotiate rather than to impose certain plants.

A revolution in the ways that children are reared can lead to profound changes ssin the structure of a civilization or a culture. However, this revolution is not likely to take place in a world in which parents are too busy and in which too few will try to get at the basics of child development through a book like this.

Understanding the above points is much more important than providing little vignettes here and there to keep the reader amused. This book is not designed to be a best seller. I don't apologize for not entertaining the reader more. This is serious educational business, not popular entertainment. Unfortunately, this book is not for everyone as noted earlier. It is for the parent who reflects and thinks creativel about how to apply important principles which foster full development. The difference between entertainment and education is simple. The goals are different, whether one is talking about parenting or about children's learning. With entertainment, the child is not expected to develop in a particular way. Education, on the other hand, is designed to "lead" the child's mind toward certain cultural areas in ways that may seem natural on the surface.

STRATEGIES FOR PARENTING

Ownership & Control

All children misbehave. And, they learn what buttons to push in order to drive their parents to distraction (creativity?). When discipline becomes an issue, call attention to the act, not the child. Parents need to keep the person and the behavior separate. Never call children names like "don't be stupid" or "you are slow" etc… Parents should never attack a child's personality as it attempts to be developed, but rather *strengthen* the little person with strokes which prevents problem behaviors. You may criticize the behavior, explaining why it is not acceptable, but never criticize the individual child. Avoid referring to the child as lazy, slow or hyperactive. Labels do not help development, and what is more such labels force the child to carry extra "emotional baggage" for a long time. The truth of the matter is that we do not know what kind of person the child is to be just yet, and she does not know either. Children should be free to choose and to change their minds over time. So, try to focus on the positive and extinguish the negative by ignoring. Never use negative stereotypes.

With a young child, you can use distraction as a strategy. If you are clever enough, you can do the same with an older one. For example, don't focus on the silliness of rap music and the virtues of your agenda. Rather focus attention on something the child does that is useful or creative. If you rarely see the child engage in an activity that is useful, find something. Look for an activity from which the child can learn, rather than saying "not this" and "you can't do that." Be consistent but don't get angry either. Remember that the child is just trying to find out what person she will be. Divert her attention to something that is novel, or that she is trying to do well.

If the behavior pattern is not useful or appropriate, simply take away your eye contact, your interest, your verbal interaction so that the message is, to put it bluntly, "this behavior is not going to get it with me." Let your actions speak louder than words and convey a message that you will not support or attend to certain types

Chapter 5: Strategies for Parenting Intelligently

of behaviors. Don't fall into the criticism trap in which you are frequently adding corrective or disapproving comments spurred on by the child's poor behavior. Focus on the positive more than on the negative. By doing so, you are helping the child to discriminate between what works and what doesn't without turning him/her off to you or to what you want him/her to do. You will notice that when parents criticize a child's taste for music and then suggest a better type, the child rarely buys into it. If they criticize a child's action and suggest a better option, the child may oblige them at that moment but only to get them off his back. Or he may overindulge his taste just to aggravate his parents. Remember the goal: to guide your child to be at the top of the class, to be creative or to enjoy certain art forms.

With preschoolers, use negotiation (Premack principle). If they agree to do what you want, then you will then agree to let them do so much of what they want. Even with older children, this principle can be used consistently to help the child to explore certain areas and to build work habits. Eventually, they learn to self-reinforce after making an intellectual effort.

Through discrimination learning, you can orient your child to many of the interests that will later pay off in terms of achievement as well as increasing familiarity and self-confidence. You can use discrimination learning to orient children towards science, the arts, sports, or whatever you want them to like and enjoy later in life. Here is how discrimination learning works. First, you observe your child's behavior, which is related to the target, or goal that you desire. For instance, your six year old asks: "Why do stars twinkle?" Pay attention to the child's innocent question as if she were a budding scientist. Orient the child by co-researching the problem with her. As a parent, notice that how you handle this question is a lot more important than what the answer is. The child needs to be praised for this interest and then some concepts can begin forming in her mind, like distance, light or numbers. You notice that this particular question could be related to an overall goal we call science, scientific thinking or interest and motivation in science. Take advantage of the teachable moment.

Second, you reinforce the behavior strongly by giving your undivided attention, showing pleasure, respect and responding in a partial manner. Nurture the question and the questioning behavior by responding in an informative way yet raising related questions or providing additional information. Do not give a simple yes or no answer. For example, you might say; "I'm not sure, I think it is because the stars are so far away. Have you ever heard of scientists using the term light years? I think it has to do with the millions of miles between us and them". You can leave it at that if that is all the child wants to do with the question at the moment. As this episode represents one learning trial among many, your child has recorded the behavior and your response pattern. Over time, the child knows that such questions are going to be met with approval and respect. Other questions like "Why do I have to go to school today?" should not get much of a response from you. After several such trials, the child learns to discriminate the behavior patterns that lead to prime time with mom and dad (and those that do not). Perhaps your child doesn't know that the context, which you have chosen to reinforce, is science necessarily, but you do. You have made a decision to reinforce a certain class of behaviors that approximate your goal. You do so, strongly and frequently at first, until the child begins developing a sense of mastery. For example, you might comment with a grandparent present about how Erin is really interested in astronomy, or how David is getting "real proficient" in Spanish. Later, you slack off on the reinforcement a bit and only provide it every other time, then every fourth time and so on until such behavior patterns become more sophisticated and you provide reinforcement randomly. And, the child discriminates between subjects or questions, which will recruit parents into learning conversations and those, which will not.

Logical Consequences

Surely, you need to use logical consequences when the child is out of line. Logical consequences are different from punishment in that they are predictable, while punishment is arbitrary. The child knows from past discussions what consequences will follow his decision to misbehave. The consequences are logical in that they are related to the reason why the behavior is inappropriate. If Mickey steals x from Tom, then besides returning x and apologizing, Mickey will have something taken away for a period of time. If the child is grounded or placed in a time out situation, make sure that the child has choices to select from and to work on independently. This way the child is still learning while something else is being removed.

Making Learning a Routine

Give children little assignments as soon as language development allows you to direct behavior (age 2 and up). Even earlier, you can ask your toddler to look for a familiar object, for example: "Where is the Kitty?" Establish a routine, a pattern, or a way of doing educational things with your child on a regular basis. Make learning familiar. With older children, you can orient them to the learning of reference skills. Look for a specific country on a map, a globe, or in the dictionary. Advance reading and writing skills by giving your child suggestions and encouraging all types of small efforts. Your child is always trying to master some understanding of the world. Your child is always engaged in scanning and responding to the environment. Redirect your child's behaviors in ways that can result in learning and positive reinforcement. Remember you are the one who is guiding the child's mind. You are programming the computer. Be sure to do so in a way that fits your child's style and personality. Children vary in how they respond. I can't really say to you, the reader, "do these things" and expect all your children to respond the same, even when they are of the same age and sex. You understand your child better than anyone else does.

The Spiral Curriculum

Intelligent parenting also means that you should have a master plan, a general scheme with which to develop various areas of expertise in your child, to organize the environment for the child and to sequence new learning. A culture organizes a lot of the experiences for children. For example, in school they are to learn to read, write, learn about other countries, etc. When they are about to finish high school, a number of skills are supposed to have been mastered. However, as you know, you can't count on schools alone to do the job. Insuring that Johnny will be able to read, write and balance a checkbook takes more than just schooling.

The family serves as an agent of culture in organizing what children become exposed to in the long run. However, the role of family in the child's mental development is much more fundamental. Yours is the master plan. From your child's earliest years, you can and should organize the environment for the child using the main principles of development and learning. For example, develop a cognitive strategy or employ a discovery/learning game. Parents need to work with the child in several ways. First, they should organize activities, which will prepare the child not only to do well in school but also to profit maximally from school. You, the parent, need to organize preschool activities so that the child qualifies for advanced, gifted and other programs. Once, again, if you want a very intelligent child, you must actively foster that intelligence from the cradle.

Second, once in school, children's development needs to be "boosted" regularly through parent's own patterns of interactions and special activities. Based upon the style and interests of your child, you must try to maintain certain avenues or channels to provide a gradual input of concepts that fall together in a special ordered fashion. These can be concepts in basic areas like science, geography, anthropology, astronomy, math or art. Any one of these areas can be considered a curriculum. The gradual input is crucial. You must decide what inputs are most useful as your child develops over time and as his mind changes in representing the world. So your job is to provide for this gradual building of knowledge—the spiral curriculum—matched to the particular stage of your child's mental development. Think of which areas seem most feasible and responsive to the child's wants and needs and the types of building blocks or experiences that you would facilitate for the child.

So the strategy of using a spiral curriculum with your child means that you arrange (whenever possible) for new pieces of information to be provided to your child in an interesting fashion. You revisit and expand on past inputs regularly from one year to the next. What you are doing is supporting the development of certain areas or aspects of culture in your child's mind. Remember, intelligence is based on one's representation of the world, what is in it, what works, and how accurately and completely the mind manipulates symbols, and categories (which is called thinking).

Back to Control

Sometimes a child will be doing something careless like throwing rocks and endangering himself or others. Instead of shouting something like: "Charles. Stop that, you are going to hurt somebody." Think of a useful way in which he can exert his energy. Maneuver him to get something for you that will lead to something fun later on. Or ask his help with something else, like figuring out how many liters are in a gallon, while you prepare a fuel mix for the lawn mower. It is better for a parent to spend a little time trying to redirect behavior than to put him into a time out situation in which no learning takes place. Such creative discipline is increasingly important if the young person's anger arises.

Distract the child from the useless and attract him to the useful. If you must use time out, expand on time out. Make sure that there is some educational stimulation available. Time out is punishment in disguise, and parents should not have to use it much if they are parenting intelligently. Punishment is totally useless in the development of intelligence, and using it more so than positive reinforcement is a sign that the parent is out of control and needs professional help.

Response Cost

Children should be given choices, which they can act upon in order to feel a connection between what they choose to do and the consequences. Sometimes children need to learn to behave intelligently and perhaps to experience some form of punishment in the process. But this outcome should be based upon a clear rule system that has been established cooperatively. Your child should know ahead of time what the cost of an intentional misbehavior is going to be. This approach is called response cost. Disrupting a serious adult conversation for a self-centered goal may be handled with a warning. Afterwards, the response cost may be one hour early bedtime but this is entirely up to the child to decide after the warning is issued, and the child is reminded of the cost.

Another approach is to offer the child the choice of a behavior that may lead to something positive. For example, Sue is a six-year-old who insists on harassing her younger brother. She can choose to stop and to select the next interesting activity or to go to her room early where there are books to read. Either choice is likely to leave learning as a possibility. Standing her in a corner for five minutes will not. Hitting her would be a dumb act. Parents should never hit children, unless life-

Chapter 5: Strategies for Parenting Intelligently

threatening situations are involved, for example like pushing a smaller child into a busy street. Children must understand the need for consequences when they choose to act out. However, they can participate in choosing a more pleasant consequence as long as they comply.

Catch the Child Doing Good (CCDG)

It is a good idea to go out of your way and to find something that the child can do well. Catch him being good. Divert attention from negative, useless behaviors and direct it toward more interesting things. Try to avoid power struggles with your child, in which you both lose. However, do not hesitate to be firm and deal with trouble consistently, with reason and without anger. Set children up for success by giving them roles, responsibility and time to follow simple directions. Remember that you are the programmer of the routines that the child will learn to execute and the concepts that he will master. The main thing for parents to know is avoid the criticism trap. Many parents and teachers believe that they are good teachers, because they know more than the child, and thus they can help the child to learn efficiently. Unfortunately, they are so eager to catch the child's mistakes that they typically engage in a "corrective feedback" mode, which is a turn off for children. Children are most likely to enjoy and to pursue an area when there is more positive than negative feedback. If you analyze what constitutes corrective feedback or critiques, it appears most like punishment which is aversive. If an aversive pattern then is established around music or science lessons, the child will be less like to pursue that field. Surely corrective feedback is necessary and an important aspect of teaching. But the point here is that the ratio of positive to negative feedback should be at least two to one. The smart parent realizes that the child's confidence and self-esteem is on the line. The "right" answers are not as important as the child's attitude towards learning in a particular field. The child's brain has a register of experiences which accumulates over time, and the child is aware of whether a certain activity is likely to be fun. For one child, art may have a high ratio of positive reinforcers, while for another child there may be a low ratio of positive experiences. Positive experiences become connected in the mind leading to what are called sets or expectancies. The first child considers herself good in art, and the other child does not have this feeling. A child's disposition is affected in subtle ways that are often not noticeable for years to come. A set is formed over time. Such sets explain how and why some children are more advanced than others in certain areas.

In sum, parents need to be aware of children's behavior patterns and reinforce often those patterns which are related to developing expertise and mastery. Corrective feedback should not effect the child's interest and motivation in a given area. If you are careful to do this for one zone or area, such as science, then the child will have a more positive set or attitude towards that type of "intelligence" in the future. As a result, it is more likely that she will be more ready to profit from school activities in that subject and thereby, the child advances intellectually (meaning she becomes a high achiever) and is motivated.

Grandma's Rule

Another strategy for intelligent parenting is to observe behaviors or activities which the child enjoys doing often. If a child likes to use the phone, to help to make dessert or to play soccer, then any of these can be used as "carrots" to increase activities which occur less often, such as studying or cleaning up her room. It may be that, for a certain child, going out with dad on Saturdays to the hardware supply store is fun. This is a reinforcer that can be used right after the child does study, or gets a good school report.

So when parents are not sure what will attract a child, the rule of thumb is to watch for current activities which have a high frequency and which you can facilitate. You should not consider such strategies as bribes, rather such activities represent a straight forward contract between the child and the parent. Make it clear that excellent reports from school automatically lead to some privileges. Contractual agreements work much better than waiting for grades to drop and then adding criticism or punishment to future attempts at negotiation.

What sorts of things can parents do to facilitate the spiral curriculum and to help the child to obtain ownership and control? Take for example, a toddler. You can ask him to name or mark things that "belong together." You can ask the child to let you know when he has found four things he can do with the same toy, and then ask for three more. Have him sort objects according to a new category like solid or liquid, human, plant or animal, and shapes and colors. Keep reworking the concepts so that a challenge often remains for the child. The main object here is for you to take time to structure parts of the day for vigorous interaction with the child. I don't mean that you have to be on top of the child prodding answers. Rather, show her that you are willing to interact and give her attention for certain types of things. These then will be the areas that represent growth of interests and knowledge. Have her practice what she has learned and to state what she has learned in different ways.

Provide for a variety of ways in which the child can demonstrate new learning. Help the child to generalize what has been learned by encouraging her to apply a new learning to different situations. For example, a nine-year-old learns what pollution is in one particular instance (car exhaust) and how it makes the air we breathe hurt us. You can help her to strengthen and to transfer the concept to other pollutants.

Or another example, if she has just learned about reptiles, lead her so that she can figure out ways in which these animals are different from mammals. Keep at the task until she can form a rule. For example, reptiles usually hatch from eggs

Chapter 5: Strategies for Parenting Intelligently

which are laid on land. As you are beginning to see, structuring the environment in which the child will grow calls for you to think of yourself as a designer. You need to arrange for interesting things to appear and to fascinate the child as much as possible. If your child is getting into trouble by messing up your bookcase, find a better setting for exploration to occur. Don't wait for the child to get into trouble to interact. Interact before that happens and arrange the situation so that what he does will not cause you to scold or to punish.

Teach children cooperation. For example, you could say "While you do this and that, I am going to make so and so. Let me know when you are finished." In this way, you create an expectancy or a reason to perform the activity because the child understands that cooperation in this task will lead to doing something fun like hitting ball at a park or going to the lake.

As another strategy, encourage your child to teach others what is being learned. Such an activity helps to consolidate intellectual skills. This is one of the reasons why first born children are usually more advanced than middle siblings in some areas.

Although routine TV watching can be a mind numbing experience for children, it also can serve as a spring board. Again, the child needs to know what is expected or that learning is an ongoing activity in the home, and that they may be involved in an educational experience at any opportunity. If they are watching a TV show, ask them to summarize what happened and gently help their thought to become expressed clearly and economically. Make it a game. "What did Mr. Rogers teach you today?" Or, "What was the most important thing for you in that story?" Remember that you are causing the child to think about things that often would go by unnoticed. It is somewhat easier to use this intellectual tool with children in middle school. It is easy to help them become abstract in their thinking or less concrete. Show them how certain statements may even have double meanings. Help them to become critical of the information that they are receiving.

Modeling

I take this opportunity to discuss modeling as its own entity. As you are well aware, children, in play, are continually using imitation. Even some animals imitate, as is the case when a lion cub imitates his mother's stalking stance, or a young bird is taught to peck for worms by his father. Imitation or modeling is a key tool to teaching learning related activity patterns. If they want an intelligent child, the parents should be actively involved in reading, in problem solving and in discussions which contain logic and skills in problem solving. If they want their child to advance in music, then parents should be involved in listening to music or playing an instrument. If you, as a parent, want your child to be skilled in math, then model searching for games that require math skills and play them often. But remember, first there must be an established positive relation between the child and the model.

Modeling is one of the most important ways in which values, attitudes and complex behavior patterns are learned by your child. The nice thing about learning through imitation is that most of the time you do not need to reinforce the child directly. Secondly, the child can learn difficult skills all in one swoop. Generally, children imitate for three reasons. The smart parent needs to know each one and also the effects of having observed a model.

I will illustrate the first reason why a child imitates through an example. If a child is doing something, like picking up his toys, and Mom says to Grandma "Look at Bobby. He's picking up after himself just like his Dad," then Bobby is more likely to continue this "like Dad" behavior in the future (provided he and dad have a strong bond). In this case, the child did something (usually good), and another person remarks that he did it well, just like a model. Remember, a model can be real, like dad, or symbolic, like Batman.

This learning by modeling happens all the time. The point here is whether you, as a parent, can learn to harness the behavior in order to orient your child towards certain payoff areas of endeavor. For example, if your child's behavior seems to be related to scientific inquiry or to creative perspectives, then relating it to models can be very effective in supporting those "traits." You could say "Bobby is a regular Mr. Wizard." This is the smart way of using social or observational learning. Another way to use observational learning is for behavior management. Particularly with young children, a behavior or skill can be learned if it is connected to a positive role model. When your child misbehaves, you could say, "He-man would not do that to his friends" and this statement could easily stop a behavior of that sort next time.

There is a second reason why children imitate. Suppose you reward Debbie for appropriate behavior like picking up the room, and then the younger sibling (target child or the observer) goes to her toy box and puts away her toys. This younger child has performed picking up behavior or a related act, and she expects to get the same regard her older sister was given. A parent who does not pick up on this learning mechanism wastes valuable opportunities. One very important thing to keep in mind is that your child might not, probably will not imitate immediately, but wait hours, days and months to show the learning. The question here then is "are you aware?" Make it easier on yourself. Remember, children can learn to show off a behavior if a model is presented and he or she gets positive attention. And this behavior can be associated with mental development. Consider the following, your child's cousin might come for the holidays and sits down to read a book. Your child, who is not used to doing that much reading, may then read more often.

Imitation learning can go still further. If a model gets punished for being self centered or for ridiculing others, then the observing child will likely inhibit being that way. As you can see, these are effective ways of using models, particularly

Chapter 5: Strategies for Parenting Intelligently

where creative and intelligent efforts need to be supported. This second way that children imitate is in order to get something or to avoid a negative consequence. Let's consider the negative for a moment. A child learns by observation that another friend gets to leave the dinner table by acting out. Now the learner wants to get out of being stuck at the dinner table *(the context) the next evening, so she imitates the model. Later on both children try the same behavior pattern in school and they get out of class by misbehaving. What have these children learned?

So you want an intelligent child? If your child observes you writing or reading frequently, and as a result, many people ask you for advice and compliment you for your wisdom (consequence), then your child is more likely to read and write (imitating you), in the hopes that she can get a compliment. I have two questions for you. Do you read and write frequently in front of your child? And are you watching her behavior enough that you see the imitation and compliment her?

Finally, children will imitate simply because that activity makes them feel good. We have all seen instances in which children become interested and motivated when they watch a model do something, like the way a favorite and successful tennis player serves the ball or a basketball player makes the 3 point play. They imitate the serve or the shot and feel vicarious reinforcement when they do so, because they are thinking of the model whom they observed earlier. Such activities make your parenting job easier. In this case, the model does not need to be rewarded for imitation to occur. All you need to do is to provide a positive role model who says "Drugs are only used by stupid people." Your child is very likely to share that attitude and the behavior of refusing drugs in the future.

When your child observes and the above types of reinforcement are present, then three effects can be predicted: Direct imitation of what was observed, engaging in a related behavior, and holding back or showing off a particular type of behavior pattern (depending on the consequences applied to the model).

Why use praise and encouragement?

Ok, before referring the reader again to association learning theory and modeling, check this out. **TYCD=Things You Can Do**. When children receive praise and encouragement, it typically makes them feel good and as if they are valued. These meet their self-esteem needs. And in turn, these feelings become associated in an indirect, subconscious way, with whatever field or activity in which you and the child are interacting. The result is that the child wants more of these feelings. And, she is motivated to keep learning about the field of interaction, whatever it is. After all, good things happen on that "channel." Things that are good for the self-concept and one's sense of worth and mastery. Pretty soon, you will not need to motivate your child from outside as much. The child begins to find joy in achieving understanding and mastery and in discovering stuff. You merely need to confirm these enthusiasti cally. In that vein, it is important to suggest to the child that she is bright and capable, and that she is doing very well, any time she tries. This confirmation results in more effort by the child and better learning. The child lives up to the expectation, and fulfills it with ease. Remember, this expectation began as yours but ends up as hers. This style of interaction can start early and really takes off as children learn language to communicate and guide their thinking. Yes, it is language that propels thought and concept development, along with activity. After guiding thought to higher levels and leading it to action, then new learning can be translated back into language. This reinforces the new learning. Over time, this pattern produces better tools and more generic mental skills.

Positive Reinforcement (PR)

Contrary to popular thought, the key is not candy. It is not money or a smile. Positive reinforcement is a process which depends upon the individual child. It is a process that results when a child feels good after doing something. That something is likely then to occur again. What ever is used to bring about joy or interest then is called a reinforcer, which may be a smile or food but not always. A positive reinforcer is what parents use when they praise and encourage a child's efforts. The parents are in effect saying to the child: "We would like you to do more of that (what-ever it is, like a thoughtful action or remembering a historical fact).

PR is the key tool for establishing activity patterns that serve to accelerate learning, and it doesn't cost you. What happens is that parents confuse PR with stock things like candy, "good girl", or privileges. PR is more than just things which parents give out. PR is anything that, when it follows a child's action, tends to make the child to do more of it. That is, if it doesn't work to increase the child's behavior, then it is not PR, regardless of how well it works for someone else.

PR is a personal thing. For example, I've seen parents fail who give children lots of "things." Yet they can't seem to understand why the child is not motivated. For PR to work, it has to give the child a good feeling, a sense of pride, or acceptance. The main thing is that the child needs to feel valued and competent, and you can do this most often when the child's intellectual curiosity is at work.

So, you need to master this point. Here is how. First, know what PR is, see it at work, learn to use it by assessing the effect it has on behavior. Learn what turns your child on by observing. Develop a menu of reinforcers, that is, things which you can add on or have happen, after the behavior that you want to see more of occur. Parents need to have a number of options readily available. Reinforcers are what you use. Reinforcement is a process that makes the child feel valued and capable, so he wants more of the reinforcer. Remember, sometimes the good feeling and affirmation are the reinforcers.

Chapter 5: Strategies for Parenting Intelligently

Second, learn to identify patterns of behavior which your child has that relate to learning about specific fields or in general. Reserve your reinforcement, more and more, for child activities that result in learning about the world and that foster flexibility in your child's perception of the world. Now, make sure that you connect the child's learning related behaviors to "good" things that happen afterwards (PR). Once you do this regularly, then start to stretch the reinforcement out. Give the big reinforcers for more challenging events, and make their occurrence less predictable. You see, the reinforcers you use for PR can be scheduled to occur each time or at varied times, in big helpings or in little doses.

So how do you know what and when? Well, here are some rules. Whenever you catch your child trying to learn about something, drop everything and rush into the interaction. Connect the action with PR right away. Do not delay in giving your strokes. Your child's computer is programmed to do more of whatever it was that led to feel- ing good (PR). Right? So, give PR right away and initially at every occurrence. Then give PR every other time and so on, until you reach the stage at which you only pro-vide PR once in a while, at unexpected times. Consider this an example that includes modeling: Your spouse is reading a letter aloud when she encounters an unfamiliar word. She asks you for the definition, you stumble and you both figure that neither of you knows the meaning. Your child is observing all this. You "attack" the word by guessing from Latin root, while your wife goes to find a reference book. You both try to confirm the hunch. You try to learn how to use this new word in different contexts. Later on, you may catch your child going to the reference books for the first time to look up words. The prior sequence is being modeled.

Since you want more of this behavior pattern, in which your child demonstrates individual motivation and intellectual curiosity, you deliver a super comment like: "Jamie, you seem to know your stuff. I like the way you go after what you want to know. Can you explain that to me a bit more?" Here the child is getting prime time from you. Later, you weave the event into a family conversation. You stress that Jamie doesn't wait around for things to come easily. She is a go-getter. When the time comes, you will know how to say it your own way, just try to be real. In this way, you are "feeding into" the development of a self-image in which the child begins to consider herself a capable, intellectual person. Such a process can be used to capitalize on interests which your child is developing particularly if these represent areas in which you want to see more growth. In general, reserve the PR for intellectual and emotional areas of growth. I say emotional because your child needs to feel confident, respected and competent in most endeavors.

Finally, avoid using punishment and time out in ways that curtail learning. Time out involves removing the child from interaction when a behavior is unacceptable. And most certainly, make sure that learning related behaviors do not become discouraged. For example, staying up late while reading in bed is not a behavior to be punished. If a child wants to keep the light on to read at night, do not punish this behavior even though it means that the child will lose sleep. Use the natural consequences on the child until the child learns to regulate himself. That is, get the child up at the appropriate time the next morning and remind him that he chose that option.

Asking too many questions (for attention at the wrong time) should not be met with a physical time out like being removed from interaction. Rather, use extinction. When you don't want to see something occur a lot, just ignore it, distract it, divert or redirects attention. Do not waste your time getting into a power struggle. Have rules already set up through which there are consequences for good and bad behaviors. There is no need to get angry. Let the consequences do their work. If you get unnerved or irritable, you are blowing it and failing to model effective behavior patterns. Let the child choose to gain or lose from consequences that have been agreed upon earlier.

Extinction

The best way to eliminate useless behaviors and to decrease interests the child may have that interfere with the development of talents is simply to ignore them. Being critical of the child still provides attention, and often, this negative attention is better than no attention at all. Your child craves you and your attention. Your child's needs for belonging, safety and self-esteem are crucial. The intellect is not likely to be developed very far, unless these other needs are satisfied.

You need to provide for the child's emotional needs in order to prevent useless behaviors.

Even so, even when you are doing a sound job of parenting, useless or negative behaviors will be observed, like a child who manipulates. And, all children manipulate. For example, a child might be doing poorly in school, and yet, instead of studying, the kid asks his mother to allow him to go skating or to take him to friends' houses to play. The parent knows that if she refuses, the child will make it uncomfort-able for her. She may feel like a "meany," and so she gives in. Then the child rein- forces her for giving in by being more pleasant, and the climate in the home goes back to normal.

The parent accepts this manipulating event which got the child out of studying since she does not like the conflict. She soothes her own conscience by promising herself to find a tutor for the child. Yet what she does not realize is that the problem is likely to worsen, and the child's development will suffer in the long run. The parent in this case does not have the big picture. The big picture is to parent in a way that helps the child be in an advantageous position in the present and in the

Chapter 5: Strategies for Parenting Intelligently

future. The child must learn not simply to adapt but also to affect the environment in meaningful ways. This requires studying and honing intellectual skills. Rewarding a child for being a pain in the neck until he gets his way is not doing him any good. In the above case, the child's ability to develop will be affected.

Parents need to be vigilant. They need to watch for what will help to cultivate intellect and creative talents. Nothing should be preventing their child's intellectual development, not even the child himself nor his friends and classmates.

Even when schools are not stimulating, children need to surmount this and to do well. Intellectual development is not negotiable. Poor grades are a symptom. Poor grades should signal to parents that other needs are not being met. Review the chapter on motivation if your child is not adapting well to school.

More Strategies To Foster Intelligence

As a parent, you recognize that encouraging motivation in areas other than intellectual may be fine but not as crucial as motivation for developing intellectual skills and knowledge. After all, "Where there is a will there is a way." However, this last statement begs the question: "A way to what?" Going to the finest colleges? As a parent, you recognize that the way is toward total development via a focus on the intellectual. Not that going to the finest colleges is not desirable, but, that is only a means to enhance potential.

What you want your child to be able to do is to initiate and to direct a pattern of behavior that is adaptive and creative. You want your child to avoid being passive or impulsive. You want your child to reflect and think. You want to avoid a couch potato consumer mentality.

In the final analysis, being intelligent really means the ability to engage in intelligent activities, to have access to a way of being and thinking that promotes growth across one's lifetime. You need, to understand that this "payoff" requires strategies such as positive reinforcement, novelty and modeling which need to be practiced regularly and systematically.

In short, when you encourage the meeting of intelligence, creativity and motivation as a whole, you have what is considered a superior or gifted person. There is nothing in the books about parenting gifted children that does not apply to your child as well, for he is gifted (given that an intelligent context has been afforded from early on). Granted you can find 3 or 5 kids out of a hundred who have had little intentional parenting, yet they develop at a more rapid rate than most. These children manifest because there is a meeting or coincidence of "supports" for motivation, intelligence and creativity which happen to be present 3-5/100 times by chance. Your child will not have to depend upon chance as you, the parent, can improve the odds, especially when you orient development in areas that schools and society value like math, science, formal operations, etc.

Teach a second and third language. There are at least two reasons to teach another language to a child. They have to do with culture and second signals. But first, before I go into detailed descriptions, I want you to think about it. Take one minute right now, and ask yourself why this type of learning may be important, and then read on. Please remember, I did not promise to simply give you 101 ways to raise your child's intelligence. I promised to teach you how to be intelligent about mental development for your child's benefit. Through this knowledge you can and will discover thousands of other methods and techniques which are individually better suited to you. As you read, I am interacting with you and your mind as you read. Suggesting a second language is only one example of what you can do with the knowledge you gain from this book. Only after you digest this information, will you start to learn what parenting for intellectual development is all about.

Teaching a second language sharpens the child's mind. In doing so, two major advantages can be noted. First, the child benefits by entering into a second culture which speeds up the child's understanding of all cultures in the world. And, remember it is culture which makes the mind intelligent.

Without our natal culture, we would have not developed our brain's potential. When a child becomes familiarized with another culture through second language learning, new windows literally open up in the brain. The child's understanding of many aspects of reality is enhanced. This allows the child to adapt better to all kinds of new situations in life. And, adapting better is another way of saying that one becomes more intelligible about the world.

In learning a second language or second way of representing the world, the child learns to understand the first language better. She becomes less concrete about her culture's way of representing the world which means that she can develop abstract concepts more easily. It matters not if the second language is Chinese or sign language, either way, the child develops learning how-to-learn skills. For example, if the child learns Spanish she then becomes more aware of the culture that is involved in using that language. Since language mirrors thought, she gets to see how other people think by using their language. A balanced bilingual child does not just simply add a second language to the mind that already possesses the first. What happens is that the second language acquisition changes the mind into a totally different computer which differs from those of persons who use either language alone. This transformation also puts the child into a new culture of bilingual/biculturalism. From this standpoint, multilingual and multi-culturally experienced persons, even when they do not share the same culture or language, tend to see the world more alike than those with only "one handle" or way of looking at the world.

Other strategies include promoting less self-centered thought. A child who turns to the environment for stimulation tends to be quick, to understand and to form new concepts. He learns how to learn. So, provide lots of different points of view in

Chapter 5: Strategies for Parenting Intelligently

your verbal interactions. Show your child how others think and view the world.

Another strategy is to protect your investment from mediocre schools and overworked, exhausted or poor teachers. One way to do this is to use schools in ways that stay one step ahead of the child's development. Hence, you need to place your child into advanced programs, magnet schools, and gifted programs. Another strategy is to start your child off a year ahead in school.

Once parents develop a style such as the one presented in this book, the child is extremely likely to be years ahead of most peers. Anyway, the strategy then is first to serve as your child's instructor or to find an appropriate tutor system or teacher under whom your child can apprentice in ways that are consistent with what you are doing. Secondly, look for advanced programs or gifted educational classes for that grade.

Thirdly, try to enter your child into the school system at least a year ahead. As a matter of fact, there is a trend to put some students into classes which are ahead of their age level. Many elementary schools are recognizing the importance of the theory behind this book, and they are mixing first, second and third graders together in classes. This class make up makes sense, since teaching should be geared towards the child's mental level and not the age of the body. So look for progressive schools and teachers. But don't make the same mistake made by some well-intentioned parents who focus on identifying the best school. This is surely the first step, but the teacher who is to tutor your child's mind for a year is more important. How can you find a good teacher? The best way to tell is to observe potential teachers in action. Most good teachers will allow you to do this. It is the poor teacher who avoids it. A good teacher is one who is aware of the child's current level, and who discovers children's readiness and partial knowledge. Partial knowledge means that a child cannot quite tell you what a concept or skill is but knows different things about it and comes close to having mastery of it.

One of the main problems with schools is that they put children into non-natural groupings. They need to become more like home settings. Schools use age segregation typically to decide what the child will be exposed to and at what level. Same age groupings can cause some potential problems, as the teacher aims for the intelligence level of the middle of the class. This means that you need to ensure that your child learns and socializes with peers who are more advanced. However, at the same time, your child needs to explain and to show other less advanced peers what, how and why and when. We find this alternation between being the teacher and the learner in the home setting.

You see, one of the reasons first born children are typically brighter is that they not only receive more and better inputs from the family but they also get to teach much of what they have learned to younger siblings. I want to note that this doesn't mean that you can't achieve the same effect with a middle child. Of course you can. If you want to. It is all a question of process. Either you have solid, intelligent processes in your home environment, or you don't. Intelligence, self-concept, motivation and creativity are all influenced by developmental processes. I say developmental because a home environmental process may work out fine when your child is nine but not two years later. The process or your style of dealing with your child's mind needs to be adapted all the time in order to maintain the level at which the brain works and can work (which we call intelligence). The mind is developing constantly, waxing and waning and shifting gears all at the same time. What your child says, writes or reads tells you much of what goes on inside. This is why it is important to have and to use certain tools or artifacts around the house. For example, when you have a word processor in the house, the child is not only likely to learn how to use it but also to learn all kinds of knowledge that will transfer later on. Again, the best strategy is to have a solid, intelligent, supportive and warm home environment.

At home you should spoil the child and forget the rod. When it comes to information seeking, transfer or operations, let the child be free and do not penalize motivated activities. Of course, I mean spoil when it comes to certain areas that are directly or indirectly related to developing interests, skills and information as well as perseverance. A parent should avoid discouraging acts which show that a child is sticking with something or investigating a trivial aspect of the environment. It may be trivial now, but it is the process that counts most. Spoiling your child? Are you? Is it "bad?" From this perspective, it depends upon what areas you are concerned about. Letting the child throw food at guests is bad and differs from letting a child seek information from a guest.

Speaking of guests, visitors and family friends, do not forget to model or have others model what you want to see develop in your child. Do you want to see a motivated, eager child? Guess what? Look at what is going on in the home day in and day out, look at the patterns. Do you want a child who follows a series of steps before making a decision? Guess what you need to do? How about a child who likes to read and to discuss literature? I hope you are getting the picture.

Dinner Conversations

We can deal with these conversations as another type of strategy. Let's say you would like your child to appreciate and to develop a keen interest in history. What does this have to do with dinner conversations? Why ruin dinner by using it as a teaching activity? Heck, dinner interactions are most useful when you want to relax and to have fun with others. However, people do discuss and discover important things during meals. Take for example the business lunch. But why am I going

Chapter 5: Strategies for Parenting Intelligently

to stress the importance of dinner or lunch, family "sit down" meals? You are what you eat. Your mind is based on what it experiences. Experience is the food that nurtures the mind. So the point is that the parent needs to establish a pattern of conversing and exchanging with the child regularly. A natural way (and probably historically the most natural way) for this to happen is around meal times. Make time. You can begin even before the child speaks. It is the pattern that counts, because it becomes the vehicle later on. Even a toddler can reciprocate during lunch and can process sounds and meanings.

Later in the child's development, a parent who is knowledgeable needs to expose the child indirectly to events which shaped the world and the kind of life we now enjoy. Asking, "what if?" about historical events or scientific discoveries can trigger advances in the child's *Zones of Potential Development* (ZPD). It is as if you help to make an entry in a zone, which may be history, physical science, or art. Days or weeks later you bring up the subject again and take it a step further. This should remind you of the spiral curriculum. But, this is also the hidden curriculum. Later, provide the child an opportunity to verbalize from memory what he can recall about these discussions. If necessary, pretend you forgot. Elaborate and connect these topics with real life.

Another natural setting is to take a walk with your child. After toddlerhood, taking a walk after a meal or sitting on the porch create special educational moments with your growing child. During infancy, these moments are easier to construct. By the time adolescence hits, it is much more difficult to have those special times with your child. The important point is that the pattern is established. Learning does not always have to take place. But this habit, which propels the mind, is set, and perhaps compared to the environment next door, it will make a difference.

Speaking of habits, it has been noted that humans' behavior is 90% habit related. These habits develop from the micro culture around the child during the formative years. All I'm saying is that some habits or patterns are better than others for the development of the child's innate genius. This is why it is easy to raise your child's intelligence. Simply connect a lot of these home patterns to the things that are considered important in schools.

What if school ends up being boring and turns your child off? Don't despair or become negative about the state of education in your district. Here are some strate-gies: Look at this situation as an opportunity to develop your child's coping skills and maturity. The world is far from perfect. Your child needs to adapt to a variety of situations in an intelligent fashion. So getting in trouble because of restlessness or because of dull or preoccupied teachers is not smart. Encourage your child to cope with a situation like this. Ask him what are 3 things that might help the hour to go by without falling asleep? Perhaps he could help the teacher by asking for clarification or relevance in a polite way. Or, he could ask questions from time to time just to keep awake. If it is really dull, he could use the time to problem find or problem solve, do breathing exercises or write creatively, including letters to grandparents.

In sum, developing patterns of informative social interaction around one-on-one special times with a parent, uncle or neighbor are very useful. Parents can work to arrange for some of these to occur. As the child grows, use friends as resources. Anything to expand gradually the child's horizons (zones of potential development) will make the difference. After all, look at the time we wasted while growing up.

The next thing is to adapt the above to where the child is currently. This adaptation requires that parents be aware of what the child is ready for at various stages of his/her development. You already know about the early stages before school. Now let's expand your zone of potential development (ZPD) when it comes to stages of development.

Infancy and Trust

As noted in chapter three, infancy is a time when the child's basic need is to establish trust. The baby rejoices in recognizing familiar things. This is the easiest time to parent. You cannot go wrong as long as you love and provide interesting surroundings. Have the child track objects visually, connect sounds with objects, and as soon as they stop showing interest, find another object. Toys that respond back help the child to infer cause-effect relations that are important for later. Babies are mainly developing concepts which are stable at this stage and developing more memory capacity, as they experience things over and over.

Toddler's Search for Independence

Once the baby begins moving around, the environment is experienced differ-ently, and the child seeks independence and *autonomy*. Exploration goes on constantly, and you, the parent, begin to use speech to direct the child's actions. It doesn't matter that much for later intelligence, whether your child begins walking at 9 months or after a year, it doesn't matter that much for later intelligence. Locomotion leads to exploration of nooks and crannies that have a temporary value. Your toddler has discovered *legs*. How to use them in squatting, in tumbling and in kicking is most fun.If you know that the child is after establishing greater control over the environment, do not interfere at this stage. According to Erickson's psychosocial theory, if you do interfere with your child's attempts to control the environment, shame and doubt re-sult. What matters here is that shame and doubt, insecurity and anxiety over being scolded curtail mental development. This is the worst no-no for parents. You never block your child's mental development except for life threatening reasons. Avoid over protecting the child. Allow for self-feeding. Go ahead and set limits, but do so consistently and without rejecting the child. Do not blame. Rather, encourage, for you are seeing the development of self-confidence in the making. At this stage, the physical competence of the child is paramount and can be regarded as a basic level of intelligence. The toddler is indicating: "Look at x, I can do this and that with x" or "x can do y." These experiences are the basic building blocks for intelligence, and speech begins to accompany actions. Later, speech can take the place of physical actions, thus freeing the child for further action. Remember that speech utterances are thoughts. Einstein may not have begun to speak until almost age four, but he surely used speech in an abbreviated form or utterances. So while the child tests the world with his strength, legs and arms, you should provide for safety and lots of verbal stimulation. Make reading a routine. An 18-month-old can label scores of objects, thus showing that these concepts have been stored in the mind. Labeling stuff needs reinforcement and repetition. Try to elaborate on those sounds and speak clearly. The toddler goes from pointing to grunting. Anytime something is recognized, then pointing or touching leads to speech sounds. Once these sounds represent the object, the child's mental development advances. Do not pressure the child or force adult-type schooling at this point. The child is quite open to learning already. Parents need to concentrate on setting the stage.

Preschoolers Need Initiative

Preschoolers who have established trust in their surroundings and a sense of autonomy now need parental encouragement (to give heart) in order to establish their own initiative. This means that parents have to support their child when he tests his power and takes on "grown up" tasks. At this point, children have a zest for testing new things, and imitation takes on a fuller meaning than before. Play is intelligence in action, but play also often represents action that is very serious for the child. Fixing a bike is a serious project, as is making a mix for a cake. The quest for taking on responsibility is at the root of motivation. Reinforce initiative and cultivate it.

"Magical Thought"

There are no limits to what can be done now that the child has language to represent complex relations among things. A cow could become a mouse since both are known, and so is the concept of growing and shrinking. A horse could have horns or fly. Why not? Planes fly. Don't they? There could be a bunch of tiny musicians in the radio making music. Monsters can be threatening, but the Good Wizard will take care of things. The clouds may be sad and cry. Dreams are movies that happen in bed at night. With the power of language, children invent worlds of magic and generate very creative metaphors. The sky is the limit. Don't rush to end this wonderful period by imposing the rules, restrictions, and regulations that will come soon enough (The other three R's).

TYCD (Things You Can Do)
Once again, we are up to the point of strategizing...

- To encourage self-confidence, an internal sense of control and initiative, make up games in which the child takes on various roles from a familiar story. The family can act out stories and historical events that are familiar. Avoid disrupting children's activities when they are focused.
- Take children's ideas seriously and act on them. Their suggestions are important.
- Give credit for efforts even when the product of the child's initiative is unremarkable. Be patient and tolerant of mistakes and accidents and watch out for that negative body language which we adults are stuck with.
- Offer a variety of choices for games and activities so that the child feels that she has a say concerning what will happen every day. Make the choices positive even when resistance is shown.
- Don't get caught in a power struggle over eating candy or going to bed. Make the choices clear. Candy is to be provided at time a or b. The choice exists as long as there is no tantrum, later. Tie one favorite thing, like going to the park later, with taking a nap now. Do not pamper too much. Encourage the child to work her own way to get what she wants in ways that come closer and closer to good habits of work without rushing development.

Early Schooling and Concrete Thought

The name of the game for children who are entering elementary school and as late as the twelfth year (middle school) is industry. This means the child's mental development is geared towards fabricating, building, and making different things. When they are blocked or diverted from doing these things, they suffer emotionally by losing self-confidence and esteem. They lose initiative and autonomy as well, and this leads to feeling inferior. A child who feels she is less good at building or draw-ing or composing rap songs is less likely to be creative and intelligent than one who is encouraged to be enterprising and diligent. Give children a role or a task to do to develop initiative and autonomy. Then allow the child to do it independently. Around age 5-7, the mind of the child experiences a major transformation, somewhat like the one around age two when language develops. The magical, intuitive innocence of the child is transformed into a more hard-nosed, testy mode of looking at the world. The concrete minded child recognizes the order and logic of the physical world. The concrete operations lead to a model of the world that is stable, and the

Chapter 5: Strategies for Parenting Intelligently

child looks for rules in which "always, never, all, or none" can be used to show peers how much she knows. (So there.) They now understand that one element can compensate for another. Or, that one operation balances out another, like when two 12-oz sodas are poured into different shaped containers. A concrete operation is obvious when the child can "mentally" reverse the operation. Applying this to the previous example of the 12-oz soda, the child mentally "pours" the liquid from the tall thin container into the 12-oz can and does the same with the big shallow container. Then the child concludes that both containers have the same volume, thus reversing the process. Emotionally and mentally, the child wants to be competent and to do things well. A moderate amount of reinforcement is important. Give lots of it at first, then back off some, and give it more randomly. This process will help the child to become self-reliant and to have an internal sense (locus) of control. Parents of creative geniuses like Pascal, Einstein, and Madame Curie were not constantly stroking the child. Rather, the parents gave them a healthy distance to do their own thing. Let the child stay up at night and finish something, as long as she can show you that she can be responsible and that she will get up the next morning and function in school. Avoid judging what the child makes or produces by adult standards, for the child equates judgment of product with judgment of self... The risk is having the child feel inferior. Of course you did not mean to do that, but parents need to be intelligent about the stages the child goes through and about how they think and feel. Once the child has a successful track record, he is resilient and can withstand put downs and laugh them off. If you have done what is suggested in this book, chances are that your child will be labeled gifted or advanced at this stage, but remind yourself and the child that the label means little if it is not understood well. What needs to be understood is that this label is simply the result of there being a long-standing match between intelligent parenting and the child's natural genius. So now that you know a bit more about the mind of your 6-11 or 7-12 or 5-9.4 year old (age ranges vary for different zones of development), what can you do?

TYCD (Things You Can Do)
- Give children readings or experiments to complete and to report on later, particularly those that come in graded forms. Educational PC software of this type can be found in increasing abundance. If you don't have a computer, get access to one. However, you don't need one to advance reading and creative problem solving skills.
- When you discuss history, use a time line and graphs. Use three dimensions in modeling ABSTRACT concepts with which your child may have difficulty. Limit your discussion of concepts like "pluralism", "detente" or "perestroiska" until your child is ready to find these useful or interesting.

- Use tree diagrams to show how various concepts are related horizontally and vertically.
- Have your child "trade places" with a character in a book, human or animal.
- Take cartoon strips, cut them apart, and give them to the child to put in an order that makes most sense. Have him verbalize why and discuss various possibilities.
- Cut a paragraph from a story into sentences, and mix the sentences on a 3 X 5 card so that the child can put the paragraph together. Take turns doing this, so that it becomes a game. With younger children, let them read the story first. Then try a paragraph from a story you just read out loud. With older children, have them create the paragraph in a logical order that will make the game "fair." (Like Scrabble.)
- Have children recite a poem or a song in a melodramatic and exaggerated way.
- Have children "download" or outline what they know about a topic or concept (like evolution, WWII, chemistry, music types). Compare and discuss. Show how using resources around the house can help your child to be ingenious and enterprising in these learning games. This is why encyclopedias are of little use unless there are established activity patterns or routines.

How to access information is part of the literacy plant you need to foster at this stage. Show the child how to use the Spell or Thesaurus function in your PC or the subject catalog and ERIC system in the library. Learning by doing is the KEY. Doing by imitation of parents and older siblings works painlessly. Don't force. Rather, INVITE. Say, "I need to find this or that out, will you come and help me?" or "When can you do this research for me?" "What is the cost per yard of XXX?"

With all that you have read so far, I don't believe I have to tell you how you are developing various zones (ZPDs) and skills and which are which. (Does it really matter as long as patterns of activities such as these exist in your home?) You can do similar things with musical instruments or other props around your home. Make up your activities like I am doing right now.

Adolescence and Abstract Thought

The main task for early adolescents is to detach from parents and to begin sketching their own sense of self or identity. There are two main things which happen at this stage that trigger all kinds of changes. First, the body begins to change and becomes hairy and developed to the point of reproductive capacity. This forces the child to examine his physical equipment but more importantly, to become self-conscious. This consciousness comes about because the mind undergoes a final major transformation which is the beginning of adult thought and logic. When the child begins to think "as if" or hypothetically, when he thinks symbolically and is able to

Chapter 5: Strategies for Parenting Intelligently

put himself more fully into someone else's shoes, then the child becomes an adolescent. Usually adolescents are not ready for the change, and when it happens, they become very uneasy and feel very special. They feel so special in fact, that they have this hunch that they are the only ones in the world who can feel and think certain things. All of a sudden, they might feel or realize that they are emerging to become themselves. Adolescence is the first time that the child becomes free enough to go beyond what has been determined biologically and culturally. During this time she may envision new and better ways of running the world. She can perceive idealistic ways of managing schools and society, like "if everyone worked an extra five hours, there would be no poverty in the state." Or, "If people were told about the misery brought about by overpopulation, they might abstain from having children."

The child turned adolescent has a lot of vitality, when permitted, and shows great passion for various social causes, modern music, computers and other things. However, because the child's main task at this stage is to break away from her parent - derived identity, this passion is directed often towards things parents do not like. So respect the child's preferences at the time. They are fleeting anyway. And, putting them down is like putting the early adolescent down. Rather, reinforce the positive, and let the rest go, unless it is counter productive, like watching too much noneducational television. Allow space for the adolescent to establish her social and vocational identities. Allow for the brisk changes in mood, and keep up on the previous patterns of special times between parent and adolescent. Keep the channel open, build new bridges, and avoid being too close. The adolescent wants you to maintain reasonable limits, even when he argues against them. He must respect your reasons. So avoid stupid reasons like " Because I said so." or "Because I'm the parent, that is why." Instead stick patiently to a reasonable argument using statements that reflect on your feeling about the matter. Say, "When you do X it makes me feel angry (sad, uncaring, irresponsible)." Give honest reasons even when you can't agree. Adolescents can think using several factors at once. Their thinking shifts from the real or the actual (as in the prior stage) to the possible. So exploring jointly with your teen various possibilities, besides those actually observed, helps to establish flexibility and mutual understanding. A main difference between adolescents and "real adults" is that the teen is much more egocentric, in spite of the capacity to think abstractly. Simply because they have access to adult logic does not mean it will be used consistently. Many teens think that everyone should share their present concerns about ecology or justice. Adolescents also tend to think everyone is aware of them, what they are wearing and how their hair looks. This self-consciousness about their body, their intellect and their actions eases as they gain a more self-defined identity. So through these storm and stress years, the adolescents are the actors, and the parents are the supporting cast. Yes, they must rebel and that is healthy. In their quest to establish an authentic identity in the social, moral, vocational, and ideological planes, they will criticize parental values and wishes. They will also fall prey to trends in the peer group. Peers become more important than parents, for they provide mutual support to each others' experimental identities. Peer feedback is sought as the teen "tries on" new profiles, identities and personalities. If parents impose their expectations and pressure the child to be who they want him to be, they will force the teen to foreclose on that identity. Some adolescents try to avoid this "crisis" and just let the parents get their way. Such teens face an easy time at first. Later, they are headed for trouble, since what they are and what they are doing are not really what they want (but it makes mom and dad happy). So what to do? Do your best to let your teen explore and experiment, rebel and criticize, and take on the challenge with grace. Withstand assault after assault, and show some class and humor. You are who you are. You do not have to please your teen constantly so that she will love you. Your teen needs to be herself, and you must trust her and the relationship which you have forged over time. Now is when it pays off.

The parent needs to realize that a teen who experiments, questions, gets into a crisis from time to time, and contradicts himself 10 times in 5 years is OK. What you see is your child's effort not to commit to a particular identity or way of being because of you or the current clique or a particular movie. The crisis goes on as she forms a sexual and physical identity (e.g. Am I attractive? Is my nose too big? Will some one date me? Can I kiss well?) Then the crisis is about her social identity (Am I group dependent? Do I conform to Billy or whoever the leader is? Can I be a good leader in my group). The teen is trying on different personas and eventually makes a commitment to be considerate or exploitative towards others of the same and opposite sex. The crises continue into college, as they find a vocation that "is them", an ideology, a set of moral and ideological values (Republican or Democrat; Born again, Deist, Cult X) So maintain a respectful distance, and your confidence that they will prevail. Discuss non-judgmentally", if you can't, find others who can serve as a sounding board. It is at this stage that parents need to let go and to trust in what they have done during the previous years. As Kahil Gibran once wrote:

"Remember that there are no perfect parents, nor perfect families."

You do the best that you know how and try to learn to be the best parent you can be. Just remain honest and true and remember not to fall prey to the irrational idea that each crisis is your fault or his. Crises can be good if you understand, and this is why you are reading this book now and will read more of the suggested readings. Your teen will have a hard time growing to full potential if safety is not there, so avoid threats. Build self esteem as the best vaccine for adolescent problems.

Chapter 5: Strategies for Parenting Intelligently

TYCD (Things You Can Do)
To assist your teens mental development here are some things you can do:
- Ask your teen how to solve a problem (New or old) and to explain why each step is important.
- Have him recite his own poems or songs.
- Have your teen argue an issue one way and then another.
- Ask him to write a treatise on alternatives to going to school, or how to prevent abuse, sexism, racism, and wars.
- Discuss the teen's points seriously and expand by finding problems and advantages.
- Ask for book or film reports for special privileges like driving lessons, or simply say "let's make a deal, I'd like to have you do more of X because it might be important down the road. What could you do about it in exchange for Y (what the teen wants)." First get the negotiation routine down and then be increasingly more demanding in areas that the teen enjoys but have been ignored.

Formal, abstract thought is brought about by interacting with symbol systems like written or live dialogues, exciting passionate discussions and reflections on art forms and readings. Since your teen must separate from you, facilitate social interactions on intellectually stimulating subjects. Have gatherings, reading clubs, computer meetings, rehearsals for school plays and parties in your home or other settings with sharp people. Promote cooperative learning.

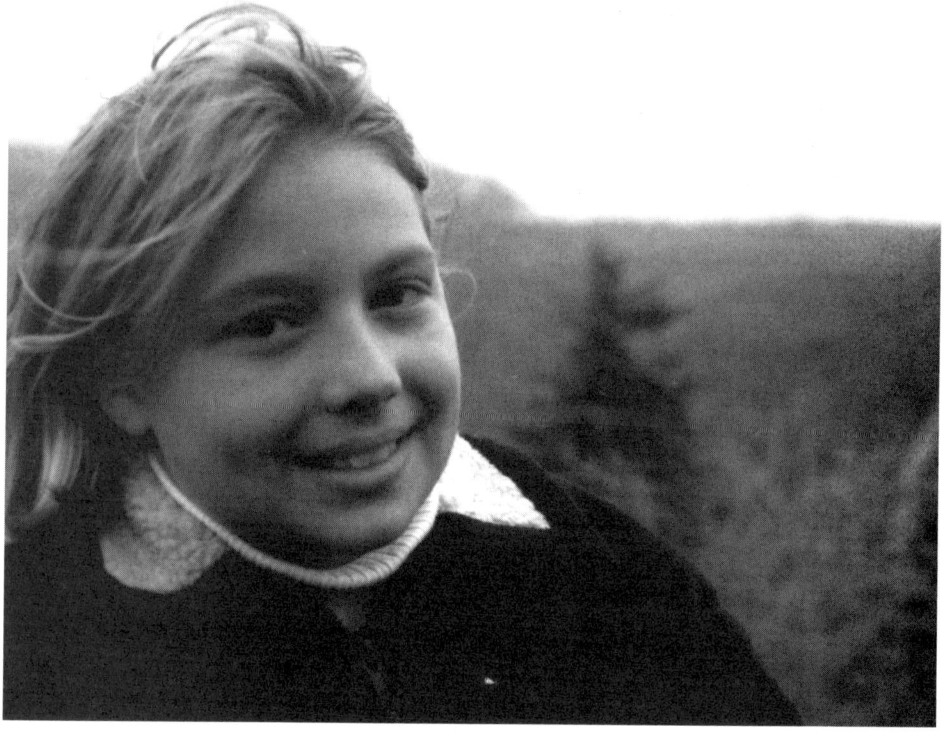

CHAPTER VI

CHILDREARING PATTERNS AND THE MIND

Life is a gift and the greatest gift is children. As Katherine Kersey wrote "Children come to us for a very short time, like packets of flower seeds, with no pictures on the cover and no guarantees. We do not know what they will look like, act like or have the potential to become. Our job, like the gardener's, is to meet their needs as best as we can: to give proper nourishment, love, attention, and caring, and hope for the best". Unlike Kersey however, I believe some gardeners are better than others in doing the job for they strive to be well informed and think while they hope.

The style parents develop to rear their children represents one of the most important influences on the development of intelligence and creativity. Childrearing style shapes a child's set towards many things and their motivation to achieve. You could probably fit into one of several patterns of childrearing psychologists talk about constantly.

A childrearing pattern is a style that parents form as they try to adapt to parenting as a way of life. Most of the time, parents do not consciously decide on which style to use for the sake of the child. Parents adopt whatever style fit their needs best. The reason childrearing style is so important is that it represents the mold that surrounds the child during the most important years. As we noted earlier, parents need to make conscious, intelligent decisions in designing the best environments for the child, including the way they will deal with various behaviors. In the past, many parents reared children in ways that were parent-centered or convenient to the adult. However, as more and more studies began to show that other patterns of childrearing were associated with better outcomes for children, many parents began going to the other extreme without really understanding why. Let's look now at the major patterns and learn how you need to develop the most responsive one for your child.

The Disciplinarian-Authoritarian Style

The autocratic/authoritarian pattern has been the standard over time. Here the kid is told what is allowed and what is not. There are nice moments but parents are always right, their feelings are more important, they don't need to explain or reason with "these brats". Their rights are few and not well respected when they get in trouble. Children in these families are at the mercy of adults' logic. They are provided with a firm structure and parental expectations are to be fulfilled.

In this type of family the child's mental development is in danger of being limited but not always. However, being told to be quiet or leave the room when the child was ready to learn something that might not come around for another 3 months is not helpful. Here parents figure that kids are well taken care of physically and what the heck, might makes right, and adult needs are most important.

The authority-oriented pattern is the most familiar to us. Many high achieving children have been raised by such parents. Yet, what does this style do to intelligence? There are some pros and many cons with it. The main problem with authoritarian childrearing is that parents tend to be rejecting of many promising initiatives by the child which are often blocked. When the child is emotionally overpowered on a daily basis two things are likely to happen. One is that the child's independence and need for autonomy is curtailed. This is very much related to areas where the child could be developing a positive self-esteem.

Also, teaching the child that power and might "make right" is not a very useful lesson. It leads to conformity and stagnation of creativity, which is the fuel for intelligence. The above type of parents also fails to show love as far as the child's needs are concerned. They do not provide as much positive reinforcement for key areas in fear of spoiling the child. The main problem with this pattern is that the parent is not very aware of the child's developmental needs. High intelligence is not likely to be cultivated systematically in such environment even when the parent does love and care. You can imagine what happens to the garden when the gardener is harsh and does not tend to growing talents. Such parents have a hostile and aggressive way about them that often touches the child so that the child is not quite sure of how secure and loved she is one day to the next. With little praise and few rights, these children are not likely to meet parental expectations to be responsible adults. If they do, it is at a tremendous socio-emotional cost.

Creative children rarely come from these type of families. This is because they need to be exposed to flexibility, and a questioning attitude about most important things. Parents who do not conform easily and share with their child why following the norm is not always wise, have creative children more often than very conforming, "Law & Order" parent types. Parents may be wrong at times and if they are not willing to discuss it or allow some input from the child, the child is deprived.

The Permissive Style

The Permissive style may appear useful if used wisely for it allows the mind to expand freely and creatively. With permissive childrearing, however, children have few responsibilities but the same rights as adults. Parents tend to let children make most decisions but often fail to model innovative ways of dealing with problems. Children in these homes would need more than a lot of freedom to be creative, they would need more reasoning and negotiating. This style tends to pamper chilren and does not prepare them for the world.

Chapter 6: Childrearing Patterns and the Mind

The Democratic Style

This brings us up to a third childrearing style which is called democratic where parents listen to objections, encourage give and take and discussions. Children assume increasing responsibilities as they develop, and live in a warm family climate where limits are set clearly and logically. This pattern is most likely to produce creative children with some variations. The erratic, off and on style of parenting is not likely to produce creativity except accidentally. You see, some children develop their creative talents in the very process of escaping uncreative and dull situations.

Your style of parenting is similar to your style of gardening. If you are alert and provide the best conditions, the results will be fantastic. The difference is that we can all afford to slip with real gardens but not with our children.

Children do need guidelines and structure but only as long as parents model creative activities or provide for mentors to do so. Your child needs a special connection with someone who is purposely fostering a special relationship that requires challenges over time. As a parent, if you can't model and challenge on the basis of a good relationship, at least provide for such to occur for your child. You see, it is critical that you make use of your child's tendency to learn by observation. Your child models whoever is there for him emotionally, caringly. If that person is sharp mathematically or talented musically, the child will inevitably try to follow in those steps. This means that a smart parent insures that creativity is observed by the child through discussion, vigorous disagreements with the norms and original perspectives of immediate and distant issues.

In sum, if you look at the histories of very creative persons you find the same thing as when you look at the histories of the most successful persons in different fields: encouragement (to give heart), motivation, self-reliance, hard work and opportunity. Do not forget humor, it is critical. The creative child uses humor but does not fancy himself as the funny clown. Humor represents the child's ability to see something from a different, unexpected perspective.

So make sure that in your home, unusual possibilities are considered, that self-direction is reinforced as well as self-responsibility and that persistence and follow-through are observed and modeled along with the humble feeling of never being too sure about why things have to be done in a certain way.

The style of interaction you develop with your child represents a key mechanism through which culture enters into your child's mind. How you rear your child influences how much is delivered and the way it affects the child's motivation and interest. Childrearing style affects how intelligent or knowledgeable your child will be and, school achievement. You could probably fit into one of 4 patterns of childrearing psychologists talk about. Let's look at other patterns of childrearing and suggest ways you may improve your own.

Reasoning/Sensitive Parent

The reasoning, sensitive parent is more oriented towards allowing the child to be his own person, even when some control is shared. The parent accepts the child without demanding something of them continually. This parent type collaborates at the drop of a hat and takes time out to "be there" for the child. The child is provided with guidance of course and the freedom is connected to consequences that are logical. Also, positive modeling of learning to take responsibility leads to many opportunities for development. The best climate for intelligence to grow is in between a free, open and loving environments as opposed to one that is often disapproving and possessive. This is where you find the most interaction between child and adult, the bridge to genius.

Inconsistent Parenting

One of the worse styles of childrearing occurs when parents show intense, infrequent attention and care and at the same time, allow the child to have a lot of unsupervised freedom. These parents tend to be immature and/or unhealthy for they are too occupied with outside concerns and relate to the child in a superficial ("sure honey..."), detached fashion. Teen parents are prone to be erratic and show little evidence of a plan to "shoot for". Of course, such parents may have, at one time, been more loving but perhaps, during a critical period in the child's development, they are neglectful. The child is then at risk for not developing many talents because they are worried about more fundamental, emotional needs that are unmet. So these children go out and try to meet basic needs and fall behind intellectually because the base, the very critical emotional base is missing. As with the authoritarian parent, rules tend to be arbitrary and there is little support for creative thinking. These parents make mistakes often in responding to the child's behavior. For example, the parent may ask the child to take more time in doing a school assignment, then whether the child does or does not, the parent ignores the behavior and seems indifferent. This is not wise in intelligent parenting.

The Protective Parent

The last direction parents can take, aside from the above is generally one where they are loving, possessive and authoritarian. These parents tend to overindulge the child at times, yet they are very protective. They rule and love the child. Rules are not discussed much together and love is withdrawn by the parent as a means of controlling the child, who is likely to become dependent and fused with the parent. Independence and freedom are the last thing these parents desire or want, for they impose themselves on most aspects of the child's life. When the child complies the parent shows love and even when they do not comply, they still indulge

Chapter 6: Childrearing Patterns and the Mind

the child, sometimes by leaving them alone. Adolescents often clash with parents of this type. Intelligence occasionally flourishes in this environment but not as much as in the freedom-oriented democratic style, where parents learn to let go and are most sensitive to the child's ever changing needs for knowing.

In all of the above patterns, remember that the child learns from observing parents so that if they are indifferent, the child learns to be so and less sensitive. As noted throughout this book, you need to develop your own style among these poles. Hopefully, you will develop an informed, intelligent parenting style that is unique. This is because you know what is desirable for the child and you know the ways to encourage certain types of development. You want to provide your child with unconditional love yet let them know clearly what is expected. The expectations change according to the child's changing abilities. There is a lot of flexibility in this climate and children eventually have a say in the development of rules. And there is no spanking unless a life is threatened and nothing else works. Even then, look into your child's eyes and do it verbally, it is more effective.

In sum, the above styles serve as a guide from which you may understand the gist of this book. Once you become better acquainted with the present model, dozens of strategies will come to you as you improve in distinguishing what is "good for the child's computer" or developing talents. In fact, you are mastering a way of parenting, a style of being with your child daily. From it, you can become more aware of how the mind develops and the infinite ways you can spark development through intelligent interactions, activities and consequences.

The first rule is not to get in the way of the child's innate drive to be a genius. The second is to create ideal conditions without pushing your own agenda. The child already has one and it is to be the best he can be. The third rule is that there are no strict rules to promote intelligence but rather just general principles that help match your input with your child's readiness to go forth. All creative and talented children have positive family environments relative to others. While the old rule was that children are to be seen not heard, now we know that is ridiculous. Active social and verbal interactions that are strategic work well and keep children involved. As you now know, parents are the first to originate and regulate thought processes in the child's mind before the child does it alone. In sum, an intelligent and positive childrearing style protects the child's genius while at the same time enhancing it.

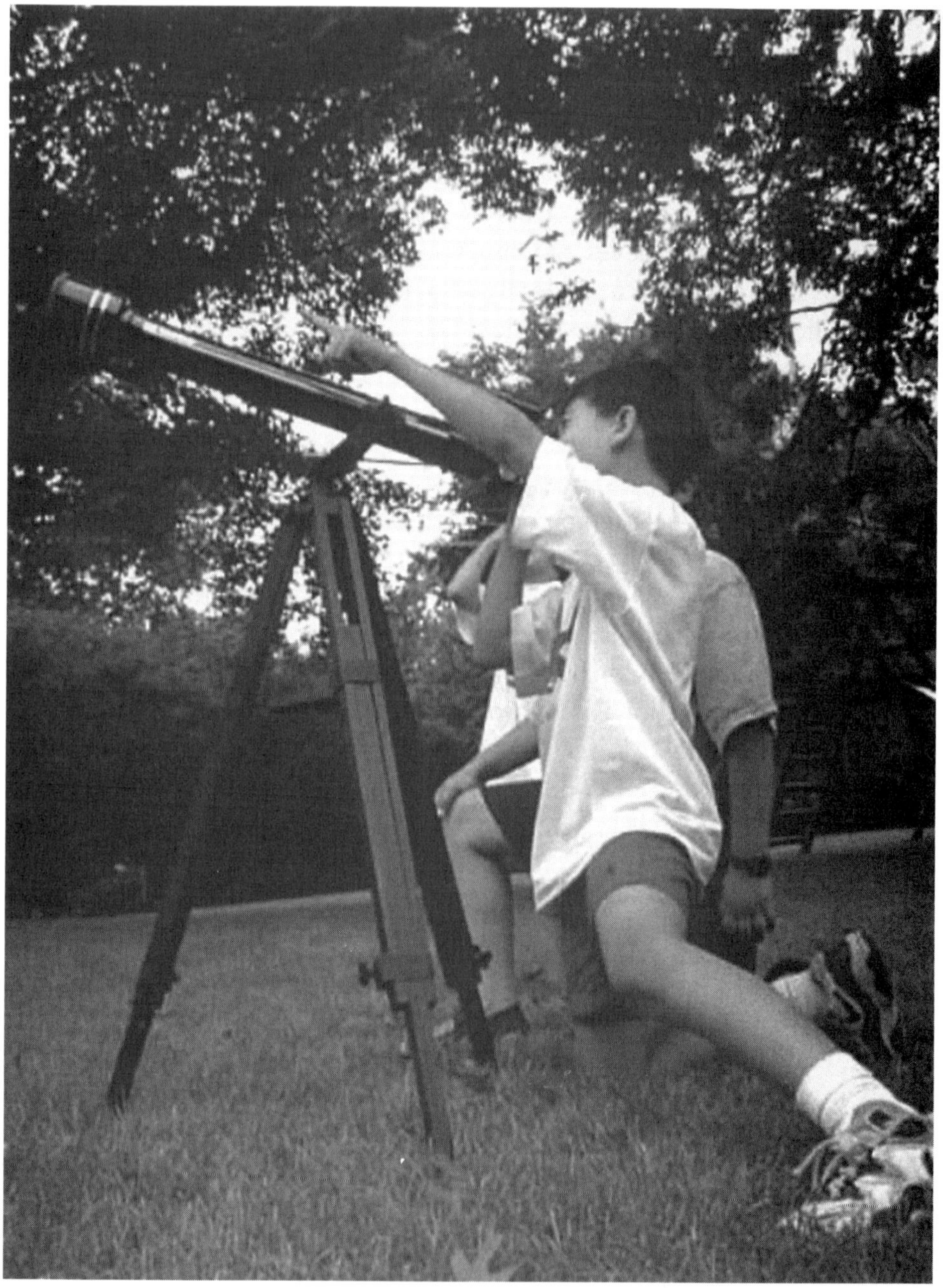

CHAPTER VII

LEARNING AND MOTIVATION

The Key to Genius

Learning how your children learn is a must for parents. Most parents and teachers do not know the keys that open the mind. Without the keys, motivation often becomes a problem. Without motivation, intelligence and creativity are for naught. A major key for developing intelligence in children is for parents to know about motivation and how to motivate children. In this chapter you will learn about:
- Different types and models of motivation.
- How motivation is related to expectations.
- How certain needs have to be met before certain motivations are possible.
- How to help your child to take self-responsibility.
- The relation of self-esteem to motivation.
- How motivation is related to intelligence and creativity.

Achievement Motivation

Let's begin with a question. How is it that some children seem "turned on" to learning, feel smart and are really advanced compared to their peers? These children are said to be achievement oriented. How do their parents manage this little miracle? Is it just that they got one of those special kids to start with? Or, are they raised by "smart parents"?

Achievement motivation gets started in the home and reflects the parents' own achievement and the way they raise their children. Achievement motivation means that children are brought up to want to achieve in general. It doesn't matter whether we are talking about chess, math, or baseball. When children achieve or become active in something, they receive internal and external reinforcement. Parents usually reinforce a pattern of achievement in the home and convey to the child how valuable doing well in a given activity is to them. The child "picks up" on this and strives hard initially in order to get some important needs met, like receiving attention, being regarded positively, and being loved. After a while, the child begins to enjoy the "achieving pattern," even when parents cease to reinforce regularly. This process is called establishing a set. The child enjoys achievement and begins to reinforce herself regularly and internally so that the behavior/attitude pattern becomes established or set as a preferred type of activity.

Children do not depend on external rewards to be smart. Children are naturally curious. They are already motivated to learn when they encounter a responsive environment. They want to achieve anyway. What parents need to do is to be aware. They need to look at the activities which the children are "into" and to connect this motivation with a zone or field of intelligence. For example, Jonathan, a 6 year old, is looking at his bike's rear wheel trying to figure what is making a rubbing noise. You can say:

a) Jon, someday you will be a great mechanic.
b) Hey, don't get your hands dirty with that grease.
c) Hey, kid do you want me to teach you about fixing bikes?
d) Observe, then say: "It isn't easy to figure out the problem. Huh? But to be good at anything, you've got to try and to go at it just like you're doing." Pat him, and go on your way.

The problem with a) is that it is connected all right but, not in the right way. You do not want to emphasize becoming a mechanic later in life because that may limit the child's career options. The next two are also inappropriate since they do not target the key aspect of the situation, which is the initiative of the child.

How Children Learn To Be Motivated

1. The mind works, quite simply, like a computer. But the mind is also tied to feelings, such as self-esteem. Whatever boosts self-esteem tends to be learned. That is a feeling just like others which makes the child belong and to feel safe and secure. Children learn when there is trust and confidence around them. This comfortable environment leads to exploration and discovery on the part of the child, which is, of course tied to learning and development.

2. The computer in the child's mind collects information, forms concepts and develops skills. It continues on in this manner until it detects an inconsistency, until an expectation is not met or not confirmed. Your child thinks a tomato is a vegetable, and then someone tells him it is a fruit. What happens inside the computer? It tells the mind "Hey, some thing isn't right in what I'm picking up. You want to do something about it kid?" Now the child's system is alert. It is energized or activated in order to try to find a balance or an explanation.

The next step is to connect some circuits so that relevant information can be examined on the "mental screen." Strategies are then selected and action taken to establish order in the system. Establishing a new order in the mind often requires learning, which in turn, produces mental development.

Children learn most when motivated. A motivation is a drive which usually has a goal or expectancy. Your child is naturally inclined to be able to do something, to stick with it, and to move towards a goal. Following this sequence leads to a sense of control or mastery in a particular area or skill. Parents can set up these sequences by paying attention and planning from time to time. Ask yourself what is most appealing to the child, and then connect it with activities that can pay off. For example, don't buy Nintendo games but rather education games.

Competence

All children are motivated to be competent. They are keen scientists. They will seek social interaction to resolve the inconsistency, the problem, the conflict or dilemma. For example, Ana is a 9 year old who insists on being informed about history. She enjoys hearing about the history of different cultures and prompts adults who have knowledge of history to talk about European nobility, royal marriages and empires. Her parents do not know why she is motivated towards that area, after all, other children might be interested in biology or math. Later you will see how this type of interest comes about through a " developmental process" based on some activities which have occurred in the environment that have a "common thread" running through them. For example, Ana's interest could stem from a film and/or a book which produced enjoyment. Of course, your own child has such drives to be competent some of the time. However, the child won't be driven to master some areas, unless you set her up to find problems or conflicts, and then show her some diverse ways to approach or resolve them.

3. To be competent, a child needs at least two things. One is self-confidence, and the other is performance skill. A child can be highly confident but have low performance skills, because these have not been developed. Such children set high goals for themselves, change them often and then blame outside factors when the feedback for their performance is negative. They externalize the blame and really do not see their part in the process, unless the outcome is positive. They are likely to say: "It ain't my fault the stupid thing would not work." Over time, an attitude becomes "set" which is not good and leads to conflicts.

Attribution of Success & Failure

Children learn lots of things, yet some are more important than others. Some of those things influence motivation a lot. How a child learns to handle outcomes in life is critical. Some children attribute success to luck or to external factors, and have a hard time accepting responsibility. When these children fail, they tend to blame external factors as well. High achievers and intelligent children, in general, attribute their success to internal factors. They attribute success or failure to effort or ability. If they fail, they try harder or try to get help in developing a skill. They may even decide to try something else in which they do have control. Parents need to pay attention to children's attributions. Ask your child from time to time why something went well or badly. Listen, and do not judge. Chances are that you will detect a pattern that sounds awfully familiar at the parental level. A lot depends upon the control patterns you have set up in the home environment.

So the first thing to do is to try to develop a pattern of attribution in your child that helps to connect outcomes to mostly internal factors. Show the child that by manipulating certain factors, different degrees of success can be achieved. This process is difficult for parents who do not share control. Such parents impose control on their children, and as a result, they tend to have externally oriented children. These parents impose chores and make demands on their children without negotiation. The environment becomes rigid and uncompromising. These are the children who end up saying "Oh what is the point. Hang it up." They quit trying and want immediate gratification, which is unlikely in most cases.

So what we are saying here is that how a child mentally interprets a situation and plans makes a big difference. You want your child to be confident and assertive. The bottom line here is to develop an attitude that, in general, goes something like this;

> *I know that not all things are under our control but of those that are, I am sure going to try to influence the outcome. Let me do all that I can, and then if it still doesn't work out, at least I tried. If I keep going this way, eventually I will succeed most of the time.*

The Parent's Role

Parents are the most important teachers and coaches of children's knowledge about the world, creativity and motivation. The parent is part of the child's culture while also being the main transmitter of culture. So when your child attempts to resolve a conflict, a mistaken notion, a fact, be there and celebrate that tiny bit of development. For you are witnessing that child has literally modified some neurons in the head. She now has a more accurate picture of the world which permits better adaptation.

Four Ways Children Learn

Children learn by:
1. association
2. consequences
3. by observation
4. by thinking and participating in informative conversations and experiences.

You can influence how your child learns certain things through each of them. All four ways influence thinking, feelings and future behavior. The power of suggestion, your expectations, and your examples make all the difference in the world.

Chapter 7: Learning and Motivation

These three provide a supercharge to the learning process. When you suggest that a child can do something and show unconditional support, the brain collaborates instead of becoming "jammed." How often do you experience fear and threatening environments which interfere with your own train of thought? There are good thoughts and useless thoughts which can influence intelligence. An intelligent child must not be burdened with fear of failure or of letting the parents down. Fear of sarcasm by siblings or parent often blocks the developmental processes that form intelligence. When a child is in the process of being fascinated by an area like music or science, some support is needed from the outside (parents and family) which reverberate in the child's mind for time to come. Self-confidence is built from others' confidence in the child. So why not harness this knowledge in order to help the child to develop excellence in various zones or areas? Well think. Try to see how you could use each of the above mechanisms or ways in helping your child to advance in some area of science, art, literature, etc. Don't wait for me to give you answers, for you already know.

Take a minute right now and check the garden. How could your child's motivation towards a useful area be supported more than it is at present? Write 3 ideas that might foster or strengthen your child's motivation. The area does not have to be academic. Do not fail by just teaching basic, school related things and nothing else. The act of sticking with something, anything, may be as important as the achievement of a particular skill in a certain area (effort and goal achievement). Perseverance or stick-with-it-ness is very important later in life when skills are also functional. Encourage your child, and expect, as a rule, that tasks will be completed. If the child takes the time to try, if you encourage the child to try, if you validate your child's effort through praise and encouragement there's no doubt that development in some area will take place. The more areas your child masters, the more he gets used to mastering things in general. This is a developmental process which takes time, just like others that produce creativity. You see, creativity, motivation and artistic talents, among others, depend upon these developmental processes which are subtle, and which in general, parents have little knowledge. Yes, I could give you examples but you would not "get it" as well as if you tried to write an example of each of the four ways now. Try it if you haven't, write down three ways to support your child's drive to, be competent in some area.

1. _____

2. _____

3. _____

Well, the above list shows what you need to do in order to motivate your child from time to time. Other ways to encourage her to verbalize or to show what she has just understood for the first time. Have her guess something by using what she knows. Remember, the answer is not as important as the process. Suggest in front of a significant person what your child is competent at.

Teach the process of thinking by using yourself as an example. Think out loud for your child. Remember your speech influences the way he thinks. How you talk about something determines how your child learns about a concept or skill. What you often talk about determines the areas in which he will learn and develop.

How well and how often you do these types of activities determines the rate at which your child's development can progress. I am suggesting that you can do a lot to start development in various areas, to resolve conflicts, to reinforce new knowledge or to show how something works. Yet remember, it is just as important to observe the preferred zones of development in your child and to respond to them creatively. The child sets the agenda, not you. How skillful you are determines how well she does or how often she comes back for more. Remember, your child is your apprentice. You can't leave his mental development up to teachers alone. They can only work with what is there, that is the mind of your child as it has developed so far. And, how your child's mind has developed may become a challenge in the classroom. For example, your child may have had the opportunity to learn at home by questioning adults continually. Is he so motivated in the classroom and confident to ask questions that the child is considered obnoxious? That is what I mean by "how." The "how" may not fit with the schoolroom environment. In this case, home based learning routines may become problematic, but remember, you shape what kind of apprentice your child is. And your child is inquisitive because there are many sorts of "experts" in the home environment to guide him. You need to establish a comfortable setting for discovery to take place frequently. Begin by asking the child about things he knows, and then move to things that he is ready to learn about.

The child eventually discriminates among different situations. He learns that when he is trying to discover or to learn, there is encouragement and "leads" or cues to follow problem solving. Parents of bright kids sense this need. They interact intelligently when the situation involves the child's development of knowledge in key areas. Key areas are those that enable the child to go on to develop accurate representations of the world in a given field that will help the child to adapt well later on as a professional.

Intelligence Comes From the Social Plane

If you want to know about the development of intelligence in your child, learn first how the internalization of what is known out there in the world takes place. This usually depends on social interaction, as that is where most of what we know comes from our culture. Then learn about your child's efforts to discover, to be creative with knowledge and to go beyond it. Anything that your child masters has it's origin outside. The child needs to develop a bond with you not just as a parent but also as a guide, a bridge to the outside world. A key way to learning then centers on question/answer episodes with your child. Do you ask your kids questions like: "Why do you think the moon changes shape over a month's period?"

Questions to ask yourself:
- Do you ask thought questions when kids are ready to understand?
- Do you ask these thought questions frequently?
- Do you ask these thought questions in a playful way?
- Do you ask these thought questions concerning stuff the child already knows something about, and perhaps he wants to know more about, so that he feels competent?

A Thought Provoking Question

What would happen if in 20 to 40 years parents were experts in helping their kids to develop their smarts? What kind of world would it be? This futuristic view isn't that unrealistic. If kids were taught parenting skills while they were in school, many social problems could be prevented. Take time to list 5 of these. Now ask your adolescent or preadolescent child: "What would happen if tomorrow's parents would be trained to be more skilled and informed about child development"? I hear so many people argue that some people shouldn't be allowed to have kids. Others say that parents should be required to have a license from the state before having kids. I believe that the answer to the problem lies in parent education, particularly if that education occurs before adolescents become parents. If we could teach them what you are learning now in this book before they become parents, their children would become the center of a more intelligent, safe, and sane society. Violence could be reduced as well as many other related problems.

Learning Mechanisms

Did you ever hear the story about Pavlov's dog salivating when a bell sounded? It seems that what Pavlov wanted to do was to get his dog subjects to salivate at the sound of the bell. But, first he started with dog food. He would put the food in front of the dogs, and they would salivate. Then he would feed the dogs. After this, he would put the food in front of the dogs and ring a bell. The dogs would salivate. Eventually the dogs would salivate whenever he rang the bell. The food did not even have to be present. In a similar situation in everyday life, a cat cuddles and acts cute when you open a food can, (As a matter of fact, even after Garfield has just eaten, he purrs and rubs against you).

What does all this have to do with kids learning? Kids respond to having the opportunity to do things which lead to feeling good. Parents can orient their child towards learning by associating games (stimuli) with learning (response). Children respond all the time, yet some spend more time responding in ways that produce learning.

What I am attempting to do here is to make classical psychological theories meaningful, so that you can understand how learning takes place. These are the four ways that children learn.

The first way of connecting the world to the mind comes from the Pavlov (A Russian scientist) experiment above and is called classical conditioning or Respondent Learning. In this process, a child is given a stimulus and he responds. The child is mostly responding to one (the original) stimulus. The trick here is to get him to respond in the same way to another thing (stimulus or trigger) like a bell or a tone of voice.

Just as a dog responds positively to food by salivating, children have a positive approach tendency for things connected with what they have learned to enjoy. They also have an avoidance tendency for stuff which they dislike. Anything associated with such "stuff" or stimuli tends to trigger a negative response.

All right. How can the parent use this basic learning mechanism? Think for a moment before I continue. Write these ideas down and then go on reading. Let's say you want Jon to enjoy history or geography. What would you do first? All right, now check what you wrote against the following:

Stimulating Activities and Models

Step 1

Think of stuff which the child responds to with gusto, things he enjoys doing often, people he responds to with enthusiasm, for example, hanging out with Uncle Harry, playing ball, watching a show, drawing, etc. These *are stimulating activities & models*. (SAMs). A model is a person your child likes a lot or looks up to.

Step 2

Pick a SAM that can be connected to what you want the child to like, for example science. (Notice here that what you want the child to like or to learn about at first does not lead initially to a favorable reaction by the child.) The child is not looking forward to being actively involved with "it." Let's call what you want the child to learn or to like enjoy the Goal Of Learning (GOL). The GOL could be an attitude, a set of concepts or skills to be learned, a strategy about how to go about doing something, or simply, the first few steps in becoming good at doing something. Here in this example "it" is science, but it could be music or math.

Chapter 7: Learning and Motivation

Step 3

If (SAM)　　(e.g. Nintendo)　...leads to or elicides a

　　　　　　　　　　　　　　　-------------------------->Positive
　　　　　　　　　　　　　　　　　　　　　　　　　　Reaction/Approach
　　　　　　　　　　　　　　　　　　　　　　　　　　from your child

　　　　　　　　　(Positive Connection)

And　Science homework (GOL)　...does not lead to a
　　　　　　　　　　　　　　　　　　　　　　Positive reaction

　　　　　　　　　(No Connection)

What could the smart parent do to get the child to like science or any other GOL? (Connect SAM with a GOL)

Make The Connection or Set It Up.

　　　If at first science problems, discussions and facts don't do much for the child, but he does enjoy watching TV you can allow him to have extra TV viewing time when science related programs come on, or you can tape or rent science programs for special occasions. Notice how the smart parent doesn't allow the child to watch TV at will. The smart parent doesn't force, but rather, gives the child a choice. Now, say the child likes to stay up late, and the only way he is allowed to do so is if he is reading or watching shows of an educational nature, what do you think will be the long term impact?. The smart parent also notices how the child enjoys learning. In this example, Kim may like to watch (more so than to read or to do). Some call this a learning style. You will find fun tests you can use to figure out how your child learns most easily. Some kids pick up information and concepts best by trying it out directly (kinesthetically), others learn visually, some listen better than others, etc.

　　　The rule for parents to learn is: Create an environment in which the SAM and the GOL appear together, or in which the GOL leads to the SAM or in which little parts of the GOL occur more and more with the SAM. Then allow for Repetition and Generalization. And most importantly, after you set up the connection and get closer and closer to the GOL, use praise, and use lots of subtle and direct positive reinforcement. Here are some ideas. When you are talking to a friend and Kim (your child) is listening, tell your friend about how well Kim is coming along in science or any other GOL. When you are asked by Kim's friends if she can go out, don't just say yes, but connect your permission with the GOL by saying something like: "Of course. Kim has been working a lot on GOL xyz this week, so she can go out." Typically, this can only work if you also reinforce immediately after GOL related behaviors are observed. For example, Kim asks you a science related question after reading, performing an experiment or viewing a film. You begin immediately by saying, "That's is a clever question. You may know more about it than I do, but I think that it is this and that..."

So catching the child at being good or active in any GOL is extremely important, because the opportunity allows you to shower the child with reinforcement and approval. (Of course, all this assumes that you and the child have a positive relation- ship.) The above description of the connection between SAM and GOL is one way of *orienting* your child toward a given intelligence, since each intelligence is made up of response patterns, attitudes, feelings about the subject, and mental skills. In sum, you are helping the child to become motivated in certain areas by providing a clear "pay off" for them. In contrast, you choose not to reinforce other areas.

Intelligence and Learning

Some people believe intelligence is what tests measure. If your child achieves a score of l30, special classes are often available that can help increase that mysterious entity we call intelligence. Most experts today agree that intelligence is not a fixed characteristic like hair color or height. Rather, it refers to a person's ability (capacity) to adapt to the environment. A child's behavior shows to some extent the degree to which that ability is present. Sometimes, parents are amazed by the insight and clever behavior (also verbally expressed ideas) of a child. They rush to the nearest psychological assessment center to find out what they have. Is he gifted? Is she overly talented and creative? What do we do now?

When parents are fortunate enough to have children like these, they tend to underestimate themselves as we will see in later chapters. An intelligent child is one that learns quickly as well as a child that has learned much and grows up in an informative, stimulating environment. A child is said to have learned much, and hence, scored very high on an I.Q. (intelligence quotient) in comparison to other children their age. The way it works in practice is as follows:

A child who learns quick seems to have a pattern or system of acquiring knowledge. This pattern develops early by having certain conditions ready in the home environment. Some children enjoy mastery, they like getting the gratification of understanding things around them and how they work. When these things are those that we adults consider useful in getting about in life, then we term this intelligent. For example, a child who guesses that the concept "double" means taking an original amount and "multiplying" or making another equal amount side by side, regardless of size is said to be intelligent if no direct teaching was present. If Sandy figures out that sent is a past tense form of send and therefore bent then would be a past tense of bend, then she is considered smart if no direct instruction took place. Parents who are available to reinforce these little miracles of learning, these "Ah-ha" experiences tend to help maximize intelligence. Such patterns help the child generalize about things and to form hypotheses, which is the basis of scientific thinking.

Intelligence then is a combination of having a sound background in certain types of knowledge and an established knack of making use of it across different tasks, especially those we prize in school.

When there is a match between what we believe is useful and what the child is able and willing to do, then there is a case of above average intelligence. What is believed to be useful? What exactly is considered to be adapting to one's environment? To be considered intelligent (above average), a child must not only have learned lots of different things but also have learned those that are deemed important in school. Similarly, when a child develops skills in thinking, a knack for figuring things, these habits need to be in areas that are considered helpful in doing well in school. Kids who excel in school are those that have an "edge" outside school. They are ready and motivated because a learning to learn skill has been established early. Their vocabulary helps them as well as liking to discover and guess.

Here are several questions you the readers should be wondering about:

a) Can a child be intelligent without necessarily being tops in school?
b) What about kids who just seem to have a lot of stuff memorized but are not all that insightful and creative?
c) What about those that do not do well in formal tests yet show they are very keen in day to day things?
d) What then makes up or defines a real intelligent kid?

Intelligence Defined

A very important question in defining intelligence is not only defining what it is but also how many types there may be. Even after decades of research, scientists argue about whether there is one general sort of intelligence, two, three, seven or more. It is known that general intelligence requires different types of abilities and information. One thing is clear, there are many skills and types of knowledge that are not tapped by intelligence tests. So a child may be smart in many things that tests are not considered and the verdict may be that intelligence is below par for that person. So, a better question is "what is the child intelligent about?". Intelligence tests measure some types of skills and knowledge that have been learned overtime in certain contexts. Many of these types are related to doing well in our society. Yet, doing well, (like becoming a millionaire), is not that highly related to intelligence tests. Strange eh?

Most millionaires are not that intelligent in traditional tests, and many people that have very high I.Q. scores do not seem to be doing that extremely well economically, emotionally and even socially. So we have a paradox here, one that requires us to define intelligence in some context to begin with, not after. Is intelligence a matter of seeing relationships among factors easily and quickly? Well, there is a context involved in any type of relationship, such as physics, economics or sports. Yet, intelligence tests tend to be OK for measuring intelligence in the contexts it was designed to assess in the beginning, - that of school contexts. The problem is that the name, intelligence test has been unhelpful and misleading because the folks who have developed tests wanted to own the whole ten yards. Rather than specifying the context they had in mind, they figured that the school context was the main one or the most important and they forgot to inform the rest of us that their definition was limited. In effect, there are as many intelligences as there are areas which have been developed in a culture. You need special combinations of skills and experiences to be intelligent in the business world, which means you know how supply and demand works and you can make fairly accurate predictions. Being good at math is not enough here. What about being an intelligent military or political strategist? Some are "better" than others. Once you define what "better" is, what being "good at" means, you begin defining intelligence, but in a context that is relative. Does this mean we should reject the value of intelligence tests? No, that would not be intelligent because a lot of work has gone into them and we can learn some things if we understand intelligence from a sound theoretical base. For example, these I.Q. tests look at many basic intellectual skills that cut across many types of contexts, and which are useful in their own right. Yet, one must keep in mind that persons can be intelligent in areas other than those covered. Some folks are very intelligent in some aspects, like navigation, but might appear inferior if given an I.Q. test. Unless you could equate everyone's background and learning opportunities, it is silly to place judgments of a person's ability and motivation. What you end up with is an estimate of how a person has responded and developed in a given environment, like in Appalachia or in a Royal family, relative to others.

What Tests Typically Measure

The ability to verbally express oneself is an important aspect of intelligence. Another one is the ability to perform tasks using visual, audio and motor skills. For example, an intelligence test requires a child to verbalize the number of weeks in a year, seasons, presidents and capitals of the world. This is just knowledge that is factual and learned directly. The ability to do this and transfer it quickly to another problem is also useful. The ability to memorize information, or numbers, as well as to figure out what is appropriate, responsible behavior in social situations are other sskills measured in these tests. Other parts of intelligence tests require children to

Chapter 7: Learning and Motivation

identify what is missing in a picture, to put puzzles together and to be quick in memorizing symbols. These skills are harder to teach directly. For example, one of these tests asks for the meaning of a proverb like "strike while the iron is hot". This requires a person to answer at a symbolic, abstract process. An answer that is too concrete and simple, like "you have to wait for the iron to get very hot before forging it", is not as sophisticated as "do it while you have a chance". Or take for example, "how is a circus like a zoo". The child needs to find a common element like animals.

Building the Base for Intelligence

The Support Systems

Have you ever asked yourself why it is that intelligent children tend to be outstanding in so many other ways? Really sharp kids feel like they have mastery over a large part of the environment around them. They have self-confidence, they have initiative and they take responsibility for a lot of what happens. How is it that they become that way?

Locus of Control

Parents can create an environment where the child learns to feel and think that no matter what he or she does, it is useless to try to change the way things are going to go. By the same token, some children learn that they can control what goes on in their lives more and more. If they don't get something they want, they keep trying until they find a way to do so. When that happens, they remember what works and what doesn't and they also learn that by trying, they can influence many things, like going on a trip.

So what does this have to do with raising intelligent kids? Well, have you ever seen kids who tell you they have given up on trying to get or do some things because they know their parents won't even discuss it. They don't show much initiative to use their minds. They don't stick to doing something until it is right. Others do and the immediate subculture makes the difference. Behind every smart kid is a support system, perhaps a poor mother or a kind uncle or teacher.

How To Develop Intelligence in Any Field

Parents can provide a family environment where certain types of intelligences become nourished beyond the norm. The norm is what your neighbors are doing with their kids. If you want your child to excel in science, it is easy once you know the theory behind how intelligence is made in any area. Once you know the secret, which is only "secret" because few people are aware of our theory, you and our child can pick and choose which type of intelligence you want to grow. Now think for a minute, what does the professional gardener do to grow the best vegetables in the state? Brainstorm with me… Do you want your child to have an opportunity to be among the top minds around? Now, you need to model after the master gardener in cultivating the best talents from your child's interaction with the culture around you. Develope general and specific types of skills, they go hand in hand.

The Secret is Activity

Intelligence is the product of activities and experiences that have been processed and absorbed in the child's mind A child may have lots of experiences in music, tennis or literature, but that doesn't guarantee a high level of intelligence in any of those areas. How many kids do you know that have had scores of lessons only to give up eventually, and even come to dislike those areas. The activity has to be processed by the child in way that meet her needs. The more expert and encouraging the process is, the further the development goes. Some situations cause the child to become more intelligent in a given area because through a lot of experiences, (particularly for which there is motivation), changes in the head literally occur. These are called changes and modifications in the mental structure of the brain. Once these changes occur, one's perception changes, you see the world and specific problems differently than before. So then, you behavior is now also different from what it was before, it is more adaptive, more economic, less error prone and guess what? The person is now regarded as more intelligent. That is rewarding to itself.

Let's take an extreme case to illustrate the point. When I lived in South America for a year, I would see these children selling all kinds of merchandise on the street. They would buy wholesale and sell on the street at retail prices that amounted to pennies. They were not literate in the formal sense of having gone to school. Yet, they could perform mathematical functions better than their peers who were going to school, at least in some complex areas. Although they did not use formal rules and symbols to compare number values, they developed other ways of representing the problem and found ways to cope with daily inflation. Their motivation to sell was to survive. In the process of daily activities which required ever changes wholesale and selling prices, dramatic changes in inflation and currency, new understandings about the field of math and economics were produced in a given context. New mental functions were developed that would not have without the activity. Unfortunately, these children who were quite advanced for their age in these skills had nowhere to go without a context that would provide for further growth. But you as a smart parent can easily see that to help develop a very intelligent child, certain things are needed. Motivation, discovery, reinforcement and more and more challenges so that intellectual development does not get stuck.

Now consider this. Assume that for whatever reason the child is motivated to learn more about something, like earning money, self esteem, recognition or respect. What can you do? What is it that you can do or arrange to have happen, so that the processing of activities in math science, music or reading modifies and expands the child's mental structure? It can be something as simple as asking "what do you see happening when 'a' follows 'b?' what is going to happen next?" or when you teach a child tennis tips like " when you hit a back hand, turn to your side and point your butt towards the ball, or exaggerate the back swing, take your racket way back." Such pointers are verbal regulations which stay with the child as they go on to repeat activities. Such rules of thumb help speed up development. And yes, frequently, the child learns to look for such tips on their own. These are called mental strategies which help solve problems.

THE SECRET IS SOCIAL INTERACTION

Self-esteem is the key to development. Use positive reinforcement around those activities that you would like your child to be interested in and do so genuinely. If you have learned anything in this chapter, it is to value the whole child regardless of performance. This is the base. Then provide special strokes for selected efforts and activities. There is no seven or twelve step plan to motive or teach intelligence. You simply need to put into practice what you now know and put your best foot forward. You are in control. You are now motivated and this is how you instill the will to learn for learning's sake. The mind is a wonderful thing to develop, nothing comes close to it. Develop your own style to promote and assist your children's natural intelligence and emerging talents. Nurture these by orchestrating lots of meaningful activities.

Summary

Children who come from privileged, rich families are not any smarter than those from modest backgrounds. Heredity has very little to do with intelligence unless a defect in the brain's structure is involved. Intelligence is the ability to adapt to the environment. So if the environment is complex, so must be one's mind. If the environment has many dimensions, then intelligence must be multidimensional. Intelligence is a social construct that is defined culturally. A mind needs the tools that can be useful in a culture. This is the software of the mind. You do not inherit intelligence but rather, you develop it in the contexts that come in contact with the child. What you inherit is the hardware, which means that as a human, you have tremendous potential if conditions meet your potential. Race has no more to do with intelligence than the length of one's hair. Intelligence develops with the aid of teachers as well as in spite of them. Schools can only be as effective as the child's home environment. Yet, a lot has to do with what we mean by the home environment and hopefully, you will develop a clearer understanding of this as you review this book and those upon which this one is based.

When intelligence is coupled with motivation and creativity, a genius is created. A superior mind can be designed, particularly since it is mostly by chance that genius occurs in the world. This doesn't mean you as a parent can't try to develop your child's talents when he is ready. Remember it is not a question of forcing but rather following your child's natural pace.

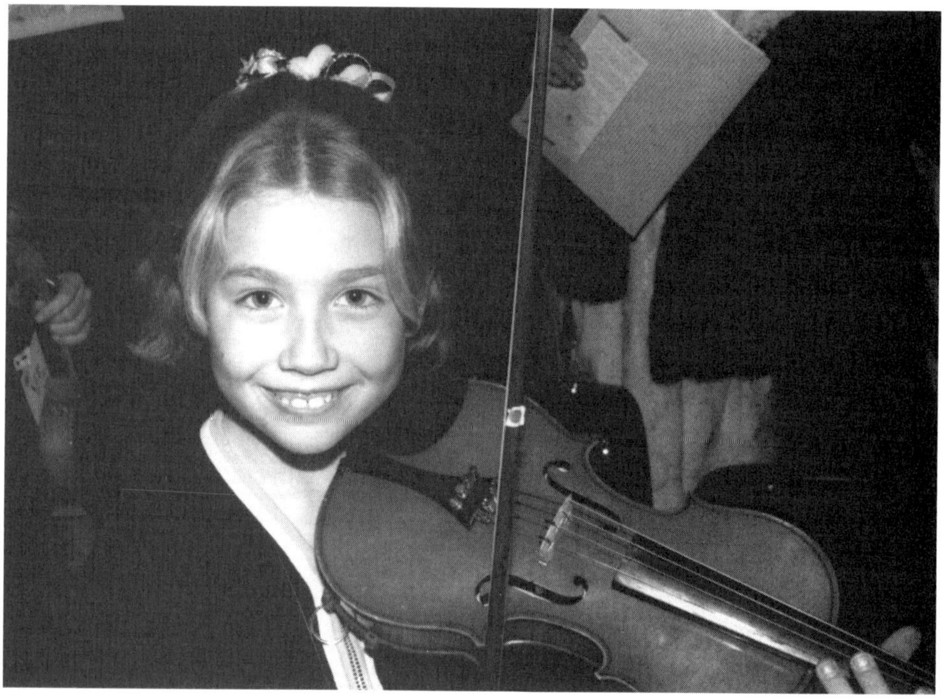

CHAPTER VIII

CREATIVITY AS INTELLIGENCE IN ACTION

A Most Unique Relationship
   F: "By the way, do you have any real reason for wanting a car?"
      (All right, all together now, let's sing out his answer)
   C: "To go places" (says child)
How refreshing it would be if a child told his father that he wanted a car for robbing banks.
   From Bill Cosby's Bestseller *Fatherhood*

Creativity is one of those human traits that is difficult to define, yet it ranks way on top of the list in terms of human values. We may think of creativity as intelligence in action or the engine behind the intelligent application of talent. Creativity is most difficult to define and to measure, more so than most people think. Imagine a teacher concluding that one child is more creative than another simply because he draws a lot or makes up stories. Some folks are fooled into thinking that a creative child is one who talks a lot and comes up with all kinds of answers that attract attention. Later on, you will learn that creative children are not after attention for attention's sake only. They tend to be nonconforming and imaginative. And yes, they do try different responses out all the time, since their minds are very flexible.

What one person thinks is evidence of creativity another person may not. Values enter into this area, as they do with all aspects of intelligence. One definition of creativity concerns the ability to invent, to think of new possibilities and angles in discovering a problem and then to solve the problem systematically. Now you will notice that in order to find a problem, one must be intelligent in the first place. In fact, people of less-than- average intelligence are rarely creative because creativity requires considerable intelligence in recognizing discrete events. Your child needs to be aware of what the world around is like before she can act on it or rearrange it. On the other hand, some extremely "intelligent" children do not seem very creative at all. Typically, these children are consumers and not producers of knowledge, inventions or innovations. They memorize facts and follow directions well. Creativity needs to be understood in terms of processes and especially in it's practical applications. Applications can be observed in various domains such as those associated with such creative geniuses as Einstein, De Vinci, Cervantes, Goethe, Edison, and Bell.

Dr. Pedro R. Portes Ph.D.

When does creativity start?

Many folks believe that creativity is something that some kids have and that others do not have. Few realize that this trait is developed over a lifetime in "special" home environments. Some people believe that, if creativity is stifled in the first decade of life, it is too late to try to develop creativity later on. Let's get some myths out of the way.

First of all, all children are born creative (assuming that a normal, healthy brain is available). For creativity to emerge, the child needs to have "intelligence" about the world surrounding her and to have an increasing number of concepts and skills readily available. You see, creativity is actually no more than intelligence being "played with"; experimented with freely. It emerges naturally in the toddler stage as the child plays with known objects and relations. Creativity is intensified in the mind of three and four year olds as they experience the fastest growth period of their mind. That is the period from age two on to full time study in a formal elementary school setting. Why does it seem that both intelligence and creativity reach a high level during the preschool years? The answer is because of language development, during which time human speech serves as a tool to nourish mental growth. The capacity to understand and to adapt to the world with speech allows for more and more complex "intelligence" to be processed by the child. During this interval, the child is going to try to deal creatively with all sorts of new stimuli without any premeditated goal in mind. He is just flowing with it. This is The Early Creativity Phase which eventually leads to The Goal Phase of concrete uses of creativity.

In the Early Phase, creativity runs rampant and imagination knows no limit. It is a magical period for children who believe all is possible. Later, as the mind evolves into a more finely tuned computer with greater capacity, some limits become evident, and the child becomes a rule bound thinker. To play with rules in mind requires having specific goals like a child who makes up a story in order to pretend he is reading the text in a good book. The story actually sounds good, it is creative and results from the child's own will. In our society, children must let go of the "goal-free" phase when they enter school. School represents a socialization process through which young minds are trained to exercise newly developed functions (or concrete operational tools) mostly in the service of predetermined curricular goals. During this phase, most children are at risk for a derailment of creativity in favor of the more goal-oriented skills that society demands. Although both goals can be easily attained, often children are placed in environments where learning is considered acquiring knowledge for the sake of the grades and approval and fooling around with concepts and ideas is discouraged. Such environments reward mostly practical regurgitations of what has been learned and they put down "nonsense" stuff or activities initiated by the child which are not regarded as being purposeful.

Chapter 8: Creating as Intelligence in Action

But, that is just the point. Creativity is just that, fooling around with new knowledge and problems and looking for any number of uses or angles just for the heck of it, freely. So don't undermine it. Creativity is a pattern of saying to yourself "what could I do with that idea?" or asking routinely "what can this thing be used for? There is no specific goal or purpose at first. The process is much more like developing an art form which later in life might become useful (once the mind becomes even better equipped with more intelligence). So as was recommended before, parents need to design, to develop and to maintain a supportive and special environment in order for creativity to thrive during the school years. Teachers need to be creative, to open themselves and not to feel easily threatened.

If parents support the child's constant attempts to engage in creative uses of objects, then the child begins to find very original possibilities. If parents model novel ways of dealing with problems, the child will feel inclined to do the same.

The relation between creativity and intelligence is *most* interesting:

1. Highly creative and intelligent children vary a lot in their behavior, sometimes acting quite mature and other times they act more childish.
2. Highly creative but less intelligent children are in conflict with teachers and others, including themselves. At times, if the feedback from others to conform is too strong then they feel inadequate or unworthy. They perform beautifully, however, when there is low stress and some encouragement.
3. Children, who are very intelligent, but not very creative, tend to be hooked on school. They strive hard for top grades in traditional areas that have, in the past, been well reinforced. They are out to please the teacher.
4. Finally, children who possess low intelligence, and creativity tend to avoid school stress by using defensive strategies as in "down playing" the importance of knowing about various topics or not caring to learn and be active in certain challenges.

Is Creativity Learned?

As before, many folks believe creativity to be something that you are either born with or not. Some believe that it is passed on from parent to child biologically. However, what we do know is that the cognitive environment which parents provide makes all the difference in the world, and the child's own activity.

There is ample evidence that extremely creative and talented persons come from very special family environments. Take for example Pascal, a great mathematician and philosopher. He had extraordinary upbringing which included the finest tutors. Such people were provided with very special environments as they developed.

Certain parental attitudes and behaviors appear critical in nurturing creative children who hunger for challenges. Such parents are able to pace activities and to model problem-solving strategies which the child observes continually as a feature of the environment. She then copies and modifies these activities to her own advantage. In order to understand what is important for parents to know and to do first requires a clear idea of what is considered creative. A child is likely to be creative when he or his home environment possess some of these traits or activities:

- Social rituals are often disregarded
- Producing things that require original effort is preferred over playing games or watching TV
- A strong sense of self is present, so that others' criticism or praise is not that important. Rather, creative persons have their own standards of evaluation. What is important is whether one's work satisfies and fully expresses oneself.
- Creative persons have "a standing quarrel" with the world. They are not satisfied with what society does and how it does it. They are always thinking, analyzing, diverging from the obvious perceptions and pushing for more intelligent ways of doing things.
- While they know what it takes to do well in life, (like those who have very high intelligence scores) creative persons choose to cut their own paths and to have a less predictable approach to life.
- They remain open minded, never rigid except to be nonrigid.
- In the home, at least one parent is creative, typically self employed, and encourages risk taking and looking for different ways of doing things.
- Hard work and little social popularity accompany the creative person. Discipline is evident in their work habits. While there is some inspiration and wonderful insight, most of the time is dedicated to work. Sometimes it's the other way around.
- They often are fascinated by simple phenomena which may lead to important breakthroughs. For example, when a faster vehicle passes you when you are traveling at a slower rate, it may seem as if you are standing still. This simple perception "clicked" for Einstein and the theory of relativity was developed.
- Creative students do not like to be kept busy, just because the teacher wants kids to stay out of trouble. (Interesting ideas are often judged to be inappropriate by teachers, as they are bothersome and interfere with discipline.)

Finally, the creative person's flexibility allows them to blend both reflective and impulsive learning styles. A home environment that supports and encourages the above mentioned traits is the key. You want to encourage creativity as a special plant in your child's garden. It is special because creativity can go with high intelligence in any area. This means that you have to be extra careful and protect the child from dull school environments in which creativity is often sacrificed or totally stifled by the end of the elementary school years. You should try to keep an open mind about things at home and to question the why's and wherefore's of stuff routinely. You invite the child to create possible solutions, to troubleshoot situations ("Well, if you go to Kathy's house and stay overnight Friday, how are you going to deal with that history project?") You need to respect your child's ideas regardless of how impractical they seem at the time.

Creativity defined

The ability and flexibility to identify or to think of various uses for things spontaneously, to see unique, original possibilities, and to shift from one way of looking at a problem to another constitutes creativity. Creativity is the highest form of intelligence or what we consider to be intelligence in action. This general definition includes music, puzzles, math, science and similar activities. Any unique and unusual approach to a problem should be reinforced by parents. (*See the prior chapters.) Unusual ways of thinking and approaching things and sticking to a problem until some progress is made are very important activities to reinforce for they build confidence and sound work habits. The ability to postpone immediate gratification and pleasure and to wait until one has reached a partial or full solution to a task is involved in creative work.

In sum, children who attempt numerous yet different, and sometimes very original solutions, are said to be creative. Although at first they may do so for strokes from others, after a while, they become self motivated. Being a self-starter, a person who is "intrinsically" motivated, to a great extent, is part of being smart. It is not only important to acquire particular knowledge but also to do so often and freely, out of interest and curiosity. So parents need to set up conditions where the child's initiative and agency can come shining through. Your daughter, for example, really wants to have a particular product. You respond by being open and supportive of any initiative. You say you will entertain ideas and suggestions on how to find the means to get at the desired goal. To cultivate agency, you make her participate, become active in developing means. Rather than giving the product to the child, brainstorm, negotiate, exchange information. Only then should you be ready to help out.

One of the problems with nurturing creativity concerns the issue of deciding what is practical. If we know that extremely smart persons have family environments that deliver lots of challenges and that provide a lot of guidance and love, then why don't we make creative environments a must in our schools? Because we value conformity more?

As a second problem, it is hard to measure creativity. Tests of this sort are not often reliable and valid in predicting or identifying who is going to contribute to the world. Creativity is also likely to be stifled early during the elementary grades. Teach-ers often cannot or will not allow psychological freedom for individuals to express themselves and to receive helpful feedback. Often, we cannot handle the free expression of little kids and fail to recognize how they arrive at clever little insights that we take for granted. Often we do not have the time to allow for discovery learning that is adult guided and requires messy, untimely experimentation by children. Children have few rights, and the truth is that adults have not yet agreed to allow and provide for as many opportunities for the development of creativity as intellectual skills. Yet, this is an area that if people wanted to make the investment, could lead to a better world. Instead, we value uniformity, obedience and tradition. As a result of not very intelligent school systems, teachers and principals, many intelligent children get turned off early. School personnel often resent their creativity and use it as a source of criticism. Most school personnel are not creative or tolerant of it.

I do not mean to say that school professionals are insensitive, or purposefully punitive, rather that they are often not intelligent or knowledgeable about intellectual development and creativity. This situation comes about, probably, because they are not trained well in their own college preparation (or before). A school pressures to conform eventually lower the child's self esteem and will to achieve in school. Consider the following case:

> Mike is a bright child in 6th grade who is an early maturer. His parents have raised him in an intelligent way and permitted him to ask questions and to comment on most things. Typically, he gets A's on all subjects in the advanced special class. As he enters 7th grade, his grades drop to C's, D's and even an F. His teacher dislikes his questioning of the teaching philosophy of the school. He argues that the classes are dull and useless.
>
> He becomes discouraged and gets to the point at which he does not care about anything in school. This leads to a cycle in which he falls into the teacher's criticism trap over and over. The parents have to be called in for meetings. The parents are torn between being consistent about supporting an open, questioning attitude and the pressure from school to simply follow the program, after all, the school knows all that is needed for Mike. Now, on top of poor school performance, creative processes are penalized, self-esteem is lowered and motivation is reduced.

Chapter 8: Creating as Intelligence in Action

Another problem is that a lot of creative children do not always produce what is valued. You see so many children who use their talents in a negative or seemingly useless way. Parents wonder yet do not realize that creative talent requires a responsive, dynamic environment. Many parents do not know how we learn. Given this lack of understanding, it is difficult to imagine the changes that would be required in Mike's case. We tend to overlook creative thought in children as being silly or inappropriate. As a result, children feel forced to say and do what is expected to avoid negative feedback. That is too bad, because creativity is necessary in developing really smart children. A major problem is that we cannot tell ahead of time who is going to make a valuable contribution in an area that we feel is worthy. For example, artists like VanGogh, Munch, and Goya were extremely creative, ahead of their time, and paid a tremedous price for their originality. They were recognized and praised only after their death.

It is well known that The Flat Earth Society was not very nice to people who attempted to show that the earth was round. Some original inventions like the internal combustion engine, solar and nuclear energy were not and are not very popular with some. Although it would take creativity to learn to work together and eliminate world hunger and preventable diseases, unfortunately we still tend to value other types of creativity such as weapons technology.

Setting Up Your Child To Be Creative

How does your child learn a strategy that might appear useful in creative problem solving? Let's suppose the following:

Your spouse is reading a letter and encounters a word he does not understand. He asks you for a definition, and you both figure that neither one knows the meaning. Your child is observing. One of you "attacks" the word by guessing from its root in Latin (for example, synectics). The other goes to confirm the definition in a reference book.

You try to confirm the hunch. You try to learn how to use it in different contexts. O.K. That is the sequence that is being modeled. Later on, you may catch your child going to the reference books for the first time. Since you want more of this behavior pattern, one in which there is individual motivation and intellectual curiosity (it does not matter what the word or fact is), you deliver a super comment like "Jamie, you seem to know your stuff, I like how you go after information you want." Or, "Can you explain that to me a bit more?"

Here the child is getting prime time from you. Later, you weave the situation into a family conversation, stressing that Jamie doesn't wait around for things to come easily. She is a go getter. This is feeding into a developing self-image through which the child begins to consider herself a capable intellectual person.

Do this for interests that are developing in your child, especially for areas in which you want to see more growth. Reserve the PR for intellectual and emotional areas of growth. I say emotional, because your child needs to feel confident, respected and competent in most endeavors.

Encourage your child to try out multiple solutions and to think of all kinds of uses for things. In doing so, mental strategies are developed, like sorting by color, size, position etc.

Finally, avoid using punishment and time out in ways that curtail learning. Time out involves removing the child when a behavior is unacceptable. Make sure that learning related behaviors do not become discouraged. Staying up late while reading in bed, or asking questions at the wrong time should not be punished. If a child wants to keep the light on to read at night, do not punish. Use natural consequences until the child learns to regulate himself. For example, get him up the next morning and remind him that he chose that option.

Asking too many questions (for attention at the wrong time) should not be met with a physical time out like being removed. Rather, use extinction. When you don't want to see something occur a lot, just ignore it, distract it, divert attention or redirect it. Do not waste your time getting into a power struggle. Have rules already set up by which there are consequences for good and bad behaviors. No need to get angry. Let the consequences do their work. If you get unnerved or tangled, you are blowing it and failing to model effective behavior patterns.

Remember, time out is a form of punishment since it is a consequence that takes the child away from where she wants to be. If used too much, it can send the wrong message, such as the child feeling unworthy because he is often punished. Always leave the child with some options that encourage her development.

How to develop creativity

There are many things parents can do to promote creativity. More importantly, there are a lot of things they should keep from doing to allow children to develop. Just as with intelligence, it is very important to design and to maintain a special environment for your child's brain. A good image to have is that of a gardener who cultivates flowers.

One aim parent's can have is to develop confidence (see section on self-esteem) and verbal skills in their children. Games like "Let's think about all the different things we can do this weekend when we go camping" or 20 Questions are helpful in developing mental strategies. The game 20 Questions helps children hone their logical skills and classification of things in the world. Here is how you play it with children as young as four years of age:

You invite them to guess what it is that you are thinking about, which you write down on a piece of paper. You think of something or somebody that exists in

Chapter 8: Creating as Intelligence in Action

the world, your child soon learns to ask " is it a plant, a mineral or a person" as a way to narrow it down. If it is a person, then you could be asked " male or female, old or young, someone I know personally or not... etc". You start out by trying to guess what the person has written first, and you have 20 questions to ask before you "lose" the game, then the other person tries it. You'll soon find that young children learn very sharp questioning skills from those which they are exposed to during previous games.

The way you ask open-ended questions, encourage unusual answers and reinforce the child makes a big difference. How you respond after the child responds makes an even bigger difference. Can you understand why?

Creativity is present when children are comfortable using certain problem finding and solving skills, or rules of thumb. They apply these to a number of different problems and learn to become more systematic and expert in the process of creativity. Remember, the child needs to hear creative thought verbalized, see original input and sense things in diverse ways. Parents can use a four-step model to build the bases for creative thought:

1. Make sure that the child fully understands the problem and the idea that choosing the best of several alternatives is the objective.
2. Help to find major solution strategies, like dividing the problem into different categories for generating solutions. Do this before or after some brainstorming. This step helps the child generate a guiding strategy to "brainstorm under." Let's say the problem is part of a discussion you are having with Erin about selecting a sport she can stick to for a long time and that would be enjoyable and have some benefits too. The solution categories for #2 above might be:
   A. Sports that are individual or group based, or both.
   B. Those that are expensive and require much training, and those that do not.
   C. Those that produce injuries often, and those that are safest.
   D. Those that make the most money if you excel and so on.
3. Have the child list various alternatives under each solution category or strategy, such as various sports that could be related to making the most money or those that produce the most or least injuries.
4. Finally, help the child to go from the analyses of solution strategies and alternatives to the evaluation of the top ones. Here, the child learns to discard the impractical options and to put the remaining ones under good, better and best categories. Help base this evaluation on certain explicit values, like personal ones or cultural ones or even grandma's. This is how you get the flexibility going, by encouraging different perspectives and role-taking.

The Big Picture

There is one fact that is revolutionary, yet simple; a fact you now know is true. This fact is that intelligence develops because of interaction with other people in which key information and learning are originated.

Yet we tend to hold on to the belief that creativity is already in the head at birth. But I ask you: Why should creativity be any different? Regardless of how much we have, what is measured through tests, talent in creativity or intellectual genius is primarily a product of learning from others and of the "patterns of coincidences" relating what the child is ready to grasp and what the environment provides the child at that moment. Since we know that individual differences in I.Q. are primarily a reflection of differences in past and present person-environment interaction, then w can get on with the business of how to maximize the development of intelligence. Once again, let one say that the business of measuring how much intelligence or creativity a child has is somewhat silly or arbitrary, since intelligence is fixed culturally unless there is an organic deficiency. The issue then is one of going beyond the question of how much learning a child has experienced. You should move on to the more critical problem of determining what your child is ready to learn next across a number of different areas. Parents can and should provide the environment for bringing out children's natural creativity. Like intelligence, creativity is a trait that is already within your child.

The Family Backgrounds of Creative Persons

Parents who nurture the development of creativity in their children are generally successful and those children later contribute much to society. Parents who do not make it their business to enhance the development of creativity are unlikely to have creative kids in the long run, even when the child tries. Needless to say, parents who stifle creativity by being rigid and inflexible doom the child to being mediocre. Children's creativity needs to be fostered by parents' own creativity and modeling. In studies which track the development of creative people over time, it turns out that people such as Thomas Edison, Madam Curie, Albert Einstein, Galileo, and others who have made significant discoveries all had supportive home environments. Their parents gave license to be imaginative, to experiment, to argue and to test hunches. Their parents gave them unconditional confidence and freedom to think, to consolidate and to test for feedback.

Consider the following. Do you think that the most creative persons had very touchy-feely, always- available parents who gave them a lot of warmth and who were very attentive to every need?

Not really. Instead, these parents tended to be a bit aloof at times, allowing the child to be independent and to try things out on her own. Certainly, they provided lots of guidance and were glad to serve personally or through tutors as "resource centers" for the child, but they also knew when to back off.

These parents were also not very conforming themselves. They had disagreements with other adults. They had a different point of view on many subjects. They second- guessed rituals and standard ways of doing things when no good reasons were apparent. In effect, these parents modeled being flexible and taking various points of view on many issues. They were a bit rebellious in their own right. They worked independently and were self-reliant. These parents felt that they were responsible for most of what happened to themselves, thus believing that they had control over many of life's situations. In sum, their children on a regular basis "pickedup" a certain freedom of thought from watching the parent and identifying with him or her. Just as in some micro cultures, it is ok to be loose physically, in the above case, the flexibility and comfort level is psychological. From that place, creative activity can occur based upon a sound intellectual and emotional foundation. When your child asks questions, be ready to serve him with answers that help him to think. Watch your tone. Respect your child and treat him as a serious adult student. Don't over do it. Let him discover on his own by giving strategic help. For example, your child asks when will the family be going on vacation. You could answer directly, "July 10-19" or you could play with her 8 year old mind by asking her something like "When did Dad say he would ask for some time off yesterday evening?" Yes, make the child work and think about factors related to the question. Keep it challenging by being attentive to where she is in her development.

A preschool child is most creative. Anything is possible in his world. He has not learned certain rules of logic and fully meaningful concepts, so he seems to be off course, in a cute way, much of the time. He is still discovering very basic concepts like what being late is, or being rich, or even being a scoundrel. Preschool kids think from one specific instance to another without getting the big picture, unless somehow the connection is made. Make the connection and then challenge the child to practice making the connection in another setting. Encourage him to be creative by using what he knows and allow him to think a while alone, and praise the effort and not the answer that is correct. Any answer that comes close to the actual one will help to establish a creative, self-motivated set. Correct solutions will come on their own and are not that important. What is most important is the process of thinking, how the child goes about it and how, in the course of various attempts, certain problem finding and problem solving strategies are formed.

In sum, psychology has approached creativity in terms of individuals having it or not having it. Like intelligence, such experts think creativity is pretty much "built-in" at birth. Yet, we must also consider creativity in terms of products or achievements displayed by the child and the modeling and supportive processes behind it.

What is behind the creative child? What in the environment tends to produce creativity in your child, or help to nourish it? First of all, although we have been talking about how important bonding and love is during the first 2-3 years, be careful about overdoing it. The style exhibited by parents of really creative children has been viewed as being not "too close" to the child. These parents are seen as somewhat aloof or distant at times. This style doesn't mean the love is not there, rather on the contrary, the love is expressed through parental demonstration of respect for the child as an individual being. Afterall, the child is a visitor in your home, an organism independent of you, who is in the process of pulling away from being too dependent. This is a healthy process. Emotionally, the child gets more independent. Mentally, they become less-self centered and more objective.

Parents of creative children are often a bit "wild" and have a fun attitude about most things. They do not conform a lot, nor are they over protective. Such parents have their own way of looking at things. They are independent, and they think independently. This is part of the reason why their children learn to be independent thinkers. Around these parents, the children observe flexible ways of doing things, of looking at things. They have a parent who is not bent on having things so and so. The parent gives the child space and time to discover and to interact with things and people, and to practice what mental skills and concepts the child is currently "on". These parents get excited at finding new ways and new angles. They may even disagree or rebel about stuff in front of the child. Then the child imitates. This is why schoolteachers do not like creative kids later on. They are the ones with the strange answer and the ones that don't fit. They see or interpret the problem differently. There is no ridicule or discouragement like telling the child, "You've been trying that too long. Let's go now. Dad is waiting." If possible, be permissive, let her go at it, only later to come to you when she is ready. This is how you help the child to build that "stick to it-ness" that many refer to as motivation or perseverance. The creative child challenges and disagrees with the teacher, and often gets "burned." As a parent, don't always side with the teacher, but rather focus on the issue.

Once your child leaves preschool, it is really important to not let schools stifle or reduce creativity. Schools, even universities, are typically not "in synch" with creative individuals or approaches, because these institutions themselves are not that creative. The school institutions that have the courage to do things differently, or to simply try new things are frequently the ones in the forefront. What if your child's school is rigid? Work positively with the teacher in order to provide the child with opportunities and tasks that permit creative work. Don't get stuck getting into conflict with school people, rather win them over. Then help your child to manage situations creatively and to see that if he plays it "smart" the typical stifling of creativity can be reduced.

Chapter 8: Creating as Intelligence in Action

The best way to deal with school situations is to share with your child an honest and clever strategy. For instance, it may be that he dislikes a course or a teacher's approach. Your job is to help him to find a creative way to avoid getting entangled. Tell your child that this present school problem is very much like life in general. The key is to find a way "to beat them at their own game." This means that you expect the child to do well in that class or in school in general, whether he likes it or not. Doing this is a skill in itself, and he needs to practice working in frustrating, undesirable conditions. You discuss ways that can help in this regard such as flexible strategies and brainstorming how to get past this and other hurdles. Become an ally towards this end, and conspire to find ways that are adaptive. In return for high grades, ask your child for short and long term things he'd like to have or to do, then make these come about as the child "takes care of business." At the same time, provide alternative educational channels to keep the development of various talents at a challenging pace outside school. That's right. Do not count on schools or teachers to cultivate the child as well as you have. If you want exceptional talents to come through, you need to make it happen yourself by having the experiences, mentors and activities happening when necessary. Protect your investment. It is your child's number one investment too.

In sum, children learn to be creative by observing creativity in their sociocultural environment. They have models for actions, feelings and thoughts in their nonconforming, intelligent parents who give them just enough rope to not hang themselves. The parents provide an interesting, varied environment, and use it to encourage interaction and the internalization of those interactions in the head.

Teachable Moments

You will notice that sometimes your are more clear headed than others, more able to pick up on things that are going on around you. Some folks talk about biorhythms and time periods when you are more motivated to learn. Well, as we have noted, your child has peak moments during the day, that is times when they are more ready than usual to develop further. With babies, often after waking up and feeding, they are delightful to interact with. They are programmed to recognize and to develop a concept of whatever keeps coming up out there, and you, the parent, are the one who does so most often. But then, other things need to be present and activated.

Children will set the agenda for developing their smarts. You only need to be alert to their readiness and to be patient. My ten month old has learned over twenty concepts just by the establishment patterns whereby objects are pointed to, a word or phrase is verbalized and fun exists. How does the parent know if the baby has the concept? You ask the baby "where is the object" and the baby looks for it or points to it. The word represents part of reality. That reality is reviewed regularly and serves as a bridge to learning new concepts. Once the child learns to talk, new challenges are provided. The creative child will often run to you with a new "discovery" which is so simple that most people think it is nothing that great. So what if Jimmy noticed something so obvious. But when encouragement is provided anyway because you place more importance on the processes than the product (an obvious, simple observation), the child is likely to continue doing so. And guess what? Most important discoveries occur that way, a simple observation gets connected with a flexible mind that brings up "several screens" and history is made.

For example, noticing that kids exposed to cowpox did not get smallpox led to the discovery of a lifesaving vaccine. Or, noticing that a bucket of water which had a whole in the bottom produced a stream of water which conducted light led to the discovery of fiber optics which will make copper wire obsolete soon. In order to find the most teachable moments, pay attention to your child's underlying meanings and not just the surface statement. Praise the effort, the act of discovery, the inquiring, "dissatisfied", questioning mind.

So at this point, you should be clear with regard to a couple of main ideas about creativity. First, it will not emerge unless intelligence has been fully developed. This means that creativity needs to be fostered as if it were (and as it is) intelligence in action. Secondly, parents need to be patient and sharp in allowing the child to engage in guided and unassisted activities that promote discovery and elicit discussion. To do this effectively, parents need to develop a style of being which nurtures the child's mind throughout the formative years. More about this idea in the next section and in chapter VI.

CHILDREARING PATTERNS AND CREATIVITY

You could probably fit into one of 4 patterns of childrearing as noted earlier. A childrearing pattern is a style that parents adopt as they try to adapt to parenting as a way of life. Most of the time, parents do not consciously decode on which style to use for the sake of the child. Parents adopt whatever style fit their needs best. The reason childrearing style is so important is that it represents the mold that surrounds the child during the most important years. As we noted earlier, parents need to make conscious, intelligent decisions in designing the best environment for the child, including the way they will deal with various behaviors. In the past, many parents reared children in ways that were parent-centered or convenient to the adult. However, as more and more studies began to show that other patterns of childrearing were associated with better outcomes for children, many parents began going to the other extreme without really understanding why. Let's look at the major patterns and learn how you need to develop the most responsive one for your child.

The first is the autocratic/authoritarian pattern which has been the standard over time. Here the kid is told what goes and what does not. There are nice moments

Chapter 8: Creating as Intelligence in Action

but parents are always right, their feelings are more important, they don't need to explain or reason with "these brats". Their rights are few and not well respected when they get in trouble. Children in these families are at the mercy of adults' faulty logic. They are provided with a firm structure and parental expectations are to be fulfilled.

Creative children rarely come from these types of families. This is because they need to be exposed to flexibility, and a questioning attitude about most important things. Parents who do not conform easily and share with their child why following the norm is not always wise, have creative children more often than very conforming, "Law & Order" parent types. Parents may be wrong at times and if they are not willing to discuss it or allow some input from the child, the child is deprived.

With Permissive childrearing (the second type), children have few responsibilities but the same rights as adults. Parents tend to let children make most decisions but fail to model innovative ways of dealing with problems. Children in these homes would need more than a lot of freedom to be creative, they would need more reasoning and negotiating.

This brings us to a third childrearing style which is called Democratic/Permissive, where parents listen to objections, encourage give and take and engage the children in discussions. Children assume increasing responsibilities as they develop, and live in a warm family climate where limits are set clearly and logically. This pattern is most likely to produce creative children with some variations.

The Erratic, off and on style of parenting is not likely to produce creativity except for accidentally. You see, some children develop their creative talents in the very process of escaping uncreative and dull situations.

Your style of parenting is similar to your style of gardening. If you are alert and provide the best conditions, the results will be fantastic. The difference is that we can all afford to slip with real gardens but not with our children. Note the section in Chapter VI that describes some of these styles and gives suggestions for developing a most intelligent one. The Democratic/Permissive style is best if used wisely for it allows the mind to expand freely and creatively. Children do need guidelines and structure but only as long as parents model creative activities or provide for mentors to do so.

Your child needs a special connection with someone who is purposefully fostering a special relationship that requires challenges over time. As a parent, if you can't model and challenge on the basis of a good relationship, at least provide for this to occur for your child. You see, it is critical that you make use of your child's tendency to learn by observation. Your child models whoever is there for him emotionally, caringly. If that person is sharp mathematically or talented musically, the child will inevitably try to follow in those steps. This means that a smart parent insures that creativity is observed by the child through discussion, vigorous disagreements with the norms and original perspectives of immediate and distant issues.

In sum, if you look at the histories of very creative persons you find the same thing as when you look at the histories of the most successful persons in different fields. En-couragement (to give heart), motivation, self-reliance, hard work and opportunity all contribute to creativity. Do not forget humor, it is critical. The creative child uses humor but does not fancy himself as the funny clown. Humor represents the child's ability to see something from a different, unexpected perspective.

So make sure that in your home, unusual possibilities are considered, that self-direction is reinforced. Self-responsibility and that persistence and follow-through are observed and modeled along with the humble feeling of never being too sureabout why things have to be done in a certain way.

Don't follow a given pattern of childrearing, invent your own.

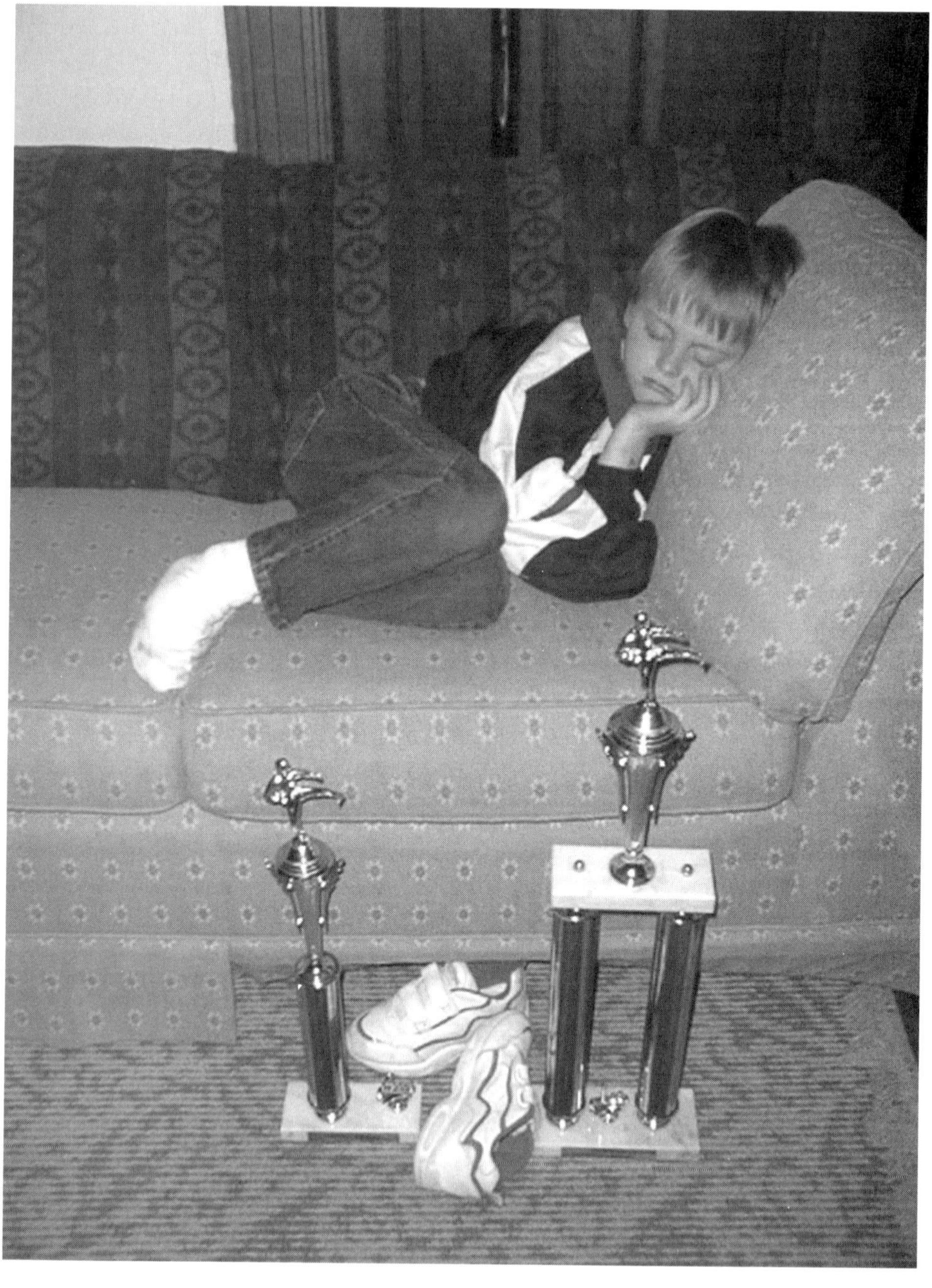

CHAPTER IX

CONCLUSIONS

"One step at a time and you will establish the patterns, and as intelligences unfold in your child, you remain alert and complement the child in an endless ballet, you lead and be led."

So now you have mastered some key concepts about how to raise your child's intelligence by thinking about the design of the garden in which your child's mind is cultivated. Parents' own intelligence is the key, the key to unlocking the potential already present in the child. This potential is realized through intelligent patterns or styles of interaction, or routines that become conditioned early on. Through them, the learning rate is accelerated effortlessly, like a ballet, because the mind of the child can handle a lot more than we think. It is all in the how it is presented.

The best thing you have done to make your child excel intellectually is become more knowledgeable yourself. You do this by reading this book and others and thinking about developing your own style, one that fits your family and in which there is freedom to experiment. You do this by reviewing the ways that children learn and the conditions that most favor learning. You see, most parents are not very clear on the mechanisms through which children learn. Remember, a child is always recording what goes on just like a camera, with time and space associations built also through consequences (real or imagined) and modeling. Learning by thinking with tools like speech, reading, or computers also leads to development.

The more that is learned, the more you advance development and what can be learned tomorrow. Remember, development unfolds at the rate at which it is started and maintained, so do a bit each day and it will add to more than what money saved can do in the long run. You have also learned that presenting important aspects of a skill or concept in many modalities to your child (visually, reading to him/her, having him/her read, draw, represent or enact, taste, smell, and touch) helps advance intelligence.

Do not overlook the power of expectations and suggestion, put both to work for your child in a playful, relaxed way. Everyday, build on you child's self esteem by challenging and inviting activities that the child is ready to handle. Not too easy but not too hard. Be there and model and encourage.

Do not be overly concerned about getting so much knowledge into your child regularly. Rather, let the child set the agenda as much as possible. You do what you do. You teach at natural opportunities like the dinner table, after shutting the TV off, or at the campsite. The main thing is to set up routines that serve to bridge minds. Your child needs to be able to look back and remember many of the direct social interactions parents used and set up for novel skills and knowledge to be introduced and woven. Don't just teach history but why history is useful and helps think about things intelligently. I look back and remember so many lessons now that at the time were just conversations between parents and friends. Remember that a lot of growth can take place in your child's areas of potential development simply by observing others carry out clever arguments. This means that an intelligent parent is not totally child focused but rather has and develops a network of interesting friends and activities. These routines may be occasional but represent a gathering of minds that children can use as a frame of reference later on. Parents do not need to do it all directly. Simply arrange for the conditions of learning to surround the child.

One of the most important things you need to have learned from this book is that parents who:
- Arrange for certain activities to occur.
- Facilitate exposure to a broad range of concepts and ideas.
- Monitor the child's actual and potential development, tend to have very sharp and advanced children.

When your child asks about how gas is stored in a bottle, or why wars are fought and so many other neat questions, you now know that the answer is not what matters. Process is more important than content. The long-term goal is not just to teach skills and strategies, logic and content. Rather, to instill a motivated set, and an intrinsic love of learning. The will to learn and master a given challenge is made easy by parents who can show that mastery of any area can be achieved, who provide the conditions that respond to the child's inclinations. How the child comes to know is critical. It does not have to be abstract or academic either. For example, build a room and create the conditions for calculating the materials needed for a square footage. Paint a picture and experiment with styles and textures. Do these things when the child is interested in interacting with you. Consult, ask for opinions, let them "guesstimate".

What matters is that in these teachable, prized, golden moments, you have an opening through which you can enrich and accelerate development. Use them. How you go about helping the child's mind arrive at an answer that meets their expectation to varying degrees at that moment and primes it to learn some more. This is how you can parent intelligently.

Verbalize your thoughts to your child even if the child is not able to grasp it all. For example, point out stuff as you go like "gasoline gets stale and won't be good for a motor to use if it has sat in the tank too long". This can be the beginning of the concept of volatility. Or note in a country fair "those carnival barkers seem fun but they take people's money. They are tricksters that fool honest people like you and me". This comment will "be heard" in the mind of the child later in time. Parenting intelligently means that you understand how activity, self-esteem, creativity, motivation influence the development of higher intelligence. With young children, encourage creativity and the sense of conquest. Anything is possible and can be understood. Then challenge your child's current level. First check it out. Then open the window and give the child something to "chew on" for a while. Let the child consolidate and ponder on a given idea for a while (a day, week or years), then move on to another zone. Remember that intelligence is multifaceted, just like the world. It is all right there in front of the family. The question is whether you are now beginning to see it. The big picture can't be achieved by "how to" techniques and exercises alone. If you want your child to advance, then you do the same. Read, take classes, write and always process out loud. Use the tool that forges the mind, literacy. The spoken or written word reverberates in the mind and makes it expand. Even when you don't know the answer, you can use the curiosity that is part of the child's nature to teach him/her how to think, and use resources and persist until some things are made clear. Even when you arrange for others to provide the answers or use certain resources like books and field trips, what matters is the process.. You show the child that regardless of the question, usually you will respond with interest, and show a way to move closer and closer to understanding the world. The child's intelligence will tend to grow as they try to get closer to you, they will ask questions often not only because it really is important for them but also as a way to engage you in discussion.

So, just as you learned about association theory (GOL) in chapters before, the child's quest for nurturing, positive self esteem, attention and respect from you needs to be connected with areas of knowledge and skill in processing information.

Remember that the use of models is most effective in teaching not only intellectual skills but also attitudes about various areas.

Intelligence Is Basically Related:

1) **Excelling At Learning How To Learn**
2) **Having An Ideal Context That Delivers It All In A Way That Is Matched To The Individual (Creativity Is More The Application Of The Process Of Learning How To Learn)**
3) **Motivation Is The Other Cornerstone Of Genius. The Will To Learn And Master The Challenge Is Crucial To The Child.**

What do children have to do, generally speaking, in the formative years? What are the main tasks for the child you need to be most aware of for intelligence to progress? Two things are most important. One is to gradually build in their mind increasingly accurate representations of the world. In the first dozen years, children build in their brain a mini replica of the world as mediated by their culture. But how they construct a view of the world is just as important in terms of motivation and self-esteem. They absorb their culture and capture all the skills that amplify the knowledge base of the culture. For example, in learning to speak, read and write or compute, they gain access to tons of data that needs to be sorted by the brain. They learn how to sort by learning sorting skills from parents, like when they say "now this is important, remember it for later" or "don't worry about that" or when the data is related to other experiences. Children relive the history of man. They go through stages where they are very primitive. They spend a couple of years in the Stone Age without the tools of culture. The simple types of intelligence are bound by the senses and what the body can do. Then pointing and objects that serve as signs begin to reflect intelligence. Learning trials are recorded in a memory that grows in capacity and functions. My 16 month-old can't wait to get his hands on my computer keyboard as I write. (Should I get bothered and get bent out of shape because I lose track of the project?). It is very likely that he will want to be computer literate soon. (So I practice what I suggest in a previous chapter, I reinforce him/her off and on to keep the interest there). This begins by sensori-motor associations being built in a stable context.

Once they reach two and three years of age, language development amplifies their minds in what seems like a year a minute. They now have access to what the culture has preserved over the years. Once they master reading (another tool), another window opens, and now the brain begins absorbing culture at a higher level. Mastery in a foreign language opens up other windows and allows for valuable comparisons between two cultural symbol systems and ways of life. Computer literacy may begin with NINTENDO but should not end there. Learning about numbers is another way that helps to represent the world. As parents help children master these symbol systems, they teach thinking skills, creative ways of doing things with information. The meaning of words should be a weekly staple food for the mind, so make the time and play whichever wordgame the child likes. As the child's mind becomes better "equipped" with fuller and more meaningful concepts, their behavior appears more and more intelligent and creative. It is important to allow the child to have psychological freedom, so that they can express themselves without fear of ridicule or being embarrassed. Remember that the behavior you see reflects what the mind is busy sketching and what it has already sketched. Sharpen and focus as well as go off on tangents with the sketches revealed by your child. Children's intelligence and creativity grows when parents provide for emotional safety and security. How often have you seen parents try to show off their kid's talents to company when the child is reluctant. How often do parents use little threats to control behavior?

This brings us to the second most important point. Just as intelligence is being born during the formative years, self-esteem is also being formed, which determines the degree of self-confidence later on. Here is where the intelligent parent learns about the child's social, emotional and psychological needs as they develop a firmer sense of self. Without self-esteem, intelligence is compromised, it can't develop fully. As you try to facilitate the growth of superior intelligence in your child, make sure that self-esteem needs are not forgotten. The two types of development go hand in hand. Otherwise, intelligence will not be as easily manifested in life. This is because before one becomes concerned with intellectual matters, one's socioemotional needs must be satisfied, and this is true only if security needs are guaranteed. The child who is abused and neglected cannot be intelligent, nor have positive self-esteem. There is a hierarchy where some things must be attended to before others can go very far. You have probably heard of this hierarchy from A. Maslow, who noted the order of how people develop themselves fully as humans by having certain needs met.

Some Final Tips:

- **Complementing school learning.**

If your child is in school already, begin to develop your own enrichment agenda based on your child's own interests. Do not rely on teachers or schools to do the job of developing the most special environments that support growth in different areas.

- **For Daycare**

By the time your child is a year and a half, it is time to provide him/her with some peer socialization. Bring other kids in or take yours to where others play just to get acquainted. Visit and observe the most highly recommended daycares and focus on the philosophy of the staff or the place in general. Review credentials of staff and have them describe how certain goals are pursued on a regular basis. Ask them to show you what they do when a child is upset. Ask how they think intelligence is developed. Look for semi structured activities that are likely to foster mental or language development. Contrary to what most people think, a daycare is not just a place to drop off the child on a regular basis. Daycare is a subculture that helps form your child's mind. So make sure that besides being safe and clean, daycare provides for educational activities and individual attention and guidance. A caretaker ideally needs to know what your child is in the process of learning and what can follow next. The caretaker needs to know what is going on in the child's stage of development so that freedom of expression and verbal guidance is provided and frustration is reduced.

- **When to develop a second language**

Your child comes ready to learn many different languages very early on. Success depends on what the environment delivers and employs on a regular basis. Imagine growing up in a place like Luxembourg where various languages are used and heard regularly. The child has little problem dealing with this situation compared to older children. If both parents are monolingual, it is wise to expose children to a foreign language after the first language is established by exposing them during preschool and immersing them during elementary school. If one parent is a native speaker of a second language and is in regular contact with the child, all or nearly all communication should be in that language for the child while the other parent (who is most fluent in the other language) maintains communication consistently in the other system.

- **Cultural experiences**

So the fundamental base of intelligence is in nurturing your child's self esteem so that there is no question that love will be provided regardless of the intellectual progress that is made. The other thing to remember is that besides the tasks above, intelligence is in the air between you and your child. It is an interactive process between the world and the child and later, between the child's developed and developing intellectual functions. As you may have noted, this book presents a way of parenting. Although you have learned some specific techniques, what will most help your children become more intelligent are the developmental views that you now have of intelligence. Now nothing can stop your child from reaching his potential.

- **Selecting Schools**

When visiting a school, trust your eyes. What you see is generally what your child is going to get. Observe. Teachers should talk to small groups of children or individual youngsters; they shouldn't just lecture. Children should be working on projects, active experiments and play; they shouldn't be at their desks all day filling in workbooks. They should be actively engaged, dictating and writing their own stories or reading. The classroom layout should have reading and art areas and space for children to work in groups. Artwork should be created by freehand, not just color or paste together adult drawings. Most importantly, watch the children's faces. Are they intellectually engaged, eager and happy? If they look bored or afraid, they probably are.

- **Children's High Achievement is Linked to Your Lifestyle**

High achieving students come from socially competent and effective families. The families look for ways to establish home/school collaboration. The conditions for high achievement cut across family income, education, ethnic background

Chapter 9: Conclusions

and whether the family is a two-parent or single-parent household. The overall climate in the family tend to reflect these elements.

Optimism should be a part of the household. Communicate high expectations to children, including praise, admiration and respect. Future orientation, dreams of success for the future, for each child and the family as a whole; should be openly discussed. Hard work is modeled, seen as the key to success, individual effort, inner motivation and commitment are a part of this. Avoid idleness, but teach children to relax with wholesome activities and educational programs. Plan for at least 20 home-based learning hours per week (broadly defined to include reading, hobbies, games, sports, family outings, jobs, writing, science projects, art, music, etc). Establish clear household rules, follow them consistently, insist on shared responsibility for chores. Contact teachers to check on school progress, and to plan activities at home that complement, learning at school.

- **Become a Homework Consultant**

Homework is "in", insist on it. Though the debate of its merits continues, education reform, public polls, and changing demands of schools all point to a new interest in homework as an extension of learning. Time spent on learning cumulates and makes future learning easier, study habits are established. What should you do about homework, other than provide a quiet space and quiet time. Many families exhausted from fighting the homework battle need to examine their role, as that of a consultant. Like a consultant in the business world, the parent-consultant helps on request, negotiates ways for helping, advises but does not take over, checks task demands relative to children's competence level. Use ownership to in place responsibility on the child to do the homework, say, "Remember it is not my job to get the work done, some kids get too much help and get the idea that someone besides them is responsible , I'll help when you need help."

You cannot make your child do the work using punishment and verbal put-downs, you will blow it. But you can provide the right environment with natural consequences over which the child has some choice, like no television, games, or other distractions during homework hours. Establish a regular time everyday evenings when you will consult and be available. This will lend continuity from one day to the next. If no school homework is expected, derive your own. Some may argue that if your child does not finish the homework, he or she will have to face the consequences at school and that you must not try to protect your child from the natural consequences of irresponsibility, but prevention is best. Do not allow this to happen in the first place. Consequences at home are usually more effective than those given in school. Use a positive tone during your consults. Short breaks are advisable when either of you feels frustrated. Focus praise mostly on your child's successes, effort and acquisition of skills building your child's self-esteem authentically. Encourage your child to develop his or her own system of rewards for achieving learning goals. Develop a rewards menu, it may include spending extra time with you, staying up late to watch special TV shows. This helps your child develop self-motivation. Avoid anger and fighting. Advocate for your child in the school. Monitor your child's homework assignments. If you uncover a perpetual pattern of boring, repetitive and unchallenging mimeographs below your child's abilities - intervene immediately and speak with the teacher.

- **Helping Your Youngster Achieve in School**

How can parents encourage a youngster to study and learn? Just because your child spends time on homework doesn't mean the time is well spent. If you suspect that your youngster isn't giving his best, the problem probably is motivation. If effort is there but results don't follow, he may be lacking study skills. Here are some excellent tips for youngsters from elementary through high school who need help in either area. Teach your child organize. This can be discussed during a meal to see what needs to be done. Show how to use a calendar and a priority list for making an assign-ment easier by planning steps. Find out what time of day your child does his best work, and adjust study time accordingly. Don't send your child to his room to study alone. He might prefer to work in the same room with you. Eliminate distractions whenever possible. Turn off the TV and stereo. Clear an area and encourage your child to work on one assignment at a time. Suggest that your child start on the toughest subject first, while his energy level is high. It's usually more successful than starting with an easy task. Help your child set study goals. Ask him/her to study 5 spelling words, for example, or locate six state capitals on a map. The more specific the goals, the better.

Teach your child positive self talk, how to talk to himself positively when concentration lags. Instead of, "I'll never finish this chapter," the thought might be, "Only 10 pages to go - I can make it." Tell your child not to let obstacles become excuses to stop work. If your child gets hung up writing an assignment because they know that they are having difficulty with spelling, tell him/her to just write the paper first for the ideas and that both grammar and spelling can be looked over later. Show your child how to divide a big project into smaller, more easily tackled segments . For example, a report on the presidents can be broken down into sections on each president. Encourage your child to respect deadlines. He will have to cope with them throughout his life. Use rewards (not bribes) when appropriate. If he finishes on time, play a favorite game.

Have your child notice title headings, introductions, summaries, review questions, and charts before tackling readings. Read in small chunks, asking questions about what's just been read in successive longer chunks ("How would my life have been different in Stargate times?"). Teach your child to use mapping techniques. Map the main idea in a passage and supporting details as the hub and spokes of a wheel.

Chapter 9: Conclusions

Most shortcuts involve maximizing time. Have your child explain something recently learned, make an educated guess, spell or solve a developmentally appropriate puzzle when traveling in the car, waiting at the doctor's. Have him/her learn songs and learn tricks to memorize rote stuff. Ask child to elaborate, to find the unusual, make hunches, compare to prior experiences in sustained interactions. These ongoing practices that then provide bridges or shortcuts to what schools expect.

In sum, early in life, vigorous, huge quantities of interaction are critical. Verbal interactions help the brain develop connections upon which functions of intelligence are built. Beside providing large doses of social interaction in the pre-school years, make quantity lead to quality of interaction. Provide for sequential, step-by-step experience that makes your child aware that there is more to know about anything and everything. Start them reading, writing, and composing before the age of five, but don't sweat the small stuff. After age six or seven, the brain matures and you can begin to expect a little more accuracy from your child. Above all be sensitive and proactive in rousing the child's mind, throughout his/her youth, and it will stick with them for a lifetime.

Dr. Pedro R. Portes Ph.D.

BIBLIOGRAPHY & RESOURCES

The following resources and references have been compiled for your use so that you may continue a lifelong learning process. Once you understand the main ideas of how to develop your child's intelligence and creativity, the resources below can be helpful in setting up useful activities and games. Many of the readings below will interact with your own intelligence and give you sound ideas to design the garden of talents for your child. Use a routine in which you learn to seek each reference or book (not always an easy task) with your child and skim the text for interesting information. By doing this, you may get a fuller use of this book.

Budd, Linda. (1990) . Living with the Active Alert Child: Groundbreaking Strategies for Parents. New York: Prentice Hall.
This book provides hundreds of practical ideas for coping with high-energy children (not specifically focused on ADHD).

Cole M., & Cole N. (1994) . The Development of Children. Scientific American Books.
Excellent textbook that covers it all! A must sourcebook for the college educated parent.

Coles, Gerald. (1989) . The Learning Mystique: A Critical Look at "Learning Disabilities." New York: Ballantine.
A well documented assault on the assumptions about learning disabilities.

Children's Television Workshop (1989) . Parents' Guide to Raising Kids Who Love to Learn. New York: Prentice Hall.
Sensible guide to learning at home and at school.

Dinkmeyer, Don, & McKay, Gary D. (1989) . The Parent's Handbook. Circle Pines, MN: American Guidance Service.
(Publisher's Building, Circle Pines, MN 55014) Practical workbook.

Dunham, R. M., Kidwell, J. S., & Portes, P. R. (1995) . Do the seeds of accelerative learning and teaching lie in a behavioral carrier wave? Journal of Accelerated Learning and Teaching: Vol. 20. (pp. 53-87).

Elkind, David. (1981) . The Hurried Child. Reading. MA: Addison-Wesley.
Describes the stress of growing up fast.

Feldman, David Henry. (1986) . Nature's Gambit. New York: Basic Books.
A ten-year study of six child prodigies reveals much about the interaction of individual talent with family and cultural support systems.

Feldman, S. S., & Wentzel, K. R. (1990) . Relations among family interaction patterns, classroom self-restraint and academic achievement in preadolescent boys. Journal of Educational Psychology: Vol. 82 (pp. 813-819).

Gallimore, R., Goldenberg, C. N., & Weisner, T. S. (1992) . The social construction of subjective reality of activity settings: Implications for community psychology. American Journal of Community Pscychology.

Gardner, Howard. (1985) . Frames of Mind. New York: Basic Books.
Builds a case for the theory of multiple intelligences.

Goertzel, Victor, & Mildred G. (1962) . Cradles of Eminence. Boston: Little, Brown and Co.
A fascinating study of 400 eminent men and women of the twentieth century. Sheds light on the formative forces that gave rise to their accomplishments.

Greenfield, Patricia Marks. (1984) . Mind and Media: The Effects of Television, Video Games, and Computers. Cambridge, MA: Harvard University Press.
Excellent readable review of the research on the effects of television and other media on children, emphasizing their positive role in learning.

Griffin, P., & Cole, M. (1984) . Current activity for the future: The zo-ped. In B. Rogoff and J. V. Wertsch (Eds.), Children's learning in the "ZPD" (pp. 45-65). San Francisco: Jossey-Bass.

Hart B., & Risley, T. (1995) . Meaningful Differences in the Everyday Experience of Young American Children. Baltimore: Paul Brookes publishing.

Henderson, B. B. (1991) . Describing parent-child interaction during exploration: Situation definitions and negotiations. Genetic, Social and General Psychology Monograph: Vol. 117(1) (pp. 77-89).

Hess, R. D., & Shipman, V. (1965) . Early experience and the socialization of cognitive modes in children. Child Development: Vol. 36 (pp. 377-388).

Holt, John. (1986) . Teach Your Own: A New and Hopeful Path for Parents and Educators. New York: Dell.
A description of the homeschooling movement with practical advice on dealing with legal issues, creating a curriculum, & schooling.

Inhelder, B., & Piaget, J. (1958) . The growth of logical thinking from childhood to adolescence. New York: Basic Books.

Judy, Stephanie. (1990) . Making Music for the Joy of It. Los Angeles: Jeremy P. Tarcher.
A course in enhancing your own musical abilities and interests as an adult.

Karpov, Y. & Bransford, J.D. (1995). L.S. Vygotsky: The doctrine of empirical and theoretical learning. Educational Psychologist: Vol. 30 (pp. 61-66).

Laosa, L. M. (1981). Parent-child Interaction: Theory, Research and Prospects. R.W. Henderson (Ed.), New York Academic Press, 1981.

Laosa, L. M. (1982). School, occupation, culture and family: The impact of parental schooling on the parent-child relationship. Journal of Educational Psychology: Vol. 74 (pp. 791-827).

Lappe, Frances Moore. (1985). What to Do After You Turn Off the T.V. New York: Ballantine.
A practical book of activities families can engage in after making a conscious decision to limit or end television watching.

Lavin, Paul. (1989). Parenting the Overactive Child: Alternatives to Drug Therapy. Lanham, MD: Madison Books.
Describes some of the drawbacks of medication for hyperactivity and offers nondrug solutions, including behavior modification, cognitive therapy, and diet control.

Mander, Jerry. (1978). Four Arguments for the Elimination of Television. New York: Morrow Quill.
Delivers substantially more than four arguments, including the negative impact of artificial light, suppression of the imagination, manipulation through advertising, program bias, sensory deprivation, and hypnotic effects.

Marjoribanks, K. (1984). Occupational status, family environments and adolescents' aspirations: The Laosa model. Journal of Educational Psychology: Vol. 76 (pp. 690-700).

Marjoribanks, K. (1987). Ability and attitude correlates of academic achievement: Family-group differences. Journal of Educational Psychology: Vol. 79 (pp. 171-178).

McGuinness, Diane. (1985). When Children Don't Learn. New York: Basic Books.
Reviews research suggesting that the concepts of hyperactivity and attention deficit disorder lack empirical support and tend to pathologize kids.

Moll, L. (1990). Vygotsky and education: Instructional implications and applications of sociohistorical psychology. Cambridge, MA: Cambridge University Press.

Montessori, Maria. (1973). The Secret of Childhood. New York: Ballantine.
One of Montessori's clearest expositions of her philosophy and method. See also her books below.

Montessori, Maria. . The Absorbent Child and The Discovery of the Child.
Don't miss these books!

Newman, D., Griffin, P., & Cole, M. (1989). The construction zone: Working for cognitive change in school. Cambridge, MA: Cambridge University Press.

Oakes, Jeannie. (1985). Keeping Track: How Schools Structure Inequality. New Haven, CT: Yale University Press.
This book discusses the history of tracking in America.

Palincsar, A. M., & Brown, A. L. (1984). Reciprocal teaching of comprehension-fostering and comprehension monitoring activities. Cognition and instruction: Vol. 1 (pp. 117-175).

Perry, Susan K. (1990). Playing Smart: A Parent's Guide to Enriching Offbeat Learning Activities for Ages 4-14. Minneapolis: Free Spirit Pub.
Full of games, puzzles, and activities designed to stimulate your child's inquiring mind in areas such as logic, photography, psychology, cultural diversity, and scientific investigation.

Portes, P. R. (1988). Mother-child verbal interactions and children's ability levels. Roeper Review: Vol. 11 (pp. 106-110).

Portes, P. R. (1991). Assessing children's cognitive environments through parent-child interaction: Estimation of a general zone of proximal development in relation to scholastic achievement. Journal of Research in Education: Vol. 23(3) (pp. 30-38).

Portes, P. R., Dunham, R. M., & Williams, S. (1986). Preschool intervention, social class and parent-child interaction differences. Journal of Genetic Psychology: Vol. 147(2) (pp. 241-257).

Richards, M. C. (1980). Toward Wholeness: Rudolf Steiner Education in America. Middletown, CT: Wesleyan University Press.
An excellent introduction to Waldorf education. Includes a directory of major Waldorf schools and teacher training programs around the country.

Rogoff, B., Malkin, C., & Gilbride, R. (1984). Interaction with babies as guidance in development. In J. V. Wertsch and B. Rogoff (Eds.), Children's learning in the "zone of proximal development" (pp. 31-44). San Francisco: Jossey-Bass.

Schuster D. H., & Gritton, C. E. (1986). Suggestive Accelerative Learning Techniques (SALT): Theory & Applications. New York: Gordon & Breach.
Well worth the investment, provides many useful teaching methods and the best description of Lozanov's work.

Singer, Dorothy G., Singer, Jerome L., & Zuckerman, Diana M. (1990). Use TV to Your Child's Advantage: The Parent's Guide. Washington, DC: Acropolis.
Provides parents with answers to questions about the potentially damaging effects of television, as well as advice on how to use television to promote growth and understanding in children.

Skolnick, J., Langbort, C., & Day. L. (1982). How to encourage girls in math and science (pp. 137-138). Prentice Hall.

Steiner, Rudolf. (1971). *The Four Temperaments.* New York: Anthroposophic Press, Inc.
Outlines Steiner's theory of four behavior styles (choleric, phlegmatic, sanguine, melancholic) and how they manifest in children's lives. Other books by Steiner include The Kingdom of Childhood and Education as an Art.

Strenio, Andrew J., Jr. (1981). *The Testing Trap.* New York: Rawson, Wade Publishing Inc.
Explores the limitations of standardized tests, describes how they pervade our lives, and how to cope with them.

Suzuki, Shinichi. (1982). *Nurtured by Love: A New Approach to Education.* Pompana Beach, FL: Exposition Press of Florida.
The founder of the Suzuki Talent Education Program describes his philosophy of learning.

Tharp, R. G. & Gallimore, R. (1988). *Rousing minds to life: Teaching, learning and schooling in social context.* Cambridge: Cambridge University Press.

Valsiner, J. (1984). Construction of the zone of proximal development in adult-child joint action: The socialization of meals. In B. Rogoff & J. Wertsch (Eds.), *Children's learning in the zone of proximal development* (pp. 65-76). San Francisco: Jossey-Bass.

Valsiner, J. (1987). *Culture and the development of children's action.* New York: Wiley.

Vygotsky, L. S. (1978). *Mind in society. The development of higher psychological functions.* Cambridge, MA: Harvard University Press.
The key to my book, integrates all the others listed here. Also Thought and Language edited by Kozulin (Cambridge Press). This book shows you the role of language in advancing intelectual thought. Don't miss these in particular.

Vygotsky, L. S. (1984). *Thought and Language.* Cambridge, MA: MIT Press.

Weisner, T. S., Gallimore, R., & Jordan, C. (1988). Unpackaging cultural effects on classroom learning: Hawaiian peer assistance and child-generated activity. *Anthropology and Education Quarterly: Vol 19* (pp. 327-353).

Wertsch, J. V., Minick, N., & Arns, F. J. (1989). The creation of context in joint problem solving: A cross cultural study. In B. Rogoff & J. Lave (Eds.), *Everyday cognition: Its development in social context* (pp. 151-171). Cambridge, MA: Harvard University Press.

Wertsch, J. V. & Stone, C. A. (1985). The concept of internalization in Vygotsky's account of the genesis of higher mental functions. In J. V. Wertsch (Ed.), *Culture, communication, and cognition: Vygotskian perspectives* (pp. 162-179). NY: Cambridge University Press.

Whiting, B., & Whiting, J. (1980). *Children of Six Cultures.* Cambridge, MA: Harvard University Press.

Winn, Marie. (1985) . The Plug-In Drug: Television, Children and the Family. New York: Penguin.
  A classic on the dangers of television watching among children. See also her follow-up book, Pulling the Plug on the Plug-In-Drug: Helping Your Children Kick the TV Habit.

Zady, M. F. (1994) . Home and school interactions in the zone of proximal devlopment: Their relation to activity-based science and aptitude. Dissertation Abstracts International: Vol. 55(07), 1819A.

Dr. Pedro R. Portes Ph.D.

Organizations

Active Parenting
810 Franklin Ct. Suite B.
Marietta, GA. 30067.

These publishers are active in the field of parenting and certification through regional workshops.

Family Resource Coalition
(312) 726-4750.
230 N. Michigan Avenue, Room 1625
Chicago, IL 60601

Network of support groups designed to strengthen the family bond. Provides books and other printed materials.

Holt Associates
(617) 864-3100
2269 Massachusetts Avenue
Cambridge, MA 02140

Founded by John Holt, this organization promotes home schooling, publishes a monthly newsletter called Growing Without Schooling.

National Homeschool Association (NHA)
(206) 432-1544
P.O. Box 58746
Seattle, WA 98138

Nonprofit organization formed to support the home schooling movement.

American Montessori Society (AMS)
(212) 924-3209
150 Fifth Avenue
New York, NY 10011

Professional association that certifies teachers in the Montessori method. This organization has tended to modernize Montessori's approach so that it is in line with contemporary American Educational philosophy.

Association Montessori International USA
(415) 861-7113
P.O. Box 421390
San Francisco, CA 94102-1390

Like the AMS, this is a professional association that trains and certifies Montessori teachers. Its philosophy has been considered to be the more traditional of the two major Montessori associations.

Making Kids Smarter: 2nd Edition

Association of Waldorf Schools of North America
(413) 528-3455
17 Hemlock Hill Road
Great Barrington, MA 01230.

A loose affiliation of Waldorf schools. This association does not train teachers but provides information about different teacher training programs and Waldorf schools around the country.

American Montessori Society (AMS)
(212) 924-3209
150 Fifth Avenue
New York, NY 10011

Professional association that certifies teachers in the Montessori method. This organization has tended to modernize Montessori's approach so that it is in line with contemporary American Educational philosophy.

Hearthsong
(800) 325-2502
P.O. Box B.
Sebastopol, CA 95472

Mail-order supplier of Waldorf-oriented books, toys, art supplies, games, musical.

Nienhuis-Montessori USA
(415) 964-2735
320 Pioneer Way
Mountain View, CA 94040

Mail-order supplier of Montessori materials for use at home or school. Free catalog.

North American Montessori Teacher's Association
(216) 371-1566
2859 Scarborough Road
Cleveland Heights, OH 44118.

Publishes directory of Montessori schools nationwide.

St. George Book Service
P.O. Box 225
Spring, Valley, NY 10977

Books on Waldorf education available by mail, including The Waldorf Parenting Handbook.

National Association of School Psychologists
(301) 608-0500
8544 Colesville Road, Ste. 1000
Silver Spring, MD 20910

Advocates delabeling of children with special needs. Write for their "Rights without Labels" guidelines and information about alternatives to labeling.

Dr. Pedro R. Portes Ph.D.

GLOSSARY:

Abstract thought - The ability to think symbolically, to hypothesize and ask "what if" questions (this usually occurs in adolescence.) The ability to employ general categories and think about various instances of a concept.

Closed-ended questions - Questions that require a simple yes or no response.

Cognitive strategy - A plan of action to solve a problem or find a problem to solve, usually a trick that others teach you, a tool for the mind.

Concrete thought - A child recognizes the order and logic of the physical world. Their concrete operation leads to a model of the world that is stable, and the child seeks rules in which "always, never, all, or none" can be used. Thinking about the world in ways that involve in not devating from rules.

Creativity - Thinking fluently and flexibly about relationships among objects/people, original ways of looking at things.

Culture - Environments where growth takes place, both micro and macro, like the family, workplace, neighborhood, nation where routine activities take place using particular tools, signs, language, customs

Discovery Learning - Learning based using your child's own insights and knowledge with minimal direct instruction, transfer of ideas from one situation to another and discovering rules and strategies to problemsolve

Extinction - When you do not want to see a behavior occur, ignore it, distract it, divert or redirects attention, but don't reward it with attention, giving in etc.

Extrinsic Rewards - Money, privileges, compliments, candy and other stimuli that modify behavior

GOL - Goal of Learning, skills in an aspect of culture you try to select for your child to get excel in by associating it with SAMs

Hidden curriculum - Activities that have subtle educational value in the home or arranged by parents like games, plays, using media

Infant Intelligence - Refers to a set of sensory motor abilities that are largely fixed by biological and prenatal conditions. (See Chapter III)

I.Q. (Intelligence Quotient) - The number of right answers on a standard test divided by age times a constant

Intrinsic Reinforcement - When the child begins to enjoy certain challenges and performs activities for fun with minimal extrinsic rewards

Locus of Control - A belief that one has control over life, tasks through effort or established competence, (versus good luck, bad luck and assorted excuses)

Making Kids Smarter: 2nd Edition

Negative Reinforcement - Making a behavior occur more frequently by providing relief from pain and discomfort

Open-ended Questions - Questions that require an amplified explanation, seeks additional information.

Positive Reinforcement - A process of strengthening a behavior, results when a person feels good or receives something good after doing something. If that action is likely to occur again. With your child the stimulus you or others provided was positive

Reinforcer - Something that makes a behavior more frequent, it can be used to bring happiness or interest. It can be a word of praise, candy, a sticker, a trip to the park, etc... It is a reward. (Could be positive or negative reinforcement, see Chapter V)

Respondent learning (theory) - Classical conditioning, learning to respond to some new thing like you would to another thing that is already pretty well established. Like learning to enjoy playing music (new thing) as a result of liking and feeling like by a teacher or parent or just being close to this person. Some like animals because they are nice and cuddly and end up being veterinarians.

Self-Esteem - How you feel about your self concept or how you think of yourself

Learning Set - A set is a predisposition or attitude in approaching something. It can be a negative set or a positive mindset that influences attention and motivation, and thus performance. (see Chapter II)

Social learning (theory) - Learning by modeling after others, observing models and acting accordingly

Spiral Curriculum - Organizing the learning environment so that new learning is structured in a sequential manner. Adding on new knowledge in a logical sequence. Building on to the learning experience, (asking "what if questions" and following up days later and taking it a step further.

Stimulating Activity and Model (SAM) - A simulus that your child responds to favorable, like dad, a pet, or camping; a strategy to guide your child's learning based on their prior sets

Stimulus-response learning - Basic learning of attitudes and behaviors by connecting activities with consequences-

Symbol Systems - 2 types (1st) sensorimotor learning, dog bites leads to fear of many animals; (2nd) type involves learning by reading, listening to stories using language and signs

Verbal Regulation of Complex Learning - When others use language to guide your thinking about things you would take a longer time figuring out.

Zone of Proximal Development (ZPD) - An aspect of development that is in transition, undergoing change so that errors still occur but can be easily corrected, an area of learning that requires sensitive help before the person catches on and becomes self-regulated in their thinking. In making an approximation as to what your child(ren) already knows in a given area or skill and what he or she needs next in the process of learning, you tap the ZPD. An educated guess as to where your child is developmentally in order to add on new skills or knowledge. (see Chapter II, The Parent-Child Interaction Study)

Dr. Pedro R. Portes Ph.D.

Gift Idea

To Order Copies of Making Kids Smarter (2nd Ed)
Send $15.00 check or money order to:

Portes Books / Butler Publishing
2202 Ardsley Road
Louisville, Ky 40207
email: prport01@athena.louisville.edu

Check us out on the Internet:
http://www.louisville.edu/~prport01

To Arrange for a presentation or speaking engagement with the author, call
(502) 852-0630
fax (502) 852-0629
